MznLnx

Missing Links Exam Preps

Exam Prep for

Essentials of Corporate Finance

Ross, Westerfield, & Jordan, 5th Edition

The MznLnx Exam Prep is your link from the texbook and lecture to your exams.
The MznLnx Exam Preps are unauthorized and comprehensive reviews of your textbooks.

All material provided by MznLnx and Rico Publications (c) 2010
Textbook publishers and textbook authors do not particpate in or contribute to these reviews.

MznLnx

Rico
Publications

Exam Prep for Essentials of Corporate Finance
5th Edition
Ross, Westerfield, & Jordan

Publisher: Raymond Houge
Assistant Editor: Michael Rouger
Text and Cover Designer: Lisa Buckner
Marketing Manager: Sara Swagger
Project Manager, Editorial Production: Jerry Emerson
Art Director: Vernon Lowerui

Product Manager: Dave Mason
Editorial Assitant: Rachel Guzmanji
Pedagogy: Debra Long
Cover Image: Jim Reed/Getty Images
Text and Cover Printer: City Printing, Inc.
Compositor: Media Mix, Inc.

(c) 2010 Rico Publications
ALL RIGHTS RESERVED. No part of this work covered by the copyright may be reproduced or used in any form or by an means--graphic, electronic, or mechanical, including photocopying, recording, taping, Web distribution, information storage, and retrieval systems, or in any other manner--without the written permission of the publisher.

Printed in the United States
ISBN:

For more information about our products, contact us at:
Dave.Mason@RicoPublications.com

For permission to use material from this text or product, submit a request online to:
Dave.Mason@RicoPublications.com

Contents

CHAPTER 1
Introduction to Financial Management   1

CHAPTER 2
Financial Statements, Taxes, and Cash Flow   16

CHAPTER 3
Working with Financial Statements   29

CHAPTER 4
Introduction to Valuation: The Time Value of Money   43

CHAPTER 5
Discounted Cash Flow Valuation   49

CHAPTER 6
Interest Rates and Bond Valuation   56

CHAPTER 7
Equity Markets and Stock Valuation   74

CHAPTER 8
Net Present Value and Other Investment Criteria   84

CHAPTER 9
Making Capital Investment Decisions   91

CHAPTER 10
Some Lessons from Capital Market History   99

CHAPTER 11
Risk and Return   108

CHAPTER 12
Cost of Capital   118

CHAPTER 13
Leverage and Capital Structure   128

CHAPTER 14
Dividends and Dividend Policy   137

CHAPTER 15
Raising Capital   146

CHAPTER 16
Short-Term Financial Planning   154

CHAPTER 17
Working Capital Management   165

CHAPTER 18
International Aspects of Financial Management   178

ANSWER KEY   189

TO THE STUDENT

COMPREHENSIVE

The *MznLnx* Exam Prep series is designed to help you pass your exams. Editors at *MznLnx* review your textbooks and then prepare these practice exams to help you master the textbook material. Unlike study guides, workbooks, and practice tests provided by the texbook publisher and textbook authors, *MznLnx* gives you **all** of the material in each chapter in exam form, not just samples, so you can be sure to nail your exam.

MECHANICAL

The MznLnx Exam Prep series creates exams that will help you learn the subject matter as well as test you on your understanding. Each question is designed to help you master the concept. Just working through the exams, you gain an understanding of the subject--its a simple mechanical process that produces success.

INTEGRATED STUDY GUIDE AND REVIEW

MznLnx is not just a set of exams designed to test you, its also a comprehensive review of the subject content. Each exam question is also a review of the concept, making sure that you will get the answer correct without having to go to other sources of material. You learn as you go! Its the easiest way to pass an exam.

HUMOR

Studying can be tedious and dry. MznLnx's instructional design includes moderate humor within the exam questions on occassion, to break the tedium and revitalize the brain

Chapter 1. Introduction to Financial Management

1. _____ is an area of finance dealing with the financial decisions corporations make and the tools and analysis used to make these decisions. The primary goal of _____ is to maximize corporate value while managing the firm's financial risks. Although it is in principle different from managerial finance which studies the financial decisions of all firms, rather than corporations alone, the main concepts in the study of _____ are applicable to the financial problems of all kinds of firms.

   a. Cash flow
   b. Gross profit
   c. Special purpose entity
   d. Corporate finance

2. _____ is the branch of economics that studies the dynamics of exchange rates, foreign investment, and how these affect international trade. It also studies international projects, international investments and capital flows, and trade deficits. It includes the study of futures, options and currency swaps.

   a. International finance
   b. ABN Amro
   c. A Random Walk Down Wall Street
   d. AAB

3. In economics, the concept of the _____ refers to the decision-making time frame of a firm in which at least one factor of production is fixed. Costs which are fixed in the _____ have no impact on a firms decisions. For example a firm can raise output by increasing the amount of labour through overtime.

   a. 529 plan
   b. 4-4-5 Calendar
   c. Long-run
   d. Short-run

4. A _____ is a regulated professional who buys and sells shares and other securities through market makers or Agency Only Firms on behalf of investors.

   While the term _____ is still in use, it is more commonly referred to as simply 'broker', 'registered rep' or simply 'rep'-- shortened versions of the official FINRA designation 'Registered Representative'. This designation is obtained by an individual passing the FINRA General Securities Representative Examination and being employed ('associated with') a registered Broker-dealer also called a brokerage firm; the firm is typically a FINRA 'member' firm.

   a. Portfolio manager
   b. Purchasing manager
   c. Day trader
   d. Stockbroker

5. An _____ is an economic concept that relates to the cost incurred by an entity (such as organizations) associated with problems such as divergent management-shareholder objectives and information asymmetry. The costs consist of two main sources:

   1. The costs inherently associated with using an agent (e.g., the risk that agents will use organizational resource for their own benefit) and
   2. The costs of techniques used to mitigate the problems associated with using an agent (e.g., the costs of producing financial statements or the use of stock options to align executive interests to shareholder interests.)

   Though effects of _____ are present in any agency relationship, the term is most used in business contexts.

   The information asymmetry that exists between shareholders and the Chief Executive Officer is generally considered to be a classic example of a principal-agent problem. The agent (the manager) is working on behalf of the principal (the shareholders), who does not observe the actions of the agent.

a. AAB
b. ABN Amro
c. A Random Walk Down Wall Street
d. Agency cost

6. In business and accounting, _____s are everything of value that is owned by a person or company. The balance sheet of a firm records the monetary value of the _____s owned by the firm. The two major _____ classes are tangible _____s and intangible _____s.
   a. EBITDA
   b. Income
   c. Asset
   d. Accounts payable

7. In economics, business, and accounting, a _____ is the value of money that has been used up to produce something, and hence is not available for use anymore. In business, the _____ may be one of acquisition, in which case the amount of money expended to acquire it is counted as _____. In this case, money is the input that is gone in order to acquire the thing.
   a. Sliding scale fees
   b. Fixed costs
   c. Marginal cost
   d. Cost

8. In finance, _____ is the ability of an entity to pay its debts with available cash. _____ can also be described as the ability of a corporation to meet its long-term fixed expenses and to accomplish long-term expansion and growth. The better a company's _____, the better it is financially.
   a. Solvency
   b. Political risk
   c. Capital asset
   d. Mid price

9. A _____, securities analyst, research analyst, equity analyst, or investment analyst is a person who performs financial analysis for external or internal clients as a core part of the job.

An analyst studies companies and other entities to arrive at the estimate of their financial value. It is normally done by analyzing financial reports, aided by follow-up interviews with company representatives and industry experts.

   a. Purchasing manager
   b. Stockbroker
   c. Portfolio manager
   d. Financial analyst

10. _____ refer to services provided by the finance industry.

The finance industry encompasses a broad range of organizations that deal with the management of money. Among these organizations are banks, credit card companies, insurance companies, consumer finance companies, stock brokerages, investment funds and some government sponsored enterprises.

   a. Cost of carry
   b. Financial instruments
   c. Delta hedging
   d. Financial services

11. A _____ is a professionally managed type of collective investment scheme that pools money from many investors and invests it in stocks, bonds, short-term money market instruments, and/or other securities. The _____ will have a fund manager that trades the pooled money on a regular basis. Currently, the worldwide value of all _____s totals more than $26 trillion.

Chapter 1. Introduction to Financial Management 3

Since 1940, there have been three basic types of investment companies in the United States: open-end funds, also known in the US as _____s; unit investment trusts (UITs); and closed-end funds.

   a. Mutual fund
   c. Net asset value
   b. Trust company
   d. Financial intermediary

12.   A _____ is a fungible, negotiable instrument representing financial value. They are broadly categorized into debt securities (such as banknotes, bonds and debentures), and equity securities; e.g., common stocks. The company or other entity issuing the _____ is called the issuer.
   a. Tracking stock
   c. Securities lending
   b. Security
   d. Book entry

13.   _____, authored by professors Benjamin Graham and David Dodd of Columbia Business School, laid the intellectual foundation for what would later be called value investing. The work was first published in 1934, following unprecedented losses on Wall Street. In summing up lessons learned, Graham and Dodd chided Wall Street for its myopic focus on a company's reported earnings per share, and were particularly harsh on the favored 'earnings trends.' They encouraged investors to take an entirely different approach by gauging the rough value of the operating business that lay behind the security.
   a. 4-4-5 Calendar
   c. Security analysis
   b. Stock valuation
   d. Growth stocks

14.   In political science and economics, the _____ or agency dilemma treats the difficulties that arise under conditions of incomplete and asymmetric information when a principal hires an agent. Various mechanisms may be used to try to align the interests of the agent with those of the principal, such as piece rates/commissions, profit sharing, efficiency wages, performance measurement (including financial statements), the agent posting a bond, or fear of firing. The _____ is found in most employer/employee relationships, for example, when stockholders hire top executives of corporations.
   a. 4-4-5 Calendar
   c. Principal-agent problem
   b. 7-Eleven
   d. 529 plan

15.   The free _____ of a public company is an estimate of the proportion of shares that are not held by large owners and that are not stock with sales restrictions (restricted stock that cannot be sold until they become unrestricted stock.)

The free _____ or a public _____ is usually defined as being all shares held by investors other than:

- shares held by owners owning more than 5% of all shares (those could be institutional investors, 'strategic shareholders,' founders, executives, and other insiders' holdings)
- restricted stocks (granted to executives that can be, but don't have to be, registered insiders)
- insider holdings (it is assumed that insiders hold stock for the very long term)

The free _____ is an important criterion in quoting a share on the stock market.

To _____ a company means to list its shares on a public stock exchange through an initial public offering (or 'flotation'.)

- Open market
- Outstanding shares
- Market capitalization
- Public _____ loat
- Reverse takeover

a. Golden parachute
b. Float
c. Trade finance
d. Synthetic CDO

16. An _____ (often called organization chart or organigram(me) or organogram(me)) is a diagram that shows the structure of an organization and the relationships and relative ranks of its parts and positions/jobs. The term is also used for similar diagrams, for example ones showing the different elements of a field of knowledge or a group of languages. The French Encyclopédie had one of the first _____s of knowledge in general.

a. AAB
b. A Random Walk Down Wall Street
c. ABN Amro
d. Organizational chart

17. _____ is the planning process used to determine whether a firm's long term investments such as new machinery, replacement machinery, new plants, new products, and research development projects are worth pursuing. It is budget for major capital, or investment, expenditures.

Many formal methods are used in _____, including the techniques such as

- Net present value
- Profitability index
- Internal rate of return
- Modified Internal Rate of Return
- Equivalent annuity

These methods use the incremental cash flows from each potential investment, or project. Techniques based on accounting earnings and accounting rules are sometimes used - though economists consider this to be improper - such as the accounting rate of return, and 'return on investment.' Simplified and hybrid methods are used as well, such as payback period and discounted payback period.

a. Preferred stock
b. Financial distress
c. Shareholder value
d. Capital budgeting

18. In finance, _____ refers to the way a corporation finances its assets through some combination of equity, debt, or hybrid securities. A firm's _____ is then the composition or 'structure' of its liabilities. For example, a firm that sells $20 billion in equity and $80 billion in debt is said to be 20% equity-financed and 80% debt-financed.

Chapter 1. Introduction to Financial Management

a. Market for corporate control
b. Rights issue
c. Book building
d. Capital structure

19. In economic models, the _____ time frame assumes no fixed factors of production. Firms can enter or leave the marketplace, and the cost (and availability) of land, labor, raw materials, and capital goods can be assumed to vary. In contrast, in the short-run time frame, certain factors are assumed to be fixed, because there is not sufficient time for them to change.
   a. 529 plan
   b. 4-4-5 Calendar
   c. Long-run
   d. Short-run

20. _____ is a financial metric which represents operating liquidity available to a business. Along with fixed assets such as plant and equipment, _____ is considered a part of operating capital. It is calculated as current assets minus current liabilities.
   a. 4-4-5 Calendar
   b. Working capital
   c. 529 plan
   d. Working capital management

21. Decisions relating to working capital and short term financing are referred to as _____. These involve managing the relationship between a firm's short-term assets and its short-term liabilities. The goal of _____ is to ensure that the firm is able to continue its operations and that it has sufficient cash flow to satisfy both maturing short-term debt and upcoming operational expenses.
   a. 4-4-5 Calendar
   b. Working capital
   c. Working capital management
   d. 529 plan

22. _____ is the balance of the amounts of cash being received and paid by a business during a defined period of time, sometimes tied to a specific project. Measurement of _____ can be used

- to evaluate the state or performance of a business or project.
- to determine problems with liquidity. Being profitable does not necessarily mean being liquid. A company can fail because of a shortage of cash, even while profitable.
- to generate project rate of returns. The time of _____s into and out of projects are used as inputs to financial models such as internal rate of return, and net present value.
- to examine income or growth of a business when it is believed that accrual accounting concepts do not represent economic realities. Alternately, _____ can be used to 'validate' the net income generated by accrual accounting.

_____ as a generic term may be used differently depending on context, and certain _____ definitions may be adapted by analysts and users for their own uses. Common terms include operating _____ and free _____.

_____s can be classified into:

1. Operational _____s: Cash received or expended as a result of the company's core business activities.
2. Investment _____s: Cash received or expended through capital expenditure, investments or acquisitions.
3. Financing _____s: Cash received or expended as a result of financial activities, such as interests and dividends.

Chapter 1. Introduction to Financial Management

All three together - the net _____ - are necessary to reconcile the beginning cash balance to the ending cash balance. Loan draw downs or equity injections, that is just shifting of capital but no expenditure as such, are not considered in the net _____.

a. Cash flow
b. Shareholder value
c. Corporate finance
d. Real option

23. _____ or financing is to provide capital (funds), which means money for a project, a person, a business or any other private or public institutions.

Those funds can be allocated for either short term or long term purposes. The health fund is a new way of _____ private healthcare centers.

a. Funding
b. Proxy fight
c. Product life cycle
d. Synthetic CDO

24. The institution most often referenced by the word '_____' is a public or publicly traded _____, the shares of which are traded on a public stock exchange (e.g., the New York Stock Exchange or Nasdaq in the United States) where shares of stock of _____s are bought and sold by and to the general public. Most of the largest businesses in the world are publicly traded _____s. However, the majority of _____s are said to be closely held, privately held or close _____s, meaning that no ready market exists for the trading of shares.

a. Federal Home Loan Mortgage Corporation
b. Protect
c. Depository Trust Company
d. Corporation

25. A _____ is a party (e.g. person, organization, company, or government) that has a claim to the services of a second party. The first party, in general, has provided some property or service to the second party under the assumption (usually enforced by contract) that the second party will return an equivalent property or service. The second party is frequently called a debtor or borrower.

a. Creditor
b. NOPLAT
c. False billing
d. Redemption value

26. In the commercial and legal parlance of most countries, a _____ or simply a partnership, refers to an association of persons or an unincorporated company with the following major features:

- Created by agreement, proof of existence and estoppel.
- Formed by two or more persons
- The owners are all personally liable for any legal actions and debts the company may face

It is a partnership in which partners share equally in both responsibility and liability.

Partnerships have certain default characteristics relating to both the relationship between the individual partners and (b) the relationship between the partnership and the outside world. The former can generally be overridden by agreement between the partners, whereas the latter generally cannot be.

Chapter 1. Introduction to Financial Management 7

The assets of the business are owned on behalf of the other partners, and they are each personally liable, jointly and severally, for business debts, taxes or tortious liability.

a. Federal Home Loan Mortgage Corporation
b. General partnership
c. The Depository Trust ' Clearing Corporation
d. First Prudential Markets

27. _____ is a concept whereby a person's financial liability is limited to a fixed sum, most commonly the value of a person's investment in a company or partnership with _____. A shareholder in a limited company is not personally liable for any of the debts of the company, other than for the value of his investment in that company. The same is true for the members of a _____ partnership and the limited partners in a limited partnership.
a. Personal property
b. Limited liability
c. Sarbanes-Oxley Act
d. Beneficial owner

28. A _____ is a form of partnership similar to a general partnership, except that in addition to one or more general partners (GPs), there are one or more limited partners (_____s). It is a partnership in which only one partner is required to be a general partner.

The GPs are, in all major respects, in the same legal position as partners in a conventional firm, i.e. they have management control, share the right to use partnership property, share the profits of the firm in predefined proportions, and have joint and several liability for the debts of the partnership.

a. Limited liability company
b. Leverage
c. Limited partnership
d. Fund of funds

29. A _____ is a type of business entity in which partners (owners) share with each other the profits or losses of the business undertaking in which all have invested. _____s are often favored over corporations for taxation purposes, as the _____ structure does not generally incur a tax on profits before it is distributed to the partners (i.e. there is no dividend tax levied.) However, depending on the _____ structure and the jurisdiction in which it operates, owners of a _____ may be exposed to greater personal liability than they would as shareholders of a corporation.
a. Partnership
b. Fiduciary
c. National Securities Markets Improvement Act of 1996
d. Clayton Antitrust Act

30. _____ is a voluntary contract between two or among more than two persons to place their capital, labor, and skills, and corporation in business with the understanding that there will be a sharing of the profits and losses between/among partners. Outside of North America, it is normally referred to simply as a partnership agreement.
a. Express warranty
b. Economies of scale
c. Economic depreciation
d. Articles of Partnership

31. A sole _____, or simply _____ is a type of business entity which legally has no separate existence from its owner. Hence, the limitations of liability enjoyed by a corporation and limited liability partnerships do not apply to sole proprietors. All debts of the business are debts of the owner.
a. Just-in-time
b. Free cash flow
c. Product life cycle
d. Proprietorship

32. In the most general sense, a _____ is anything that is a hindrance, or puts individuals at a disadvantage.

Before we discuss the financial terms, we should note that a _____ can also have a much more important slang meaning.

This is best described in an example.

a. Liability
c. Limited liability
b. Covenant
d. McFadden Act

33. The _____ are the primary rules governing the management of a corporation in the United States and Canada, and are filed with a state or other regulatory agency. The equivalent in the United Kingdom and various other countries is Articles of Association.

A corporation's _____ generally provide information such as:

- The corporation's name, which has to be unique from any other corporation in that jurisdiction. As part of the corporation's name, certain words such as 'incorporated', 'limited', 'corporation', (or their abbreviations) or some equivalent term in countries whose language is not English, are usually required as part of the name as a 'flag' to indicate to persons doing business with the organization that it is a corporation as opposed to an individual or partnership (with unlimited liability.) In some cases, certain types of names are prohibited except by special permission, such as words implying the corporation is a government agency or has powers to act in ways it is not otherwise allowed.
- The name of the person(s) organizing the corporation (usually members of the board of directors.)
- Whether the corporation is a stock corporation or a non-stock corporation.
- Whether the corporation's existence is permanent or limited for a specific period of time. Generally the rule is that a corporation existence is forever, or until (1) it stops paying the yearly corporate renewal fees or otherwise fails to do something required to continue its existence such as file certain paperwork each year; or (2) it files a request to 'wind up and dissolve.'
- In some cases, a corporation must state the purposes for which it is formed. Some jurisdictions permit a general statement such as 'any lawful purpose' but some require explicit specifications.
- If a non-stock corporation, whether it is for profit or non-profit. However, some jurisdictions differentiate by 'for profit' or 'non profit' and some by 'stock or non-stock'.
- In the United States, if a corporation is to be organized as a non-profit, to be recognized as such by the Internal Revenue Service, such as for eligibility for tax exemption, certain specific wording must be included stating no part of the assets of the corporation are to benefit the members.
- If a stock corporation, the number of shares the corporation is authorized to issue, or the maximum amount in a specific currency of stock that may be issued, e.g. a maximum of $25,000.
- The number and names of the corporation's initial Board of Directors (though this is optional in most cases.)
- The initial director(s) of the corporation (in some cases the incorporator or the registered agent must be a director, if not an attorney or another corporation.)
- The location of the corporation's 'registered office' - the location at which legal papers can be served to the corporation if necessary. Some states further require the designation of a Registered Agent: a person to whom such papers could be delivered.

Chapter 1. Introduction to Financial Management 9

Most states permit a corporation to be formed by one person; in some cases (such as non-profit corporations) it may require three or five or more. This change has come about as a result of Delaware liberalizing its corporation rules to allow corporations to be formed by one person, and states not wanting to lose corporate charters to Delaware had to revise their rules as a result.

a. Articles of Partnership
c. Articles of incorporation

b. External risks
d. Expedited Funds Availability Act

34. A mutual shareholder or _____ is an individual or company (including a corporation) that legally owns one or more shares of stock in a joint stock company. A company's shareholders collectively own that company. Thus, the typical goal of such companies is to enhance shareholder value.

a. Trading curb
c. Stock market bubble

b. Limit order
d. Stockholder

35. _____ is the imposition of two or more taxes on the same income (in the case of income taxes), asset (in the case of capital taxes), or financial transaction (in the case of sales taxes.) It refers to two distinct situations:

- taxation of dividend income without relief or credit for taxes paid by the company paying the dividend on the income from which the dividend is paid. This arises in the so-called 'classical' system of corporate taxation, used in the United States.
- taxation by two or more countries of the same income, asset or transaction, for example income paid by an entity of one country to a resident of a different country. The double liability is often mitigated by tax treaties between countries.

It is not unusual for a business or individual who is resident in one country to make a taxable gain (earnings, profits) in another. This person may find that he is obliged by domestic laws to pay tax on that gain locally and pay again in the country in which the gain was made. Since this is inequitable, many nations make bilateral _____ agreements with each other.

a. 529 plan
c. 7-Eleven

b. Double taxation
d. 4-4-5 Calendar

36. A _____ is a type of business entity: it is a type of corporation or partnership between two companies. Certificates of ownership (or stocks) are issued by the company in return for each contribution, and the shareholders are free to transfer their ownership interest at any time by selling their stockholding to others.

There are two kinds of _____. The private company kind and the open market. The shares are usually only held by the directors and Company Secretary. Debt for which they agree to be liable.

a. 529 plan
c. Joint stock company

b. Subsidiary
d. 4-4-5 Calendar

37. A _____ in the law of the vast majority of United States jurisdictions is a legal form of business company that provides limited liability to its owners. It is a hybrid business entity having certain characteristics of both a corporation and a partnership or sole proprietorship (depending on how many owners there are.) The primary characteristic an _____ shares with a corporation is limited liability, and the primary characteristic it shares with a partnership is the availability of pass-through income taxation.
   a. Financial endowment
   b. Limited liability company
   c. Pension fund
   d. Fund of funds

38. A _____ is a type of limited company in the United Kingdom and the Republic of Ireland which is permitted to offer its shares to the public.
   a. 7-Eleven
   b. 529 plan
   c. Public limited company
   d. 4-4-5 Calendar

39. In business, _____ is income that a company receives from its normal business activities, usually from the sale of goods and services to customers. Some companies also receive _____ from interest, dividends or royalties paid to them by other companies. _____ may refer to business income in general, or it may refer to the amount, in a monetary unit, received during a period of time, as in 'Last year, Company X had _____ of $32 million.'

In many countries, including the UK, _____ is referred to as turnover.

   a. Furniture, Fixtures and Equipment
   b. Bottom line
   c. Revenue
   d. Matching principle

40. _____ is a form of corporation equity ownership represented in the securities. It is dangerous in comparison to preferred shares and some other investment options, in that in the event of bankruptcy, _____ investors receive their funds after preferred stockholders, bondholders, creditors, etc. On the other hand, common shares on average perform better than preferred shares or bonds over time.
   a. Stop-limit order
   b. Stock split
   c. Stock market bubble
   d. Common stock

41. _____ is typically a higher ranking stock than voting shares, and its terms are negotiated between the corporation and the investor.

_____ usually carry no voting rights, but may carry superior priority over common stock in the payment of dividends and upon liquidation. _____ may carry a dividend that is paid out prior to any dividends to common stock holders.

   a. Follow-on offering
   b. Second lien loan
   c. Trade-off theory
   d. Preferred stock

42. _____ is the difference between price and the costs of bringing to market whatever it is that is accounted as an enterprise (whether by harvest, extraction, manufacture, or purchase) in terms of the component costs of delivered goods and/or services and any operating or other expenses.

A key difficulty in measuring profit is in defining costs. Pure economic monetary profits can be zero or negative even in competitive equilibrium when accounted monetized costs exceed monetized price.

Chapter 1. Introduction to Financial Management

a. A Random Walk Down Wall Street
b. Accounting profit
c. Economic profit
d. AAB

43. In economics, _____ is the process by which a firm determines the price and output level that returns the greatest profit. There are several approaches to this problem. The total revenue--total cost method relies on the fact that profit equals revenue minus cost, and the marginal revenue--marginal cost method is based on the fact that total profit in a perfectly competitive market reaches its maximum point where marginal revenue equals marginal cost.

a. 4-4-5 Calendar
b. Net profit margin
c. Profit maximization
d. Profit margin

44. _____ is a legally declared inability or impairment of ability of an individual or organization to pay their creditors. Creditors may file a _____ petition against a debtor ('involuntary _____') in an effort to recoup a portion of what they are owed or initiate a restructuring. In the majority of cases, however, _____ is initiated by the debtor (a 'voluntary _____' that is filed by the bankrupt individual or organization.)

a. Debt settlement
b. 4-4-5 Calendar
c. 529 plan
d. Bankruptcy

45. The _____, in terms of finance and investing, describes how the expected return of a stock or portfolio is correlated to the return of the financial market as a whole.

An asset with a beta of 0 means that its price is not at all correlated with the market; that asset is independent. A positive beta means that the asset generally follows the market.

a. Beta coefficient
b. LIBOR market model
c. Current yield
d. Perpetuity

46. _____ LLP, based in Chicago, was once one of the 'Big Five' accounting firms among PricewaterhouseCoopers, Deloitte Touche Tohmatsu, Ernst ' Young and KPMG, providing auditing, tax, and consulting services to large corporations. In 2002, the firm voluntarily surrendered its licenses to practice as Certified Public Accountants in the United States after being found guilty of criminal charges relating to the firm's handling of the auditing of Enron, the energy corporation, resulting in the loss of 85,000 jobs. Although the verdict was subsequently overturned by the Supreme Court of the United States, it has not returned as a viable business.

a. Accion USA
b. Institute of Financial Accountants
c. Information Systems Audit and Control Association
d. Arthur Andersen

47. In finance, a _____ is a debt security, in which the authorized issuer owes the holders a debt and, depending on the terms of the _____, is obliged to pay interest (the coupon) and/or to repay the principal at a later date, termed maturity.

Thus a _____ is a loan: the issuer is the borrower, the _____ holder is the lender, and the coupon is the interest. _____s provide the borrower with external funds to finance long-term investments, or, in the case of government _____s, to finance current expenditure.

a. Puttable bond
b. Convertible bond
c. Bond
d. Catastrophe bonds

Chapter 1. Introduction to Financial Management

48. _____ is subcontracting a process, such as product design or manufacturing, to a third-party company. The decision to outsource is often made in the interest of lowering cost or making better use of time and energy costs, redirecting or conserving energy directed at the competencies of a particular business, or to make more efficient use of land, labor, capital, (information) technology and resources. _____ became part of the business lexicon during the 1980s.
   a. AT'T Inc.
   b. Outsourcing
   c. Exchange Rate Mechanism
   d. OTC Bulletin Board

49. The _____ of 2002 (Pub.L. 107-204, 116 Stat. 745, enacted July 30, 2002), also known as the Public Company Accounting Reform and Investor Protection Act of 2002 and commonly called Sarbanes-Oxley, Sarbox or SOX, is a United States federal law enacted on July 30, 2002 in response to a number of major corporate and accounting scandals including those affecting Enron, Tyco International, Adelphia, Peregrine Systems and WorldCom.
   a. Sarbanes-Oxley Act
   b. Duty of loyalty
   c. Foreign Corrupt Practices Act
   d. Blue sky law

50. A _____ is an event that may occur when a corporation's stockholders develop opposition to some aspect of the corporate governance, often focusing on directorial and management positions. Corporate activists may attempt to persuade shareholders to use their proxy votes (i.e. votes by one individual or institution as the authorized representative of another) to install new management for any of a variety of reasons.

In a _____, incumbent directors and management have the odds stacked in their favor over those trying to force the corporate change.

   a. Proxy fight
   b. Forfaiting
   c. Trade finance
   d. Procurement

51. In business, a _____ is the purchase of one company (the target) by another (the acquirer or bidder). In the UK the term refers to the acquisition of a public company whose shares are listed on a stock exchange, in contrast to the acquisition of a private company.

Before a bidder makes an offer for another company, it usually first informs that company's board of directors.

   a. Takeover
   b. 4-4-5 Calendar
   c. 529 plan
   d. Stock swap

52. _____ is a fee paid on borrowed assets. It is the price paid for the use of borrowed money, or, money earned by deposited funds. Assets that are sometimes lent with _____ include money, shares, consumer goods through hire purchase, major assets such as aircraft, and even entire factories in finance lease arrangements.
   a. A Random Walk Down Wall Street
   b. AAB
   c. Insolvency
   d. Interest

53. In economics, a _____ is a mechanism that allows people to easily buy and sell (trade) financial securities (such as stocks and bonds), commodities (such as precious metals or agricultural goods), and other fungible items of value at low transaction costs and at prices that reflect the efficient-market hypothesis.

_____s have evolved significantly over several hundred years and are undergoing constant innovation to improve liquidity.

Chapter 1. Introduction to Financial Management 13

Both general markets (where many commodities are traded) and specialized markets (where only one commodity is traded) exist.

a. Delta hedging
b. Secondary market
c. Cost of carry
d. Financial market

54. The _____ is a financial market where participants buy and sell debt securities, usually in the form of bonds. As of 2006, the size of the international _____ is an estimated $45 trillion, of which the size of the outstanding U.S. _____ debt was $25.2 trillion.

Nearly all of the $923 billion average daily trading volume in the U.S. _____ takes place between broker-dealers and large institutions in a decentralized, over-the-counter market.

a. 4-4-5 Calendar
b. 529 plan
c. Fixed income
d. Bond market

55. _____ is that which is owed; usually referencing assets owed, but the term can cover other obligations. In the case of assets, _____ is a means of using future purchasing power in the present before a summation has been earned. Some companies and corporations use _____ as a part of their overall corporate finance strategy.

a. Credit cycle
b. Partial Payment
c. Cross-collateralization
d. Debt

56. The _____ is a stock exchange based in New York City, New York. It is the largest stock exchange in the world by dollar value of its listed companies securities. As of October 2008, the combined capitalization of all domestic _____ listed companies was $10.1 trillion.

a. 529 plan
b. 4-4-5 Calendar
c. New York Stock Exchange
d. 7-Eleven

57. The _____ is that part of the capital markets that deals with the issuance of new securities. Companies, governments or public sector institutions can obtain funding through the sale of a new stock or bond issue. This is typically done through a syndicate of securities dealers.

a. Peer group analysis
b. Sector rotation
c. Volatility clustering
d. Primary market

58. In the United States, a _____ is an offering of securities that are not registered with the Securities and Exchange Commission (SEC.) Such offerings exploit an exemption offered by the Securities Act of 1933 that comes with several restrictions, including a prohibition against general solicitation. This exemption allows companies to avoid quarterly reporting requirements and many of the legal liabilities associated with the Sarbanes-Oxley Act.

a. 7-Eleven
b. Private placement
c. 4-4-5 Calendar
d. 529 plan

59. _____, is when a company issues common stock or shares to the public for the first time. They are often issued by smaller, younger companies seeking capital to expand, but can also be done by large privately-owned companies looking to become publicly traded.

14 *Chapter 1. Introduction to Financial Management*

In an _____ the issuer may obtain the assistance of an underwriting firm, which helps it determine what type of security to issue (common or preferred), best offering price and time to bring it to market.

a. Initial public offering
c. Insolvency
b. Interest
d. Asian Financial Crisis

60. The _____ is the financial market where previously issued securities and financial instruments such as stock, bonds, options, and futures are bought and sold. The term '_____' is also used refer to the market for any used goods or assets, or an alternative use for an existing product or asset where the customer base is the second market

With primary issuances of securities or financial instruments, or the primary market, investors purchase these securities directly from issuers such as corporations issuing shares in an IPO or private placement, or directly from the federal government in the case of treasuries.

a. Performance attribution
c. Financial market
b. Delta neutral
d. Secondary market

61. A _____, securities exchange or (in Europe) bourse is a corporation or mutual organization which provides 'trading' facilities for stock brokers and traders, to trade stocks and other securities. _____s also provide facilities for the issue and redemption of securities as well as other financial instruments and capital events including the payment of income and dividends. The securities traded on a _____ include: shares issued by companies, unit trusts and other pooled investment products and bonds.

a. Stock Exchange
c. 4-4-5 Calendar
b. 529 plan
d. 7-Eleven

62. _____ offer, asking price is a price a seller of a good is willing to accept for that particular good.

In bid and ask, the term _____ is used in contrast to the term bid price. The difference between the _____ and the bid price is called the spread.

a. Ask price
c. Interest rate parity
b. AAB
d. A Random Walk Down Wall Street

63. The _____ is an American stock exchange. It is the largest electronic screen-based equity securities trading market in the United States. With approximately 3,200 companies, it has more trading volume per day than any other stock exchange in the world.

a. 7-Eleven
c. 4-4-5 Calendar
b. 529 plan
d. NASDAQ

64. In the United States, the Financial Industry Regulatory Authority (FINRA) is a self-regulatory organization (SRO) under the Securities Exchange Act of 1934, successor to the _____, Inc.

FINRA is responsible for regulatory oversight of all securities firms that do business with the public; professional training, testing and licensing of registered persons; arbitration and mediation; market regulation by contract for The NASDAQ Stock Market, Inc., the American Stock Exchange LLC, and the International Securities Exchange, LLC; and industry utilities, such as Trade Reporting Facilities and other over-the-counter operations.

a. 4-4-5 Calendar
b. 529 plan
c. 7-Eleven
d. National Association of Securities Dealers

16 *Chapter 2. Financial Statements, Taxes, and Cash Flow*

1. _____ is the balance of the amounts of cash being received and paid by a business during a defined period of time, sometimes tied to a specific project. Measurement of _____ can be used

   - to evaluate the state or performance of a business or project.
   - to determine problems with liquidity. Being profitable does not necessarily mean being liquid. A company can fail because of a shortage of cash, even while profitable.
   - to generate project rate of returns. The time of _____s into and out of projects are used as inputs to financial models such as internal rate of return, and net present value.
   - to examine income or growth of a business when it is believed that accrual accounting concepts do not represent economic realities. Alternately, _____ can be used to 'validate' the net income generated by accrual accounting.

   _____ as a generic term may be used differently depending on context, and certain _____ definitions may be adapted by analysts and users for their own uses. Common terms include operating _____ and free _____.

   _____s can be classified into:

   1. Operational _____s: Cash received or expended as a result of the company's core business activities.
   2. Investment _____s: Cash received or expended through capital expenditure, investments or acquisitions.
   3. Financing _____s: Cash received or expended as a result of financial activities, such as interests and dividends.

   All three together - the net _____ - are necessary to reconcile the beginning cash balance to the ending cash balance. Loan draw downs or equity injections, that is just shifting of capital but no expenditure as such, are not considered in the net _____.

   a. Corporate finance
   c. Shareholder value
   b. Cash flow
   d. Real option

2. _____, in bookkeeping, refers to assets, liabilities, income, and expenses recorded on individual pages of the so called book of final entry or ledger. Changes in _____ value are made by chronologically posting debit (DR) and credit (CR) entries to its page. Examples of _____s are cash, _____s receivable, mortgages, loans, land and buildings, common stock, sales, services provided, wages, and payroll overhead.
   a. Option
   c. Account
   b. Alpha
   d. Accretion

3. _____ is a file or account that contains money that a person or company owes to suppliers, but hasn't paid yet (a form of debt.) When you receive an invoice you add it to the file, and then you remove it when you pay. Thus, the A/P is a form of credit that suppliers offer to their purchasers by allowing them to pay for a product or service after it has already been received.
   a. Accounts payable
   c. Outstanding balance
   b. Earnings before interest, taxes, depreciation and amortization
   d. Accrual

Chapter 2. Financial Statements, Taxes, and Cash Flow

4. _____ is one of a series of accounting transactions dealing with the billing of customers who owe money to a person, company or organization for goods and services that have been provided to the customer. In most business entities this is typically done by generating an invoice and mailing or electronically delivering it to the customer, who in turn must pay it within an established timeframe called credit or payment terms.

An example of a common payment term is Net 30, meaning payment is due in the amount of the invoice 30 days from the date of invoice.

a. Income
b. Impaired asset
c. Accounts receivable
d. Accounting methods

5. In business and accounting, _____s are everything of value that is owned by a person or company. The balance sheet of a firm records the monetary value of the _____s owned by the firm. The two major _____ classes are tangible _____s and intangible _____s.

a. Income
b. EBITDA
c. Accounts payable
d. Asset

6. In financial accounting, a _____ or statement of financial position is a summary of a person's or organization's balances. Assets, liabilities and ownership equity are listed as of a specific date, such as the end of its financial year. A _____ is often described as a snapshot of a company's financial condition.

a. Statement of retained earnings
b. Statement on Auditing Standards No. 70: Service Organizations
c. Financial statements
d. Balance sheet

7. In accounting, a _____ is an asset on the balance sheet which is expected to be sold or otherwise used up in the near future, usually within one year, or one business cycle - whichever is longer. Typical _____s include cash, cash equivalents, accounts receivable, inventory, the portion of prepaid accounts which will be used within a year, and short-term investments.

On the balance sheet, assets will typically be classified into _____s and long-term assets.

a. Current asset
b. Historical cost
c. Long-term liabilities
d. Write-off

8. In accounting, _____ are considered liabilities of the business that are to be settled in cash within the fiscal year or the operating cycle, whichever period is longer.

For example accounts payable for goods, services or supplies that were purchased for use in the operation of the business and payable within a normal period of time would be _____.

Bonds, mortgages and loans that are payable over a term exceeding one year would be fixed liabilities.

a. Current liabilities
b. Net income
c. Gross sales
d. Closing entries

Chapter 2. Financial Statements, Taxes, and Cash Flow

9. _____ plant, and equipment, is a term used in accountancy for assets and property which cannot easily be converted into cash. This can be compared with current assets such as cash or bank accounts, which are described as liquid assets. In most cases, only tangible assets are referred to as fixed.
   a. Percentage of Completion
   b. Petty cash
   c. Remittance advice
   d. Fixed asset

10. _____ are defined as identifiable non-monetary assets that cannot be seen, touched or physically measured, which are created through time and/or effort and that are identifiable as a separate asset. There are two primary forms of intangibles - legal intangibles (such as trade secrets (e.g., customer lists), copyrights, patents, trademarks, and goodwill) and competitive intangibles (such as knowledge activities (know-how, knowledge), collaboration activities, leverage activities, and structural activities.) Legal intangibles generate legal property rights defensible in a court of law.
    a. A Random Walk Down Wall Street
    b. ABN Amro
    c. AAB
    d. Intangible assets

11. In economic models, the _____ time frame assumes no fixed factors of production. Firms can enter or leave the marketplace, and the cost (and availability) of land, labor, raw materials, and capital goods can be assumed to vary. In contrast, in the short-run time frame, certain factors are assumed to be fixed, because there is not sufficient time for them to change.
    a. Short-run
    b. 4-4-5 Calendar
    c. 529 plan
    d. Long-run

12. _____ are liabilities with a future benefit over one year, such as notes payable that mature greater than one year.

In accounting, the _____ are shown on the right wing of the balance-sheet representing the sources of funds, which are generally bounded in form of capital assets.

Examples of _____ are debentures, mortgage loans and other bank loans (note: not all bank loans are long term as not all are paid over a period greater than a year, the example is bridging loan.)

   a. Bottom line
   b. Deferred income
   c. Matching principle
   d. Long-term liabilities

13. _____ is the price at which an asset would trade in a competitive Walrasian auction setting. _____ is often used interchangeably with open _____, fair value or fair _____, although these terms have distinct definitions in different standards, and may differ in some circumstances.

International Valuation Standards defines _____ as 'the estimated amount for which a property should exchange on the date of valuation between a willing buyer and a willing seller in an arm'e;s-length transaction after proper marketing wherein the parties had each acted knowledgeably, prudently, and without compulsion.'

_____ is a concept distinct from market price, which is 'e;the price at which one can transact'e;, while _____ is 'e;the true underlying value'e; according to theoretical standards.

   a. Debt restructuring
   b. Wrap account
   c. Market value
   d. T-Model

14. In finance, a _____ is a debt security, in which the authorized issuer owes the holders a debt and, depending on the terms of the _____, is obliged to pay interest (the coupon) and/or to repay the principal at a later date, termed maturity.

Thus a _____ is a loan: the issuer is the borrower, the _____ holder is the lender, and the coupon is the interest. _____s provide the borrower with external funds to finance long-term investments, or, in the case of government _____s, to finance current expenditure.

 a. Catastrophe bonds
 b. Bond
 c. Puttable bond
 d. Convertible bond

15. In economics, business, and accounting, a _____ is the value of money that has been used up to produce something, and hence is not available for use anymore. In business, the _____ may be one of acquisition, in which case the amount of money expended to acquire it is counted as _____. In this case, money is the input that is gone in order to acquire the thing.
 a. Cost
 b. Sliding scale fees
 c. Marginal cost
 d. Fixed costs

16. _____ is a financial metric which represents operating liquidity available to a business. Along with fixed assets such as plant and equipment, _____ is considered a part of operating capital. It is calculated as current assets minus current liabilities.
 a. 529 plan
 b. Working capital management
 c. 4-4-5 Calendar
 d. Working capital

17. _____ is a legally declared inability or impairment of ability of an individual or organization to pay their creditors. Creditors may file a _____ petition against a debtor ('involuntary _____') in an effort to recoup a portion of what they are owed or initiate a restructuring. In the majority of cases, however, _____ is initiated by the debtor (a 'voluntary _____' that is filed by the bankrupt individual or organization.)
 a. Debt settlement
 b. 4-4-5 Calendar
 c. 529 plan
 d. Bankruptcy

18. _____ is that which is owed; usually referencing assets owed, but the term can cover other obligations. In the case of assets, _____ is a means of using future purchasing power in the present before a summation has been earned. Some companies and corporations use _____ as a part of their overall corporate finance strategy.
 a. Credit cycle
 b. Cross-collateralization
 c. Partial Payment
 d. Debt

19. In the most general sense, a _____ is anything that is a hindrance, or puts individuals at a disadvantage.

Before we discuss the financial terms, we should note that a _____ can also have a much more important slang meaning.

This is best described in an example.

a. Limited liability
c. Covenant
b. McFadden Act
d. Liability

20. _____ is a measure of the ability of a debtor to pay their debts as and when they fall due. It is usually expressed as a ratio or a percentage of current liabilities.

For a corporation with a published balance sheet there are various ratios used to calculate a measure of liquidity.

a. Operating leverage
c. Accounting liquidity
b. Invested capital
d. Operating profit margin

21. In accounting, _____ or *Carrying value* is the value of an asset according to its balance sheet account balance. For assets, the value is based on the original cost of the asset less any depreciation, amortization or impairment costs made against the asset. A company's _____ is its total assets minus intangible assets and liabilities.

a. Current liabilities
c. Pro forma
b. Retained earnings
d. Book value

22. In finance, _____ refers to the way a corporation finances its assets through some combination of equity, debt, or hybrid securities. A firm's _____ is then the composition or 'structure' of its liabilities. For example, a firm that sells $20 billion in equity and $80 billion in debt is said to be 20% equity-financed and 80% debt-financed.

a. Capital structure
c. Book building
b. Rights issue
d. Market for corporate control

23. _____ is a form of corporation equity ownership represented in the securities. It is dangerous in comparison to preferred shares and some other investment options, in that in the event of bankruptcy, _____ investors receive their funds after preferred stockholders, bondholders, creditors, etc. On the other hand, common shares on average perform better than preferred shares or bonds over time.

a. Stock market bubble
c. Common stock
b. Stop-limit order
d. Stock split

24. The institution most often referenced by the word '_____' is a public or publicly traded _____, the shares of which are traded on a public stock exchange (e.g., the New York Stock Exchange or Nasdaq in the United States) where shares of stock of _____s are bought and sold by and to the general public. Most of the largest businesses in the world are publicly traded _____s. However, the majority of _____s are said to be closely held, privately held or close _____s, meaning that no ready market exists for the trading of shares.

a. Depository Trust Company
c. Protect
b. Federal Home Loan Mortgage Corporation
d. Corporation

25. In finance, the _____ is the minimum rate of return a firm must offer shareholders to compensate for waiting for their returns, and for bearing some risk.

The _____ capital for a particular company is the rate of return on investment that is required by the company's ordinary shareholders. The return consists both of dividend and capital gains, e.g. increases in the share price.

a. Net pay
b. Residual value
c. Round-tripping
d. Cost of equity

26. _____ is the standard framework of guidelines for financial accounting used in the United States of America. It includes the standards, conventions, and rules accountants follow in recording and summarizing transactions, and in the preparation of financial statements. _____ are now issued by the Financial Accounting Standards Board (FASB).
a. Net income
b. Depreciation
c. Revenue
d. Generally accepted accounting principles

27. In accounting, _____ is the original monetary value of an economic item. In some circumstances, assets and liabilities may be shown at their _____, as if there had been no change in value since the date of acquisition. The balance sheet value of the item may therefore differ from the 'true' value.
a. Pro forma
b. Treasury stock
c. Historical cost
d. Deferred income

28. _____ is typically a higher ranking stock than voting shares, and its terms are negotiated between the corporation and the investor.

_____ usually carry no voting rights, but may carry superior priority over common stock in the payment of dividends and upon liquidation. _____ may carry a dividend that is paid out prior to any dividends to common stock holders.

a. Preferred stock
b. Second lien loan
c. Trade-off theory
d. Follow-on offering

29. A _____ is a fungible, negotiable instrument representing financial value. They are broadly categorized into debt securities (such as banknotes, bonds and debentures), and equity securities; e.g., common stocks. The company or other entity issuing the _____ is called the issuer.
a. Tracking stock
b. Book entry
c. Security
d. Securities lending

30. The _____, in terms of finance and investing, describes how the expected return of a stock or portfolio is correlated to the return of the financial market as a whole.

An asset with a beta of 0 means that its price is not at all correlated with the market; that asset is independent. A positive beta means that the asset generally follows the market.

a. Perpetuity
b. LIBOR market model
c. Current yield
d. Beta coefficient

31. In finance, _____ (or gearing) is borrowing money to supplement existing funds for investment in such a way that the potential positive or negative outcome is magnified and/or enhanced. It generally refers to using borrowed funds, or debt, so as to attempt to increase the returns to equity. Deleveraging is the action of reducing borrowings.
a. Pension fund
b. Limited partnership
c. Financial endowment
d. Leverage

32. Net income is informally called the _____ because it is typically found on the last line of a company's income statement. A related term is top line, meaning revenue, which forms the first line of the account statement.

An equation for net income in merchandising:

Net income or net loss =Revenue - Cost of goods sold - Sales discounts - Sales returns and allowances - Expenses - Minority interest - Preferred stock dividends

- a. Retained earnings
- b. Matching principle
- c. Net income
- d. Bottom line

33. _____ are the earnings returned on the initial investment amount.

In the US, the Financial Accounting Standards Board (FASB) requires companies' income statements to report _____ for each of the major categories of the income statement: continuing operations, discontinued operations, extraordinary items, and net income.

The _____ formula does not include preferred dividends for categories outside of continued operations and net income.

- a. Average accounting return
- b. Assets turnover
- c. Earnings per share
- d. Inventory turnover

34. _____, refers to consumption opportunity gained by an entity within a specified time frame, which is generally expressed in monetary terms. However, for households and individuals, '_____ is the sum of all the wages, salaries, profits, interests payments, rents and other forms of earnings received... in a given period of time.' For firms, _____ generally refers to net-profit: what remains of revenue after expenses have been subtracted.

- a. Accrual
- b. Income
- c. Annual report
- d. OIBDA

35. An _____ is a financial statement for companies that indicates how Revenue is transformed into net income The purpose of the _____ is to show managers and investors whether the company made or lost money during the period being reported.

The important thing to remember about an _____ is that it represents a period of time.

- a. A Random Walk Down Wall Street
- b. Income statement
- c. ABN Amro
- d. AAB

36. _____ is equal to the income that a firm has after subtracting costs and expenses from the total revenue. _____ can be distributed among holders of common stock as a dividend or held by the firm as retained earnings. _____ is an accounting term; in some countries (such as the UK) profit is the usual term.

- a. Write-off
- b. Furniture, Fixtures and Equipment
- c. Historical cost
- d. Net income

Chapter 2. Financial Statements, Taxes, and Cash Flow

37. In business, _____ is income that a company receives from its normal business activities, usually from the sale of goods and services to customers. Some companies also receive _____ from interest, dividends or royalties paid to them by other companies. _____ may refer to business income in general, or it may refer to the amount, in a monetary unit, received during a period of time, as in 'Last year, Company X had _____ of $32 million.'

In many countries, including the UK, _____ is referred to as turnover.

a. Matching principle
c. Bottom line
b. Furniture, Fixtures and Equipment
d. Revenue

38. In business and finance, a _____ (also referred to as equity _____) of stock means a _____ of ownership in a corporation (company.) In the plural, stocks is often used as a synonym for _____ s especially in the United States, but it is less commonly used that way outside of North America.

In the United Kingdom, South Africa, and Australia, stock can also refer to completely different financial instruments such as government bonds or, less commonly, to all kinds of marketable securities.

a. Bucket shop
c. Procter ' Gamble
b. Margin
d. Share

39. A _____ is a payment made by a corporation to its shareholder members. When a corporation earns a profit or surplus, that money can be put to two uses: it can either be re-invested in the business (called retained earnings), or it can be paid to the shareholders as a _____. Many corporations retain a portion of their earnings and pay the remainder as a _____.

a. Dividend
c. Dividend yield
b. Dividend puzzle
d. Special dividend

40. _____ is a cornerstone of accrual accounting together with revenue recognition. They both determine the point, at which expenses and revenues are recognized. According to the principle, expenses are recognized when they are (1) incurred and (2) offset against recognized revenues, which were generated from those expenses (related on the cause-and-effect basis), no matter when cash is paid out.

a. Matching principle
c. Pro forma
b. Retained earnings
d. Gross sales

41. In accounting, _____ refers to the portion of net income which is retained by the corporation rather than distributed to its owners as dividends. Similarly, if the corporation makes a loss, then that loss is retained and called variously retained losses, accumulated losses or accumulated deficit. _____ and losses are cumulative from year to year with losses offsetting earnings.

a. Matching principle
c. Historical cost
b. Generally Accepted Accounting Principles
d. Retained earnings

42. The _____ principle is a cornerstone of accrual accounting together with matching principle. They both determine the accounting period, in which revenues and expenses are recognized. According to the principle, revenues are recognized when they are (1) realized or realizable, and are (2) earned (usually when goods are transferred or services rendered), no matter when cash is received.

Chapter 2. Financial Statements, Taxes, and Cash Flow

a. Commodity Pool Operator
c. Regulation FD
b. Tail risk
d. Revenue recognition

43. _____ is a term used in accounting, economics and finance to spread the cost of an asset over the span of several years.

In simple words we can say that _____ is the reduction in the value of an asset due to usage, passage of time, wear and tear, technological outdating or obsolescence, depletion or other such factors.

In accounting, _____ is a term used to describe any method of attributing the historical or purchase cost of an asset across its useful life, roughly corresponding to normal wear and tear.

a. Matching principle
c. Bottom line
b. Depreciation
d. Deferred financing costs

44. _____ are business expenses that are not dependent on the level of production or sales. They tend to be time-related, such as salaries or rents being paid per month. This is in contrast to Variable costs, which are volume-related (and are paid per quantity.)
a. Sliding scale fees
c. Fixed costs
b. Marginal cost
d. Transaction cost

45. Depreciation methods that provide for a higher depreciation charge in the first year of an asset's life and gradually decreasing charges in subsequent years are called accelerated depreciation methods. This may be a more realistic reflection of an asset's actual expected benefit from the use of the asset: many assets are most useful when they are new. One popular accelerated method is the declining-balance method. Under this method the Book Value is multiplied by a fixed rate.

The most common rate used is double the straight-line rate. For this reason, this technique is referred to as the _____. To illustrate, suppose a business has an asset with $1,000 Original Cost, $100 Salvage Value, and 5 years useful life. First, calculate straight-line depreciation rate. Since the asset has 5 years useful life, the straight-line depreciation rate equals (100% / 5) 20% per year. With _____, as the name suggests, double that rate, or 40% depreciation rate is used.

a. Database auditing
c. Doctrine of the Proper Law
b. The Goodyear Tire ' Rubber Company
d. Double-declining-balance method

46. _____ are expenses that change in proportion to the activity of a business. In other words, _____ are the sum of marginal costs. It can also be considered normal costs. Along with fixed costs, _____ make up the two components of total cost. Direct Costs, however, are costs that can be associated with a particular cost object.
a. Transaction cost
c. Fixed costs
b. Cost accounting
d. Variable costs

47. In economics, the concept of the _____ refers to the decision-making time frame of a firm in which at least one factor of production is fixed. Costs which are fixed in the _____ have no impact on a firms decisions. For example a firm can raise output by increasing the amount of labour through overtime.

| a. Long-run | b. Short-run |
| c. 529 plan | d. 4-4-5 Calendar |

48. In accounting and finance, _____ is the portion of receivables that can no longer be collected, typically from accounts receivable or loans. _____ in accounting is considered an expense.

There are two methods to account for _____:

1. Direct write off method (Non - GAAP)

A receivable which is not considered collectible is charged directly to the income statement.

1. Allowance method (GAAP)

An estimate is made at the end of each fiscal year of the amount of _____. This is then accumulated in a provision which is then used to reduce specific receivable accounts as and when necessary.

| a. Tax expense | b. 4-4-5 Calendar |
| c. 529 plan | d. Bad debt |

49. _____ or cookie jar reserves is an accounting practice in which a company uses generous reserves from good years against losses that might be incurred in bad years.

An example of a cookie jar reserve is a liability created when a company records an expense that is not directly linked to a specific accounting period -- the expense may fall in one period or another. Companies may record such discretionary expense when profits are high because they can afford to take the hit to income.

| a. Resources, Events, Agents | b. Moving-Average Cost |
| c. Cookie jar accounting | d. Non Performing Asset |

50. _____ and earnings management are euphemisms referring to accounting practices that may follow the letter of the rules of standard accounting practices, but certainly deviate from the spirit of those rules. They are characterized by excessive complication and the use of novel ways of characterizing income, assets, or liabilities and the intent to influence readers towards the interpretations desired by the authors. The terms 'innovative' or 'aggressive' are also sometimes used.

| a. Creative accounting | b. Non Performing Asset |
| c. Controlling account | d. Debit and credit |

51. The _____ (NYSE: FNM), commonly known as Fannie Mae, is a stockholder-owned corporation chartered by Congress in 1968 as a government sponsored enterprise (GSE), but founded in 1938 during the Great Depression. The corporation's purpose is to purchase and securitize mortgages in order to ensure that funds are consistently available to the institutions that lend money to home buyers.

On September 7, 2008, James Lockhart, director of the Federal Housing Finance Agency (FHFA), announced that Fannie Mae and Freddie Mac were being placed into conservatorship of the FHFA.

Chapter 2. Financial Statements, Taxes, and Cash Flow

a. SPDR
b. General partnership
c. The Depository Trust ' Clearing Corporation
d. Federal National Mortgage Association

52. The U.S. _____ is an independent agency of the United States government which holds primary responsibility for enforcing the federal securities laws and regulating the securities industry, the nation's stock and options exchanges, and other electronic securities markets. The SEC was created by section 4 of the SEC of 1934 (now codified as 15 U.S.C. § 78d and commonly referred to as the 1934 Act.)
   a. 529 plan
   b. 7-Eleven
   c. 4-4-5 Calendar
   d. Securities and Exchange Commission

53. The term _____ describes a reduction in recognized value. In accounting terminology, it refers to recognition of the reduced or zero value of an asset. In income tax statements, it refers to a reduction of taxable income as recognition of certain expenses required to produce the income.
   a. Write-off
   b. Net profit
   c. Net income
   d. Trial balance

54. In political science and economics, the _____ or agency dilemma treats the difficulties that arise under conditions of incomplete and asymmetric information when a principal hires an agent. Various mechanisms may be used to try to align the interests of the agent with those of the principal, such as piece rates/commissions, profit sharing, efficiency wages, performance measurement (including financial statements), the agent posting a bond, or fear of firing. The _____ is found in most employer/employee relationships, for example, when stockholders hire top executives of corporations.
   a. 4-4-5 Calendar
   b. 529 plan
   c. 7-Eleven
   d. Principal-agent problem

55. _____ refers to a tax levied by various jurisdictions on the profits made by companies or associations. It is a tax on the value of the corporation's profits.

The measure of taxable profits varies from country to country.

   a. Corporate tax
   b. Proxy fight
   c. Trade finance
   d. First-mover advantage

56. _____ loans are often used by traditional moneylenders in the informal economy of developing countries. They are also used by many microfinance institutions. One reason for their popularity is their ease of use.
   a. Rural credit cooperatives
   b. Naked call
   c. Controlled foreign corporations
   d. Flat interest rate

57. In financial and business accounting, _____ is a measure of a firm's profitability that excludes interest and income tax expenses.

EBIT = Operating Revenue - Operating Expenses (OPEX) + Non-operating Income

Operating Income = Operating Revenue - Operating Expenses

Chapter 2. Financial Statements, Taxes, and Cash Flow

Operating income is the difference between operating revenues and operating expenses, but it is also sometimes used as a synonym for EBIT and operating profit. This is true if the firm has no non-operating income.

a. ABN Amro
b. Earnings before interest and taxes
c. A Random Walk Down Wall Street
d. AAB

58. In financial accounting, _____ , cash flow provided by operations or cash flow from operating activities, refers to the amount of cash a company generates from the revenues it brings in, excluding costs associated with long-term investment on capital items or investment in securities.

_____ = Cash generated from operations less taxation and interest paid, investment income received and less dividends paid gives rise to _____s per International Financial Reporting Standards.

To calculate cash generated from operations, one must calculate cash generated from customers and cash paid to suppliers.

a. Operating cash flow
b. Other Comprehensive Basis of Accounting
c. A Random Walk Down Wall Street
d. Appreciation

59. In financial accounting, a _____ or statement of cash flows is a financial statement that shows a company's flow of cash. The money coming into the business is called cash inflow, and money going out from the business is called cash outflow. The statement shows how changes in balance sheet and income accounts affect cash and cash equivalents, and breaks the analysis down to operating, investing, and financing activities.
a. 529 plan
b. 7-Eleven
c. 4-4-5 Calendar
d. Cash flow statement

60. _____ is a fee paid on borrowed assets. It is the price paid for the use of borrowed money , or, money earned by deposited funds . Assets that are sometimes lent with _____ include money, shares, consumer goods through hire purchase, major assets such as aircraft, and even entire factories in finance lease arrangements.
a. AAB
b. A Random Walk Down Wall Street
c. Insolvency
d. Interest

61. _____ is the corporate management term for the act of reorganizing the legal, ownership, operational, or other structures of a company for the purpose of making it more profitable or better organized for its present needs. Alternate reasons for restructing include a change of ownership or ownership structure, demerger repositioning debt _____ and financial _____.

a. Cross-border leasing
b. Concentrated stock
c. Restructuring
d. Day trading

62. _____ relates to the cost of borrowing money. It is the price that a lender charges a borrower for the use of the lender's money. _____ is different from OPEX and CAPEX, for it relates to the capital structure of a company.
a. Interest expense
b. A Random Walk Down Wall Street
c. AAB
d. ABN Amro

Chapter 2. Financial Statements, Taxes, and Cash Flow

63. In corporate finance, _____ is a cash flow available for distribution among all the security holders of a company. They include equity holders, debt holders, preferred stock holders, convertible security holders, and so on.

Note that the first three lines above are calculated for you on the standard Statement of Cash Flows.

   a. Free cash flow
   b. Forfaiting
   c. Safety stock
   d. Funding

64. A _____ is a party (e.g. person, organization, company, or government) that has a claim to the services of a second party. The first party, in general, has provided some property or service to the second party under the assumption (usually enforced by contract) that the second party will return an equivalent property or service. The second party is frequently called a debtor or borrower.
   a. NOPLAT
   b. False billing
   c. Redemption value
   d. Creditor

65. A mutual shareholder or _____ is an individual or company (including a corporation) that legally owns one or more shares of stock in a joint stock company. A company's shareholders collectively own that company. Thus, the typical goal of such companies is to enhance shareholder value.
   a. Stock market bubble
   b. Limit order
   c. Trading curb
   d. Stockholder

66. A _____ or bank is a financial institution whose primary activity is to act as a payment agent for customers and to borrow and lend money.

The first modern bank was founded in Italy in Genoa in 1406, its name was Banco di San Giorgio (Bank of St. George.)

Many other financial activities were added over time.

   a. 4-4-5 Calendar
   b. Black Sea Trade and Development Bank
   c. Banker
   d. Bought deal

67. _____ is a United States based company that specializes in the design, manufacture, marketing and sales of automobiles and truck tires, with additional subsidiaries that specialize in motorcycle and racing tires, as well as tread rubber and related equipment for the industry. With headquarters in Findlay, Ohio, Cooper Tire has 59 manufacturing, sales, distribution, technical and design facilities within its family of companies located around the world.

In 1941, the first year the Cooper oval trademark with the Cooper Knight head gear was registered and used.

   a. Protect
   b. FASB
   c. Governmental Accounting Standards Board
   d. Cooper Tire ' Rubber Company

Chapter 3. Working with Financial Statements

1. The institution most often referenced by the word '_____' is a public or publicly traded _____, the shares of which are traded on a public stock exchange (e.g., the New York Stock Exchange or Nasdaq in the United States) where shares of stock of _____s are bought and sold by and to the general public. Most of the largest businesses in the world are publicly traded _____s. However, the majority of _____s are said to be closely held, privately held or close _____s, meaning that no ready market exists for the trading of shares.
   a. Protect
   b. Corporation
   c. Federal Home Loan Mortgage Corporation
   d. Depository Trust Company

2. A _____ is the price of a single share of a no. of saleable stocks of the company. Once the stock is purchased, the owner becomes a shareholder of the company that issued the share.
   a. Whisper numbers
   b. Stock split
   c. Trading curb
   d. Share price

3. _____ are formal records of a business' financial activities.

   _____ provide an overview of a business' financial condition in both short and long term. There are four basic _____:

   1. **Balance sheet**: also referred to as statement of financial position or condition, reports on a company's assets, liabilities, and net equity as of a given point in time.
   2. **Income statement**: also referred to as Profit and Loss statement (or a 'P'L'), reports on a company's income, expenses, and profits over a period of time.
   3. **Statement of retained earnings**: explains the changes in a company's retained earnings over the reporting period.
   4. **Statement of cash flows**: reports on a company's cash flow activities, particularly its operating, investing and financing activities.

   a. Financial statements
   b. Statement of retained earnings
   c. Notes to the Financial Statements
   d. Statement on Auditing Standards No. 70: Service Organizations

4. In financial accounting, a _____ or statement of financial position is a summary of a person's or organization's balances. Assets, liabilities and ownership equity are listed as of a specific date, such as the end of its financial year. A _____ is often described as a snapshot of a company's financial condition.
   a. Financial statements
   b. Statement on Auditing Standards No. 70: Service Organizations
   c. Statement of retained earnings
   d. Balance sheet

5. _____, refers to consumption opportunity gained by an entity within a specified time frame, which is generally expressed in monetary terms. However, for households and individuals, '_____ is the sum of all the wages, salaries, profits, interests payments, rents and other forms of earnings received... in a given period of time.' For firms, _____ generally refers to net-profit: what remains of revenue after expenses have been subtracted.
   a. Income
   b. Annual report
   c. Accrual
   d. OIBDA

Chapter 3. Working with Financial Statements

6. An _____ is a financial statement for companies that indicates how Revenue is transformed into net income The purpose of the _____ is to show managers and investors whether the company made or lost money during the period being reported.

The important thing to remember about an _____ is that it represents a period of time.

a. AAB
c. Income statement
b. A Random Walk Down Wall Street
d. ABN Amro

7. In finance, a _____ or accounting ratio is a ratio of two selected numerical values taken from an enterprise's financial statements. There are many standard ratios used to try to evaluate the overall financial condition of a corporation or other organization. They may be used by managers within a firm, by current and potential shareholders (owners) of a firm, and by a firm's creditors. Security analysts use these to compare the strengths and weaknesses in various companies.

a. Return on capital employed
c. Financial ratio
b. Price/cash flow ratio
d. Sustainable growth rate

8. In accounting, a _____ is an asset on the balance sheet which is expected to be sold or otherwise used up in the near future, usually within one year, or one business cycle - whichever is longer. Typical _____ s include cash, cash equivalents, accounts receivable, inventory, the portion of prepaid accounts which will be used within a year, and short-term investments.

On the balance sheet, assets will typically be classified into _____ s and long-term assets.

a. Long-term liabilities
c. Write-off
b. Historical cost
d. Current asset

9. In accounting, _____ are considered liabilities of the business that are to be settled in cash within the fiscal year or the operating cycle, whichever period is longer.

For example accounts payable for goods, services or supplies that were purchased for use in the operation of the business and payable within a normal period of time would be _____.

Bonds, mortgages and loans that are payable over a term exceeding one year would be fixed liabilities.

a. Closing entries
c. Net income
b. Gross sales
d. Current liabilities

10. The _____ is a financial ratio that measures whether or not a firm has enough resources to pay its debts over the next 12 months. It compares a firm's current assets to its current liabilities. It is expressed as follows:

$$\text{Current ratio} = \frac{\text{Current Assets}}{\text{Current Liabilities}}$$

For example, if WXY Company's current assets are $50,000,000 and its current liabilities are $40,000,000, then its _____ would be $50,000,000 divided by $40,000,000, which equals 1.25.

Chapter 3. Working with Financial Statements

a. Debt service coverage ratio
b. Current ratio
c. Sustainable growth rate
d. PEG ratio

11. _____ is the field of accountancy concerned with the preparation of financial statements for decision makers, such as stockholders, suppliers, banks, employees, government agencies, owners, and other stakeholders. The fundamental need for _____ is to reduce principal-agent problem by measuring and monitoring agents' performance and reporting the results to interested users.

_____ is used to prepare accounting information for people outside the organization or not involved in the day to day running of the company.

a. 4-4-5 Calendar
b. Financial Accounting
c. 529 plan
d. 7-Eleven

12. _____ is a measure of the ability of a debtor to pay their debts as and when they fall due. It is usually expressed as a ratio or a percentage of current liabilities.

For a corporation with a published balance sheet there are various ratios used to calculate a measure of liquidity.

a. Operating leverage
b. Accounting liquidity
c. Invested capital
d. Operating profit margin

13. In business and accounting, _____s are everything of value that is owned by a person or company. The balance sheet of a firm records the monetary value of the _____s owned by the firm. The two major _____ classes are tangible _____s and intangible _____s.

a. Income
b. Accounts payable
c. Asset
d. EBITDA

14. The _____ is a bank regulation that sets the minimum reserves each bank must hold to customer deposits and notes. These reserves are designed to satisfy withdrawal demands, and would normally be in the form of fiat currency stored in a bank vault (vault cash), or with a central bank.

The reserve ratio is sometimes used as a tool in the monetary policy, influencing the country's economy, borrowing, and interest rates.

a. Wall Street Journal prime rate
b. Variable rate mortgage
c. Prime rate
d. Reserve requirement

15. In finance, the Acid-test or _____ or liquid ratio measures the ability of a company to use its near cash or quick assets to immediately extinguish or retire its current liabilities. Quick assets include those current assets that presumably can be quickly converted to cash at close to their book values.

Generally, the acid test ratio should be 1:1 or better, however this varies widely by industry.

a. Net assets
b. P/E ratio
c. Quick ratio
d. Financial ratio

16. In a _____, a company's creditors generally agree to cancel some or all of the debt in exchange for equity in the company.

These deals often occur when large companies run into serious financial trouble, and often result in these companies being taken over by their principal creditors. This is because both the debt and the remaining assets in these companies are so large that there is no advantage for the creditors to drive the company into bankruptcy.

a. Debt restructuring
b. Covestor
c. Financial Gerontology
d. Debt-for-equity swap

17. In financial and business accounting, _____ is a measure of a firm's profitability that excludes interest and income tax expenses.

EBIT = Operating Revenue - Operating Expenses (OPEX) + Non-operating Income

Operating Income = Operating Revenue - Operating Expenses

Operating income is the difference between operating revenues and operating expenses, but it is also sometimes used as a synonym for EBIT and operating profit. This is true if the firm has no non-operating income.

a. ABN Amro
b. AAB
c. Earnings before interest and taxes
d. A Random Walk Down Wall Street

18. In finance, _____ (or gearing) is borrowing money to supplement existing funds for investment in such a way that the potential positive or negative outcome is magnified and/or enhanced. It generally refers to using borrowed funds, or debt, so as to attempt to increase the returns to equity. Deleveraging is the action of reducing borrowings.

a. Limited partnership
b. Pension fund
c. Financial endowment
d. Leverage

19. In economic models, the _____ time frame assumes no fixed factors of production. Firms can enter or leave the marketplace, and the cost (and availability) of land, labor, raw materials, and capital goods can be assumed to vary. In contrast, in the short-run time frame, certain factors are assumed to be fixed, because there is not sufficient time for them to change.

a. Long-run
b. Short-run
c. 529 plan
d. 4-4-5 Calendar

20. _____ or interest coverage ratio is a measure of a company's ability to honor its debt payments. It may be calculated as either EBIT or EBITDA divided by the total interest payable.

Chapter 3. Working with Financial Statements

$$\text{Times-Interest-Earned} = \frac{\text{EBIT or EBITDA}}{\text{Interest Charges}}$$

- Financial ratio
- Financial leverage
- EBIT
- EBITDA
- Debt service coverage ratio

Interest Charges = Traditionally 'charges' refers to interest expense found on the income statement.

_____ or Interest Coverage is a great tool when measuring a company's ability to meet its debt obligations.

a. Cash conversion cycle
c. Net assets
b. Times interest earned
d. Return of capital

21. _____ is that which is owed; usually referencing assets owed, but the term can cover other obligations. In the case of assets, _____ is a means of using future purchasing power in the present before a summation has been earned. Some companies and corporations use _____ as a part of their overall corporate finance strategy.

a. Partial Payment
c. Debt
b. Credit cycle
d. Cross-collateralization

22. _____ is a financial ratio that indicates the percentage of a company's assets are provided via debt. It is the ratio of total debt (the sum of current liabilities and long-term liabilities) and total assets (the sum of current assets, fixed assets, and other assets such as 'goodwill'.)

or alternatively:

For example, a company with $2 million in total assets and $500,000 in total liabilities would have a _____ of 25%

Like all financial ratios, a company's _____ should be compared with their industry average or other competing firms.

a. Cash management
c. Capitalization rate
b. Cash concentration
d. Debt ratio

Chapter 3. Working with Financial Statements

23. _____ is a fee paid on borrowed assets. It is the price paid for the use of borrowed money, or, money earned by deposited funds. Assets that are sometimes lent with _____ include money, shares, consumer goods through hire purchase, major assets such as aircraft, and even entire factories in finance lease arrangements.
    a. Insolvency
    b. Interest
    c. A Random Walk Down Wall Street
    d. AAB

24. In finance, _____ is the ability of an entity to pay its debts with available cash. _____ can also be described as the ability of a corporation to meet its long-term fixed expenses and to accomplish long-term expansion and growth. The better a company's _____, the better it is financially.
    a. Political risk
    b. Capital asset
    c. Mid price
    d. Solvency

25. _____ is a financial ratio that measures the efficiency of a company's use of its assets in generating sales revenue or sales income to the company.

$$Asset\ Turnover = \frac{Sales}{Average Total Assets}$$

- 'Sales' is the value of 'Net Sales' or 'Sales' from the company's income statement
- 'Average Total Assets' is the value of 'Total assets' from the company's balance sheet in the beginning and the end of the fiscal period divided by 2.

- Assets turnover

    a. Inventory turnover
    b. Asset turnover
    c. Earnings yield
    d. Average accounting return

26. _____ is a list for goods and materials held available in stock by a business. It is also used for a list of the contents of a household and for a list for testamentary purposes of the possessions of someone who has died. In accounting _____ is considered an asset.
    a. Inventory
    b. AAB
    c. ABN Amro
    d. A Random Walk Down Wall Street

27. The _____ is an equation that equals the cost of goods sold divided by the average inventory. Average inventory equals beginning inventory plus ending inventory divided by 2.

The formula for _____:

$$Inventory\ Turnover = \frac{Cost\ of\ Goods\ Sold}{Average\ Inventory}$$

The formula for average inventory:

Chapter 3. Working with Financial Statements

$$\text{Average Inventory} = \frac{\text{Beginning inventory} + \text{Ending inventory}}{2}$$

A low turnover rate may point to overstocking, obsolescence, or deficiencies in the product line or marketing effort.

a. Operating leverage
b. Earnings yield
c. Information ratio
d. Inventory turnover

28. _____ is the term in economics for the amount of fixed or real capital present in relation to other factors of production, especially labor. At the level of either a production process or the aggregate economy, it may be estimated by the capital/labor ratio, such as from the points along a capital/labor isoquant.

Since the use of tools and machinery makes labor more effective, rising _____ pushes up the productivity of labor, so a society that is more capital intensive tends to have a higher standard of living over the long run than one with low _____.

a. 4-4-5 Calendar
b. Weighted average cost of capital
c. Capital intensity
d. Cost of capital

29. _____ is one of the Accounting Liquidity ratios, a financial ratio. This ratio measures the number of times, on average, the inventory is sold during the period. Its purpose is to measure the liquidity of the inventory.
a. Inventory turnover Ratio
b. A Random Walk Down Wall Street
c. ABN Amro
d. AAB

30. _____ is one of the accounting liquidity ratios, a financial ratio. This ratio measures the number of times, on average, receivables (e.g. Accounts Receivable) are collected during the period. A popular variant of the _____ is to convert it into an Average Collection Period in terms of days.
a. Return on equity
b. Sharpe ratio
c. PEG ratio
d. Receivables turnover Ratio

31. In financial accounting, _____ , cash flow provided by operations or cash flow from operating activities, refers to the amount of cash a company generates from the revenues it brings in, excluding costs associated with long-term investment on capital items or investment in securities.

_____ = Cash generated from operations less taxation and interest paid, investment income received and less dividends paid gives rise to _____s per International Financial Reporting Standards.

To calculate cash generated from operations, one must calculate cash generated from customers and cash paid to suppliers.

a. Other Comprehensive Basis of Accounting
b. Operating cash flow
c. A Random Walk Down Wall Street
d. Appreciation

32. _____ is the difference between price and the costs of bringing to market whatever it is that is accounted as an enterprise (whether by harvest, extraction, manufacture, or purchase) in terms of the component costs of delivered goods and/or services and any operating or other expenses.

A key difficulty in measuring profit is in defining costs. Pure economic monetary profits can be zero or negative even in competitive equilibrium when accounted monetized costs exceed monetized price.

    a. Accounting profit
    b. AAB
    c. A Random Walk Down Wall Street
    d. Economic profit

33. _____, Net Margin, Net _____ or Net Profit Ratio all refer to a measure of profitability. It is calculated using a formula and written as a percentage or a number.

$$\text{Net profit margin} = \frac{\text{Net profit after taxes}}{\text{Net Sales}}$$

The _____ is mostly used for internal comparison.

    a. Profit maximization
    b. 4-4-5 Calendar
    c. Profit margin
    d. Net profit margin

34. _____ is the balance of the amounts of cash being received and paid by a business during a defined period of time, sometimes tied to a specific project. Measurement of _____ can be used

- to evaluate the state or performance of a business or project.
- to determine problems with liquidity. Being profitable does not necessarily mean being liquid. A company can fail because of a shortage of cash, even while profitable.
- to generate project rate of returns. The time of _____s into and out of projects are used as inputs to financial models such as internal rate of return, and net present value.
- to examine income or growth of a business when it is believed that accrual accounting concepts do not represent economic realities. Alternately, _____ can be used to 'validate' the net income generated by accrual accounting.

_____ as a generic term may be used differently depending on context, and certain _____ definitions may be adapted by analysts and users for their own uses. Common terms include operating _____ and free _____.

_____s can be classified into:

1. Operational _____s: Cash received or expended as a result of the company's core business activities.
2. Investment _____s: Cash received or expended through capital expenditure, investments or acquisitions.
3. Financing _____s: Cash received or expended as a result of financial activities, such as interests and dividends.

All three together - the net _____ - are necessary to reconcile the beginning cash balance to the ending cash balance. Loan draw downs or equity injections, that is just shifting of capital but no expenditure as such, are not considered in the net _____.

a. Shareholder value
c. Corporate finance
b. Real option
d. Cash flow

35. In finance, a _____ is collateral that the holder of a position in securities, options, or futures contracts has to deposit to cover the credit risk of his counterparty (most often his broker.) This risk can arise if the holder has done any of the following:

- borrowed cash from the counterparty to buy securities or options,
- sold securities or options short, or
- entered into a futures contract.

The collateral can be in the form of cash or securities, and it is deposited in a _____ account. On U.S. futures exchanges, '_____' was formally called performance bond.

_____ buying is buying securities with cash borrowed from a broker, using other securities as collateral.

a. Margin
c. Share
b. Credit
d. Procter ' Gamble

36. _____ is the price at which an asset would trade in a competitive Walrasian auction setting. _____ is often used interchangeably with open _____, fair value or fair _____, although these terms have distinct definitions in different standards, and may differ in some circumstances.

International Valuation Standards defines _____ as 'the estimated amount for which a property should exchange on the date of valuation between a willing buyer and a willing seller in an arm'e;s-length transaction after proper marketing wherein the parties had each acted knowledgeably, prudently, and without compulsion.'

_____ is a concept distinct from market price, which is 'e;the price at which one can transact'e;, while _____ is 'e;the true underlying value'e; according to theoretical standards.

a. Market value
c. T-Model
b. Wrap account
d. Debt restructuring

37. The _____ percentage shows how profitable a company's assets are in generating revenue.

_____ can be computed as:

$$ROA = \frac{\text{Net Income}}{\text{Total Assets}}$$

Chapter 3. Working with Financial Statements

This number tells you 'what the company can do with what it's got', i.e. how many dollars of earnings they derive from each dollar of assets they control. It's a useful number for comparing competing companies in the same industry.

a. Receivables turnover ratio
b. Return on assets
c. Return on sales
d. P/E ratio

38. _____ measures the rate of return on the ownership interest (shareholders' equity) of the common stock owners. _____ is viewed as one of the most important financial ratios. It measures a firm's efficiency at generating profits from every dollar of shareholders' equity (also known as net assets or assets minus liabilities.)
a. Return of capital
b. Return on sales
c. Diluted Earnings Per Share
d. Return on equity

39. The _____ is a financial ratio used to compare a company's book value to its current market price. Book value is an accounting term denoting the portion of the company held by the shareholders; in other words, the company's total tangible assets less its total liabilities. The calculation can be performed in two ways, but the result should be the same each way. In the first way, the company's market capitalization can be divided by the company's total book value from its balance sheet. The second way, using per-share values, is to divide the company's current share price by the book value per share (i.e. its book value divided by the number of outstanding shares).
a. Price-to-book ratio
b. Whisper numbers
c. Stop order
d. Stock repurchase

40. In business, _____ is the total assets minus total outside liabilities of an individual or a company. For a company, this is called shareholders' equity and may be referred to as book value. _____ is stated as at a particular point in time.
a. Moneylender
b. Net worth
c. Restructuring
d. Certified International Investment Analyst

41. In economics, business, and accounting, a _____ is the value of money that has been used up to produce something, and hence is not available for use anymore. In business, the _____ may be one of acquisition, in which case the amount of money expended to acquire it is counted as _____. In this case, money is the input that is gone in order to acquire the thing.
a. Fixed costs
b. Marginal cost
c. Sliding scale fees
d. Cost

42. _____, _____ includes the direct costs attributable to the production of the goods sold by a company. This amount includes the materials cost used in creating the goods along with the direct labor costs used to produce the good. It excludes indirect expenses such as distribution costs and sales force costs.
a. Net profit
b. Goodwill
c. Cost of goods sold
d. Deferred financing costs

43. A _____ is a payment made by a corporation to its shareholder members. When a corporation earns a profit or surplus, that money can be put to two uses: it can either be re-invested in the business (called retained earnings), or it can be paid to the shareholders as a _____. Many corporations retain a portion of their earnings and pay the remainder as a _____.

Chapter 3. Working with Financial Statements

a. Dividend puzzle
c. Dividend yield
b. Special dividend
d. Dividend

44. _____ is the fraction of net income a firm pays to its stockholders in dividends:

$$\text{Dividend Payout Ratio} = \frac{\text{Dividends}}{\text{Net Income}}$$

The part of the earnings not paid to investors is left for investment to provide for future earnings growth. Investors seeking high current income and limited capital growth prefer companies with high _____. However investors seeking capital growth may prefer lower payout ratio because capital gains are taxed at a lower rate.

a. Dividend imputation
c. Dividend yield
b. Dividend puzzle
d. Dividend payout ratio

45. In the theory of capital structure, _____ is the phrase used to describe funds that firms obtain from outside of the firm. It is contrasted to internal financing which consists mainly of profits retained by the firm for investment. There are many kinds of _____.

a. Asset-backed commercial paper
c. Ownership equity
b. Adjustment
d. External financing

46. _____ or financing is to provide capital (funds), which means money for a project, a person, a business or any other private or public institutions.

Those funds can be allocated for either short term or long term purposes. The health fund is a new way of _____ private healthcare centers.

a. Product life cycle
c. Funding
b. Proxy fight
d. Synthetic CDO

47. In the theory of capital structure _____ is the name for a firm using its profits as a source of capital for new investment, rather than a) distributing them to firm's owners or other investors and b) obtaining capital elsewhere. It is to be contrasted with external financing which consists of new money from outside of the firm brought in for investment. _____ is generally thought to be less expensive for the firm than external financing because the firm does not have to incur transaction costs to obtain it, nor does it have to pay the taxes associated with paying dividends.

a. Operating ratio
c. Employee stock option
b. Underwriting contract
d. Internal financing

48. _____ indicates the percentage of a company's earnings that are not paid out in dividends but credited to retained earnings. It is the opposite of the dividend payout ratio, so that also called the retention rate.

_____ = 1 - Dividend Payout Ratio

a. Dow Jones Indexes
c. Retention ratio
b. Fair market value
d. Bankassurer

49. _____ is the maximum rate at which a company can grow revenue without having to invest new equity capital. If a company earns a 15% return on equity (ROE), it can grow 15% simply by reinvesting all the earnings in new opportunities and maintaining a stable debt to equity ratio. In order to grow faster, the company would have to invest more equity capital or increase its financial leverage.
   a. Sustainable growth rate
   b. Current ratio
   c. Return on capital employed
   d. Price/cash flow ratio

50. In finance, a _____ is a debt security, in which the authorized issuer owes the holders a debt and, depending on the terms of the _____, is obliged to pay interest (the coupon) and/or to repay the principal at a later date, termed maturity.

Thus a _____ is a loan: the issuer is the borrower, the _____ holder is the lender, and the coupon is the interest. _____s provide the borrower with external funds to finance long-term investments, or, in the case of government _____s, to finance current expenditure.

   a. Bond
   b. Puttable bond
   c. Catastrophe bonds
   d. Convertible bond

51. _____ refinancing (in the case of real property) occurs when a loan is taken out on property already owned, and the loan amount is above and beyond the cost of transaction, payoff of existing liens, and related expenses.

Strictly speaking all refinancing of debt is '_____', when funds retrieved are utilized for anything other than repaying an existing lien.

In the case of common usage of the term, _____ refinancing refers to when equity is liquidated from a property above and beyond sum of the payoff of existing loans held in lien on the property, loan fees, costs associated with the loan, taxes, insurance, tax reserves, insurance reserves, and in the past any other non-lien debt held in the name of the owner being paid by loan proceeds.

   a. Cash-out
   b. Home equity line of credit
   c. Conforming loan
   d. Fixed rate mortgage

52. _____ represents the impact on the stock price that investors would cause in reaction to a change in policy of a company.
   a. Trade date
   b. Volatility clustering
   c. Bonus share
   d. Clientele effect

53. The _____ is an expected return that the provider of capital plans to earn on their investment.

Capital (money) used for funding a business should earn returns for the capital providers who risk their capital. For an investment to be worthwhile, the expected return on capital must be greater than the _____.

   a. Weighted average cost of capital
   b. 4-4-5 Calendar
   c. Capital intensity
   d. Cost of capital

Chapter 3. Working with Financial Statements

54. _____ is a 'policy by which management devotes its time to investigating only those situations in which actual results differ significantly from planned results. The idea is that management should spend its valuable time concentrating on the more important items (such as shaping the company's future strategic course.) Attention is given only to material deviations requiring investigation.'

It is not entirely synonymous with the concept of exception management in that it describes a policy where absolute focus is on exception management, in contrast to moderate application of exception management.

a. Cash cow
b. Corporate Transparency
c. Management by exception
d. Performance measurement

55. _____ is the practice of comparing a firm's results to those of similar companies or competitors.
a. False billing
b. Peer group analysis
c. Capital guarantee
d. Trade date

56. The _____ or _____ is used by business and government to classify and measure economic activity in Canada, Mexico and the United States. It has largely replaced the older Standard Industrial Classification (SIC) system; however, certain government departments and agencies, such as the U.S. Securities and Exchange Commission (SEC), still use the SIC codes.

The _____ numbering system is a six-digit code.

a. 529 plan
b. 7-Eleven
c. 4-4-5 Calendar
d. North American Industry Classification System

57. The _____ is a United States government system for classifying industries by a four-digit code. Established in 1937, it is being supplanted by the six-digit North American Industry Classification System, which was released in 1997; however certain government departments and agencies, such as the U.S. Securities and Exchange Commission (SEC), still use the _____ codes.

The following table is from the SEC's site, which allows searching for companies by _____ code in its database of filings.

a. 529 plan
b. 7-Eleven
c. 4-4-5 Calendar
d. Standard Industrial Classification

58. _____ are financial statements that factor the holding company's subsidiaries into its aggregated accounting figure. It is a representation of how the holding company is doing as a group. The consolidated accounts should provide a true and fair view of the financial and operating conditions of the group.
a. Treynor ratio
b. Consolidated financial statements
c. Fund Accounting
d. Net operating profit after tax

59. _____ is the standard framework of guidelines for financial accounting used in the United States of America. It includes the standards, conventions, and rules accountants follow in recording and summarizing transactions, and in the preparation of financial statements. _____ are now issued by the Financial Accounting Standards Board (FASB).

a. Generally accepted accounting principles   b. Revenue
c. Depreciation   d. Net income

60. _____ is the task of determining how a business will afford to achieve its strategic goals and objectives. Usually, a company creates a Financial Plan immediately after the vision and objectives have been set. The Financial Plan describes each of the activities, resources, equipment and materials that are needed to achieve these objectives, as well as the timeframes involved.

a. Corporate Transparency   b. Financial planning
c. Management by exception   d. Performance measurement

Chapter 4. Introduction to Valuation: The Time Value of Money

1. The institution most often referenced by the word '_____' is a public or publicly traded _____, the shares of which are traded on a public stock exchange (e.g., the New York Stock Exchange or Nasdaq in the United States) where shares of stock of _____s are bought and sold by and to the general public. Most of the largest businesses in the world are publicly traded _____s. However, the majority of _____s are said to be closely held, privately held or close _____s, meaning that no ready market exists for the trading of shares.
   a. Corporation
   b. Depository Trust Company
   c. Federal Home Loan Mortgage Corporation
   d. Protect

2. A _____ is a fungible, negotiable instrument representing financial value. They are broadly categorized into debt securities (such as banknotes, bonds and debentures), and equity securities; e.g., common stocks. The company or other entity issuing the _____ is called the issuer.
   a. Book entry
   b. Tracking stock
   c. Securities lending
   d. Security

3. In finance, the value of an option consists of two components, its intrinsic value and its _____. Time value is simply the difference between option value and intrinsic value. _____ is also known as theta, extrinsic value, or instrumental value.
   a. Global Squeeze
   b. Conservatism
   c. Debt buyer
   d. Time value

4. Simply put, _____ is the value of money figuring in a given amount of interest for a given amount of time. For example 100 dollars of todays money held for a year at 5 percent interest is worth 105 dollars, therefore 100 dollars paid now or 105 dollars paid exactly one year from now is the same amount of payment of money with that given intersest at that given amount of time. This notion dates at least to Martín de Azpilcueta of the School of Salamanca.

   All of the standard calculations for _____ derive from the most basic algebraic expression for the present value of a future sum, 'discounted' to the present by an amount equal to the _____. For example, a sum of FV to be received in one year is discounted (at the rate of interest r) to give a sum of PV at present: PV = FV -- r·PV = FV/(1+r).

   a. Coefficient of variation
   b. Current account
   c. Zero-coupon bond
   d. Time value of money

5. _____ is that which is owed; usually referencing assets owed, but the term can cover other obligations. In the case of assets, _____ is a means of using future purchasing power in the present before a summation has been earned. Some companies and corporations use _____ as a part of their overall corporate finance strategy.
   a. Cross-collateralization
   b. Credit cycle
   c. Partial Payment
   d. Debt

6. _____ measures the nominal future sum of money that a given sum of money is 'worth' at a specified time in the future assuming a certain interest rate rate of return; it is the present value multiplied by the accumulation function.

The value does not include corrections for inflation or other factors that affect the true value of money in the future. This is used in time value of money calculations.

a. Discounted cash flow
c. Future-oriented
b. Future value
d. Present value of costs

7. _____ or financing is to provide capital (funds), which means money for a project, a person, a business or any other private or public institutions.

Those funds can be allocated for either short term or long term purposes. The health fund is a new way of _____ private healthcare centers.

a. Synthetic CDO
c. Product life cycle
b. Proxy fight
d. Funding

8. An _____ is an economic concept that relates to the cost incurred by an entity (such as organizations) associated with problems such as divergent management-shareholder objectives and information asymmetry. The costs consist of two main sources:

1. The costs inherently associated with using an agent (e.g., the risk that agents will use organizational resource for their own benefit) and
2. The costs of techniques used to mitigate the problems associated with using an agent (e.g., the costs of producing financial statements or the use of stock options to align executive interests to shareholder interests.)

Though effects of _____ are present in any agency relationship, the term is most used in business contexts.

The information asymmetry that exists between shareholders and the Chief Executive Officer is generally considered to be a classic example of a principal-agent problem. The agent (the manager) is working on behalf of the principal (the shareholders), who does not observe the actions of the agent.

a. ABN Amro
c. A Random Walk Down Wall Street
b. AAB
d. Agency cost

9. In economics, business, and accounting, a _____ is the value of money that has been used up to produce something, and hence is not available for use anymore. In business, the _____ may be one of acquisition, in which case the amount of money expended to acquire it is counted as _____. In this case, money is the input that is gone in order to acquire the thing.

a. Fixed costs
c. Marginal cost
b. Sliding scale fees
d. Cost

10. _____ is the concept of adding accumulated interest back to the principal, so that interest is earned on interest from that moment on. The act of declaring interest to be principal is called compounding (i.e., interest is compounded.) A loan, for example, may have its interest compounded every month: in this case, a loan with $100 principal and 1% interest per month would have a balance of $101 at the end of the first month.

a. Risk management
c. Compound interest
b. Penny stock
d. 4-4-5 Calendar

Chapter 4. Introduction to Valuation: The Time Value of Money

11. _____ is a fee paid on borrowed assets. It is the price paid for the use of borrowed money, or, money earned by deposited funds. Assets that are sometimes lent with _____ include money, shares, consumer goods through hire purchase, major assets such as aircraft, and even entire factories in finance lease arrangements.
    a. A Random Walk Down Wall Street
    b. Insolvency
    c. Interest
    d. AAB

12. The terms _____, nominal _____, and effective _____ describe the interest rate for a whole year (annualized), rather than just a monthly fee/rate, as applied on a loan, mortgage, credit card, etc. Those terms have formal, legal definitions in some countries or legal jurisdictions, but in general:

    - The nominal _____ is the simple-interest rate (for a year.)
    - The effective _____ is the fee+compound interest rate (calculated across a year.)

    The nominal _____ is calculated as: the rate, for a payment period, multiplied by the number of payment periods in a year. However, the exact legal definition of 'effective _____' can vary greatly in each jurisdiction, depending on the type of fees included, such as participation fees, loan origination fees, monthly service charges, or late fees. The effective _____ has been called the 'mathematically-true' interest rate for each year. The computation for the effective _____, as the fee+compound interest rate, can also vary depending on whether the up-front fees, such as origination or participation fees, are added to the entire amount, or treated as a short-term loan due in the first payment.

    a. A Random Walk Down Wall Street
    b. AAB
    c. ABN Amro
    d. Annual percentage rate

13. A '_____' is a 'Charge' that is paid to obtain the right to delay a payment. Essentially, the payer purchases the right to make a given payment in the future instead of in the Present. The '_____', or 'Charge' that must be paid to delay the payment, is simply the difference between what the payment amount would be if it were paid in the present and what the payment amount would be paid if it were paid in the future.
    a. Value at risk
    b. Risk modeling
    c. Risk aversion
    d. Discount

14. In economics, the _____ is the proposition by Irving Fisher that the real interest rate is independent of monetary measures, especially the nominal interest rate. The Fisher equation is

    $r_r = r_n >- >\pi^e$.

    This means, the real interest rate (r_r) equals the nominal interest rate (r_n) minus expected rate of inflation ($>\pi^e$.) Here all the rates are continuously compounded.

    a. 4-4-5 Calendar
    b. 529 plan
    c. Fisher hypothesis
    d. 7-Eleven

15. _____ is the value on a given date of a future payment or series of future payments, discounted to reflect the time value of money and other factors such as investment risk. _____ calculations are widely used in business and economics to provide a means to compare cash flows at different times on a meaningful 'like to like' basis.

The most commonly applied model of the time value of money is compound interest.

a. Present value of benefits
b. Negative gearing
c. Net present value
d. Present value

16. The _____, P(T), is the number which a future cash flow, to be received at time T, must be multiplied by in order to obtain the current present value. Thus, a fixed annually compounded discount rate is

$$P(T) = \frac{1}{(1+r)^T}$$

For fixed continuously compounded discount rate we have

$$P(T) = e^{-rT}$$

For discounts in marketing, see discounts and allowances, sales promotion, and pricing.

a. Risk premium
b. Discount
c. Risk modeling
d. Discount factor

17. The _____ is an interest rate a central bank charges depository institutions that borrow reserves from it.

The term _____ has two meanings:

- the same as interest rate; the term 'discount' does not refer to the meaning of the word, but to the purpose of using the quantity, such as computations of present value, e.g. net present value / discounted cash flow

- the annual effective _____, which is the annual interest divided by the capital including that interest; this rate is lower than the interest rate; it corresponds to using the value after a year as the nominal value, and seeing the initial value as the nominal value minus a discount; it is used for Treasury Bills and similar financial instruments

The annual effective _____ is the annual interest divided by the capital including that interest, which is the interest rate divided by 100% plus the interest rate. It is the annual discount factor to be applied to the future cash flow, to find the discount, subtracted from a future value to find the value one year earlier.

For example, suppose there is a government bond that sells for $95 and pays $100 in a year's time.

a. Discount rate
b. Fisher equation
c. Black-Scholes
d. Stochastic volatility

Chapter 4. Introduction to Valuation: The Time Value of Money

18. In finance, the _____ approach describes a method of valuing a project, company, or asset using the concepts of the time value of money. All future cash flows are estimated and discounted to give their present values. The discount rate used is generally the appropriate cost of capital and may incorporate judgments of the uncertainty (riskiness) of the future cash flows.
   a. Present value of benefits
   b. Net present value
   c. Discounted cash flow
   d. Future-oriented

19. _____ is the balance of the amounts of cash being received and paid by a business during a defined period of time, sometimes tied to a specific project. Measurement of _____ can be used

   - to evaluate the state or performance of a business or project.
   - to determine problems with liquidity. Being profitable does not necessarily mean being liquid. A company can fail because of a shortage of cash, even while profitable.
   - to generate project rate of returns. The time of _____s into and out of projects are used as inputs to financial models such as internal rate of return, and net present value.
   - to examine income or growth of a business when it is believed that accrual accounting concepts do not represent economic realities. Alternately, _____ can be used to 'validate' the net income generated by accrual accounting.

   _____ as a generic term may be used differently depending on context, and certain _____ definitions may be adapted by analysts and users for their own uses. Common terms include operating _____ and free _____.

   _____s can be classified into:

   1. Operational _____s: Cash received or expended as a result of the company's core business activities.
   2. Investment _____s: Cash received or expended through capital expenditure, investments or acquisitions.
   3. Financing _____s: Cash received or expended as a result of financial activities, such as interests and dividends.

   All three together - the net _____ - are necessary to reconcile the beginning cash balance to the ending cash balance. Loan draw downs or equity injections, that is just shifting of capital but no expenditure as such, are not considered in the net _____.

   a. Shareholder value
   b. Real option
   c. Corporate finance
   d. Cash flow

20. In finance, _____ is the process of estimating the potential market value of a financial asset or liability. they can be done on assets (for example, investments in marketable securities such as stocks, options, business enterprises, or intangible assets such as patents and trademarks) or on liabilities (e.g., Bonds issued by a company.) _____s are required in many contexts including investment analysis, capital budgeting, merger and acquisition transactions, financial reporting, taxable events to determine the proper tax liability, and in litigation.
   a. Share
   b. Valuation
   c. Procter ' Gamble
   d. Margin

21. An _____ can be defined as a contract which provides an income stream in return for an initial payment.

Chapter 4. Introduction to Valuation: The Time Value of Money

An immediate _____ is an _____ for which the time between the contract date and the date of the first payment is not longer than the time interval between payments. A common use for an immediate _____ is to provide a pension to a retired person or persons.

a. Amortization
c. Intrinsic value

b. AT'T Inc.
d. Annuity

22. In finance, _____, also known as return on investment is the ratio of money gained or lost on an investment relative to the amount of money invested. The amount of money gained or lost may be referred to as interest, profit/loss, gain/loss, or net income/loss. The money invested may be referred to as the asset, capital, principal, or the cost basis of the investment.

a. Composiition of Creditors
c. Stock or scrip dividends

b. Doctrine of the Proper Law
d. Rate of return

23. _____ is the process of decreasing an amount over a period of time. The word comes from Middle English amortisen to kill, alienate in mortmain, from Anglo-French amorteser, alteration of amortir, from Vulgar Latin admortire to kill, from Latin ad- + mort-, mors death. Particular instances of the term include:

- _____ (business), the allocation of a lump sum amount to different time periods, particularly for loans and other forms of finance, including related interest or other finance charges.
    - _____ schedule, a table detailing each periodic payment on a loan (typically a mortgage), as generated by an _____ calculator.
    - Negative _____, an _____ schedule where the loan amount actually increases through not paying the full interest
- Amortized analysis, analyzing the execution cost of algorithms over a sequence of operations.
- _____ of capital expenditures of certain assets under accounting rules, particularly intangible assets, in a manner analogous to depreciation.
- _____ (tax law)

_____ is also used in the context of zoning regulations and describes the time in which a property owner has to relocate when the property's use constitutes a preexisting nonconforming use under zoning regulations.

- Depreciation

a. Amortization
c. AT'T Inc.

b. Intrinsic value
d. Option

24. The U.S. _____ is an independent agency of the United States government which holds primary responsibility for enforcing the federal securities laws and regulating the securities industry, the nation's stock and options exchanges, and other electronic securities markets. The SEC was created by section 4 of the SEC of 1934 (now codified as 15 U.S.C. Â§ 78d and commonly referred to as the 1934 Act.)

a. 529 plan
c. 4-4-5 Calendar

b. 7-Eleven
d. Securities and Exchange Commission

Chapter 5. Discounted Cash Flow Valuation

1. In finance, the _____ approach describes a method of valuing a project, company, or asset using the concepts of the time value of money. All future cash flows are estimated and discounted to give their present values. The discount rate used is generally the appropriate cost of capital and may incorporate judgments of the uncertainty (riskiness) of the future cash flows.

   a. Discounted cash flow
   b. Net present value
   c. Future-oriented
   d. Present value of benefits

2. _____ or financing is to provide capital (funds), which means money for a project, a person, a business or any other private or public institutions.

   Those funds can be allocated for either short term or long term purposes. The health fund is a new way of _____ private healthcare centers.

   a. Funding
   b. Proxy fight
   c. Product life cycle
   d. Synthetic CDO

3. _____ measures the nominal future sum of money that a given sum of money is 'worth' at a specified time in the future assuming a certain interest rate rate of return; it is the present value multiplied by the accumulation function.

   The value does not include corrections for inflation or other factors that affect the true value of money in the future. This is used in time value of money calculations.

   a. Present value of costs
   b. Future value
   c. Discounted cash flow
   d. Future-oriented

4. _____ is the balance of the amounts of cash being received and paid by a business during a defined period of time, sometimes tied to a specific project. Measurement of _____ can be used

   - to evaluate the state or performance of a business or project.
   - to determine problems with liquidity. Being profitable does not necessarily mean being liquid. A company can fail because of a shortage of cash, even while profitable.
   - to generate project rate of returns. The time of _____s into and out of projects are used as inputs to financial models such as internal rate of return, and net present value.
   - to examine income or growth of a business when it is believed that accrual accounting concepts do not represent economic realities. Alternately, _____ can be used to 'validate' the net income generated by accrual accounting.

   _____ as a generic term may be used differently depending on context, and certain _____ definitions may be adapted by analysts and users for their own uses. Common terms include operating _____ and free _____.

_____s can be classified into:

1. Operational _____s: Cash received or expended as a result of the company's core business activities.
2. Investment _____s: Cash received or expended through capital expenditure, investments or acquisitions.
3. Financing _____s: Cash received or expended as a result of financial activities, such as interests and dividends.

All three together - the net _____ - are necessary to reconcile the beginning cash balance to the ending cash balance. Loan draw downs or equity injections, that is just shifting of capital but no expenditure as such, are not considered in the net _____.

    a. Shareholder value   b. Real option
    c. Corporate finance   d. Cash flow

5. In finance, _____ is the process of estimating the potential market value of a financial asset or liability. they can be done on assets (for example, investments in marketable securities such as stocks, options, business enterprises, or intangible assets such as patents and trademarks) or on liabilities (e.g., Bonds issued by a company.) _____s are required in many contexts including investment analysis, capital budgeting, merger and acquisition transactions, financial reporting, taxable events to determine the proper tax liability, and in litigation.
    a. Valuation   b. Share
    c. Margin   d. Procter ' Gamble

6. _____ is the value on a given date of a future payment or series of future payments, discounted to reflect the time value of money and other factors such as investment risk. _____ calculations are widely used in business and economics to provide a means to compare cash flows at different times on a meaningful 'like to like' basis.

The most commonly applied model of the time value of money is compound interest.

    a. Present value of benefits   b. Net present value
    c. Negative gearing   d. Present value

7. The terms _____ , nominal _____ , and effective _____ describe the interest rate for a whole year (annualized), rather than just a monthly fee/rate, as applied on a loan, mortgage, credit card, etc. Those terms have formal, legal definitions in some countries or legal jurisdictions, but in general:

- The nominal _____ is the simple-interest rate (for a year.)
- The effective _____ is the fee+compound interest rate (calculated across a year.)

Chapter 5. Discounted Cash Flow Valuation

The nominal _____ is calculated as: the rate, for a payment period, multiplied by the number of payment periods in a year. However, the exact legal definition of 'effective _____' can vary greatly in each jurisdiction, depending on the type of fees included, such as participation fees, loan origination fees, monthly service charges, or late fees. The effective _____ has been called the 'mathematically-true' interest rate for each year. The computation for the effective _____, as the fee+compound interest rate, can also vary depending on whether the up-front fees, such as origination or participation fees, are added to the entire amount, or treated as a short-term loan due in the first payment.

a. AAB
b. A Random Walk Down Wall Street
c. ABN Amro
d. Annual percentage rate

8. An _____ can be defined as a contract which provides an income stream in return for an initial payment.

An immediate _____ is an _____ for which the time between the contract date and the date of the first payment is not longer than the time interval between payments. A common use for an immediate _____ is to provide a pension to a retired person or persons.

a. Intrinsic value
b. Annuity
c. AT'T Inc.
d. Amortization

9. _____ is the process of decreasing an amount over a period of time. The word comes from Middle English amortisen to kill, alienate in mortmain, from Anglo-French amorteser, alteration of amortir, from Vulgar Latin admortire to kill, from Latin ad- + mort-, mors death. Particular instances of the term include:

- _____ (business), the allocation of a lump sum amount to different time periods, particularly for loans and other forms of finance, including related interest or other finance charges.
    - _____ schedule, a table detailing each periodic payment on a loan (typically a mortgage), as generated by an _____ calculator.
    - Negative _____, an _____ schedule where the loan amount actually increases through not paying the full interest
- Amortized analysis, analyzing the execution cost of algorithms over a sequence of operations.
- _____ of capital expenditures of certain assets under accounting rules, particularly intangible assets, in a manner analogous to depreciation.
- _____ (tax law)

_____ is also used in the context of zoning regulations and describes the time in which a property owner has to relocate when the property's use constitutes a preexisting nonconforming use under zoning regulations.

- Depreciation

a. Amortization
b. Intrinsic value
c. AT'T Inc.
d. Option

10. _____ is a fee paid on borrowed assets. It is the price paid for the use of borrowed money, or, money earned by deposited funds. Assets that are sometimes lent with _____ include money, shares, consumer goods through hire purchase, major assets such as aircraft, and even entire factories in finance lease arrangements.

a. A Random Walk Down Wall Street
b. Insolvency
c. AAB
d. Interest

11. An _____ is the price a borrower pays for the use of money they do not own, and the return a lender receives for deferring the use of funds, by lending it to the borrower. _____s are normally expressed as a percentage rate over the period of one year.

_____s targets are also a vital tool of monetary policy and are used to control variables like investment, inflation, and unemployment.

a. AAB
b. ABN Amro
c. A Random Walk Down Wall Street
d. Interest rate

12. In economics, the _____ is the proposition by Irving Fisher that the real interest rate is independent of monetary measures, especially the nominal interest rate. The Fisher equation is

$r_r = r_n >- >\pi^e$.

This means, the real interest rate (r_r) equals the nominal interest rate (r_n) minus expected rate of inflation ($>\pi^e$.) Here all the rates are continuously compounded.

a. Fisher hypothesis
b. 7-Eleven
c. 4-4-5 Calendar
d. 529 plan

13. A _____ is a contract entered into between which regulates the terms of a loan. they usually relate to loans of cash, but market specific contracts are also used to regulate securities lending.

They are usually in written form, but there is no legal reason why a _____ cannot be a purely oral contract (although in some countries this may be limited by the Statute of frauds or equivalent legislation).

a. Lien
b. Loan agreement
c. Royalties
d. Foreclosure

14. A _____ is an annuity in which the periodic payments begin on a fixed date and continue indefinitely. It is sometimes referred to as a perpetual annuity. Fixed coupon payments on permanently invested (irredeemable) sums of money are prime examples of these. Scholarships paid perpetually from an endowment fit the definition of _____.

a. Current yield
b. LIBOR market model
c. Stochastic volatility
d. Perpetuity

Chapter 5. Discounted Cash Flow Valuation

15. A _____ is an exchange of promises between two or more parties to do an act which is enforceable in a court of law. It is where an unqualified offer meets a qualified acceptance and the parties reach Consensus ad Idem. The parties must have the necessary capacity to _____ and the _____ must not be either trifling, indeterminate, impossible or illegal.
   a. 529 plan
   b. 4-4-5 Calendar
   c. Contract
   d. 7-Eleven

16. _____ is the concept of adding accumulated interest back to the principal, so that interest is earned on interest from that moment on. The act of declaring interest to be principal is called compounding (i.e., interest is compounded.) A loan, for example, may have its interest compounded every month: in this case, a loan with $100 principal and 1% interest per month would have a balance of $101 at the end of the first month.
   a. 4-4-5 Calendar
   b. Risk management
   c. Penny stock
   d. Compound interest

17. The _____, effective annual interest rate, Annual Equivalent Rate (AER) or simply effective rate is the interest rate on a loan or financial product restated from the nominal interest rate as an interest rate with annual compound interest. It is used to compare the annual interest between loans with different compounding terms (daily, monthly, annually, or other.)

The _____ differs in two important respects from the annual percentage rate (APR):

   1. the _____ generally does not incorporate one-time charges such as front-end fees;
   2. the _____ is (generally) not defined by legal or regulatory authorities (as APR is in many jurisdictions.)

By contrast, the 'effective APR' is used as a legal term, where front-fees and other costs can be included, as defined by local law.

Annual Percentage Yield or effective annual yield is the analogous concept used for savings or investment products, such as a certificate of deposit.

   a. ABN Amro
   b. Effective interest rate
   c. AAB
   d. A Random Walk Down Wall Street

18. _____ is typically a higher ranking stock than voting shares, and its terms are negotiated between the corporation and the investor.

_____ usually carry no voting rights, but may carry superior priority over common stock in the payment of dividends and upon liquidation. _____ may carry a dividend that is paid out prior to any dividends to common stock holders.

   a. Follow-on offering
   b. Trade-off theory
   c. Preferred stock
   d. Second lien loan

Chapter 5. Discounted Cash Flow Valuation

19. _____ are those dividends paid out in form of additional stock shares of the issuing corporation or other corporation They are usually issued in proportion to shares owned (for example for every 100 shares of stock owned, 5% stock dividend will yield 5 extra shares). If this payment involves the issue of new shares, this is very similar to a stock split in that it increases the total number of shares while lowering the price of each share and does not change the market capitalization or the total value of the shares held
   a. Stock or scrip dividends
   b. Time-based currency
   c. The Hong Kong Securities Institute
   d. Database auditing

20. A _____ is a payment made by a corporation to its shareholder members. When a corporation earns a profit or surplus, that money can be put to two uses: it can either be re-invested in the business (called retained earnings), or it can be paid to the shareholders as a _____. Many corporations retain a portion of their earnings and pay the remainder as a _____.
   a. Special dividend
   b. Dividend yield
   c. Dividend
   d. Dividend puzzle

21. A _____ is a small, short-term loan that is intended to cover a borrower's expenses until his or her next payday. The loans are also sometimes referred to as cash advances, though that term can also refer to cash provided against a prearranged line of credit such as a credit card Legislation regarding _____s varies widely between different countries and, within the USA, between different states.
   a. Payday loan
   b. 4-4-5 Calendar
   c. 529 plan
   d. 7-Eleven

22. _____ mature in one year or less. Like zero-coupon bonds, they do not pay interest prior to maturity; instead they are sold at a discount of the par value to create a positive yield to maturity. Many regard _____ as the least risky investment available to U.S. investors.
   a. Treasury bills
   b. Treasury securities
   c. 4-4-5 Calendar
   d. Treasury Inflation Protected Securities

23. A '_____' is a 'Charge' that is paid to obtain the right to delay a payment. Essentially, the payer purchases the right to make a given payment in the future instead of in the Present. The '_____', or 'Charge' that must be paid to delay the payment, is simply the difference between what the payment amount would be if it were paid in the present and what the payment amount would be paid if it were paid in the future.
   a. Discount
   b. Risk aversion
   c. Value at risk
   d. Risk modeling

24. An _____ is a loan in which for a set term the borrower pays only the interest on the principal balance, with the principal balance unchanged. At the end of the interest-only term the borrower may enter an interest-only mortgage, pay the principal, or (with some lenders) convert the loan to a principal and interest payment (or amortized) loan at his/her option.

In the United States, a five- or ten-year interest-only period is typical.

   a. Interest-only Loan
   b. AAB
   c. ABN Amro
   d. A Random Walk Down Wall Street

25. An _____ is a table detailing each periodic payment on a amortizing loan (typically a mortgage), as generated by an amortization calculator.

While a portion of every payment is applied towards both the interest and the principal balance of the loan, the exact amount applied to principal each time varies (with the remainder going to interest.) An _____ reveals the specific monetary amount put towards interest, as well as the specific put towards the Principal balance, with each payment.

- a. Adjusted basis
- b. Annual report
- c. Amortization schedule
- d. Adjusting entries

26. In financial accounting, the term _____ is most commonly used to describe any part of shareholders' equity, except for basic share capital. Sometimes, the term is used instead of the term provision; such a use, however, is inconsistent with the terminology suggested by International Accounting Standards Board. For more information about provisions, see provision (accounting.)
- a. Closing entries
- b. Treasury stock
- c. FIFO and LIFO accounting
- d. Reserve

27. The phrase _____ or bullet payment refers to one of two ways for repaying a loan; the other type is called amortizing payment or Amortization (business).

With a balloon loan, a _____ is paid back when the loan comes to its contractual maturity, e.g. reaches the deadline set to repayment at the time the loan was granted, representing the full loan amount (also called principal.) Periodic interest payments are generally made throughout the life of the loan.

- a. Refinancing risk
- b. Present value of costs
- c. Future-oriented
- d. Balloon payment

28. In banking and finance, a _____ is a loan where a payment of the entire principal of the loan, and sometimes the principal and interest, is due at the end of the loan term. Likewise for bullet bond. A _____ can be a mortgage, bond, note or any other type of credit.
- a. Modern portfolio theory
- b. Bear raid
- c. Bankruptcy remote
- d. Bullet loan

Chapter 6. Interest Rates and Bond Valuation

1. A _____ is an international bond that is denominated in a currency not native to the country where it is issued. It can be categorised according to the currency in which it is issued. London is one of the centers of the _____ market, but _____s may be traded throughout the world - for example in Singapore or Tokyo.

   a. Eurobond
   b. Interest rate option
   c. Education production function
   d. Economic entity

2. In finance, a _____ is a debt security, in which the authorized issuer owes the holders a debt and, depending on the terms of the _____, is obliged to pay interest (the coupon) and/or to repay the principal at a later date, termed maturity.

   Thus a _____ is a loan: the issuer is the borrower, the _____ holder is the lender, and the coupon is the interest. _____s provide the borrower with external funds to finance long-term investments, or, in the case of government _____s, to finance current expenditure.

   a. Catastrophe bonds
   b. Puttable bond
   c. Convertible bond
   d. Bond

3. The coupon or _____ of a bond is the amount of interest paid per year expressed as a percentage of the face value of the bond.

   For example if you hold $10,000 nominal of a bond described as a 4.5% loan stock, you will receive $450 in interest each year (probably in two installments of $225 each.)

   Not all bonds have coupons.

   a. Zero-coupon bond
   b. Revenue bonds
   c. Puttable bond
   d. Coupon rate

4. _____ is a fee paid on borrowed assets. It is the price paid for the use of borrowed money, or, money earned by deposited funds. Assets that are sometimes lent with _____ include money, shares, consumer goods through hire purchase, major assets such as aircraft, and even entire factories in finance lease arrangements.

   a. Insolvency
   b. AAB
   c. Interest
   d. A Random Walk Down Wall Street

5. An _____ is the price a borrower pays for the use of money they do not own, and the return a lender receives for deferring the use of funds, by lending it to the borrower. _____s are normally expressed as a percentage rate over the period of one year.

   _____s targets are also a vital tool of monetary policy and are used to control variables like investment, inflation, and unemployment.

   a. AAB
   b. ABN Amro
   c. A Random Walk Down Wall Street
   d. Interest rate

6. An _____ is a loan in which for a set term the borrower pays only the interest on the principal balance, with the principal balance unchanged. At the end of the interest-only term the borrower may enter an interest-only mortgage, pay the principal, or (with some lenders) convert the loan to a principal and interest payment (or amortized) loan at his/her option.

Chapter 6. Interest Rates and Bond Valuation

In the United States, a five- or ten-year interest-only period is typical.

a. AAB
c. ABN Amro
b. A Random Walk Down Wall Street
d. Interest-only loan

7. _____ is a life of security. It may also refer to the final payment date of a loan or other financial instrument, at which point all remaining interest and principal is due to be paid.

1, 3, 6 months _____ band can be calculated by using 30-day per month periods.

a. Maturity
c. False billing
b. Replacement cost
d. Primary market

8. _____, in finance and accounting, means stated value or face value. From this comes the expressions at par (at the _____), over par (over _____) and under par (under _____.)

The term '_____' has several meanings depending on context and geography.

a. FIDC
c. Par value
b. Sinking fund
d. Global Squeeze

9. In finance, the term _____ describes the amount in cash that returns to the owners of a security. Normally it does not include the price variations, at the difference of the total return. _____ applies to various stated rates of return on stocks (common and preferred, and convertible), fixed income instruments (bonds, notes, bills, strips, zero coupon), and some other investment type insurance products (e.g. annuities.)

a. 4-4-5 Calendar
c. Macaulay duration
b. Yield to maturity
d. Yield

10. The _____ or redemption yield is the yield promised to the bondholder on the assumption that the bond or other fixed-interest security such as gilts will be held to maturity, that all coupon and principal payments will be made and coupon payments are reinvested at the bond's promised yield at the same rate as invested. It is a measure of the return of the bond. This technique in theory allows investors to calculate the fair value of different financial instruments.

a. 4-4-5 Calendar
c. Macaulay duration
b. Yield
d. Yield to maturity

11. The terms _____ , nominal _____, and effective _____ describe the interest rate for a whole year (annualized), rather than just a monthly fee/rate, as applied on a loan, mortgage, credit card, etc. Those terms have formal, legal definitions in some countries or legal jurisdictions, but in general:

- The nominal _____ is the simple-interest rate (for a year.)
- The effective _____ is the fee+compound interest rate (calculated across a year.)

The nominal _____ is calculated as: the rate, for a payment period, multiplied by the number of payment periods in a year. However, the exact legal definition of 'effective _____' can vary greatly in each jurisdiction, depending on the type of fees included, such as participation fees, loan origination fees, monthly service charges, or late fees. The effective _____ has been called the 'mathematically-true' interest rate for each year. The computation for the effective _____, as the fee+compound interest rate, can also vary depending on whether the up-front fees, such as origination or participation fees, are added to the entire amount, or treated as a short-term loan due in the first payment.

- a. AAB
- b. A Random Walk Down Wall Street
- c. Annual percentage rate
- d. ABN Amro

12. _____ is the balance of the amounts of cash being received and paid by a business during a defined period of time, sometimes tied to a specific project. Measurement of _____ can be used

- to evaluate the state or performance of a business or project.
- to determine problems with liquidity. Being profitable does not necessarily mean being liquid. A company can fail because of a shortage of cash, even while profitable.
- to generate project rate of returns. The time of _____s into and out of projects are used as inputs to financial models such as internal rate of return, and net present value.
- to examine income or growth of a business when it is believed that accrual accounting concepts do not represent economic realities. Alternately, _____ can be used to 'validate' the net income generated by accrual accounting.

_____ as a generic term may be used differently depending on context, and certain _____ definitions may be adapted by analysts and users for their own uses. Common terms include operating _____ and free _____.

_____s can be classified into:

1. Operational _____s: Cash received or expended as a result of the company's core business activities.
2. Investment _____s: Cash received or expended through capital expenditure, investments or acquisitions.
3. Financing _____s: Cash received or expended as a result of financial activities, such as interests and dividends.

All three together - the net _____ - are necessary to reconcile the beginning cash balance to the ending cash balance. Loan draw downs or equity injections, that is just shifting of capital but no expenditure as such, are not considered in the net _____.

- a. Corporate finance
- b. Shareholder value
- c. Real option
- d. Cash flow

13. _____ is that which is owed; usually referencing assets owed, but the term can cover other obligations. In the case of assets, _____ is a means of using future purchasing power in the present before a summation has been earned. Some companies and corporations use _____ as a part of their overall corporate finance strategy.

a. Cross-collateralization
b. Partial Payment
c. Credit cycle
d. Debt

14. An _____ can be defined as a contract which provides an income stream in return for an initial payment.

An immediate _____ is an _____ for which the time between the contract date and the date of the first payment is not longer than the time interval between payments. A common use for an immediate _____ is to provide a pension to a retired person or persons.

a. Amortization
b. Annuity
c. Intrinsic value
d. AT'T Inc.

15. _____ is the value on a given date of a future payment or series of future payments, discounted to reflect the time value of money and other factors such as investment risk. _____ calculations are widely used in business and economics to provide a means to compare cash flows at different times on a meaningful 'like to like' basis.

The most commonly applied model of the time value of money is compound interest.

a. Net present value
b. Negative gearing
c. Present value
d. Present value of benefits

16. A '_____' is a 'Charge' that is paid to obtain the right to delay a payment. Essentially, the payer purchases the right to make a given payment in the future instead of in the Present. The '_____', or 'Charge' that must be paid to delay the payment, is simply the difference between what the payment amount would be if it were paid in the present and what the payment amount would be paid if it were paid in the future.

a. Discount
b. Risk modeling
c. Risk aversion
d. Value at risk

17. A _____ is a bond bought at a price lower than its face value, with the face value repaid at the time of maturity. It does not make periodic interest payments, or so-called 'coupons,' hence the term zero-coupon bond. Investors earn return from the compounded interest all paid at maturity plus the difference between the discounted price of the bond and its par value.

a. Bowie bonds
b. Municipal bond
c. Callable bond
d. Zero coupon bond

18. A _____ is a generic term for any bond selling for more than 100% of par value, i.e., at a price greater than 100.00, which typically occurs for high coupon bonds in a falling interest rate climate.

a. Nominal yield
b. Premium bond
c. Revenue bonds
d. Municipal bond

19. _____ is the risk (variability in value) borne by an interest-bearing asset, such as a loan or a bond, due to variability of interest rates. In general, as rates rise, the price of a fixed rate bond will fall, and vice versa. _____ is commonly measured by the bond's duration.

a. Official bank rate
b. International Fisher effect
c. Interest rate risk
d. A Random Walk Down Wall Street

20. In business, _____ is income that a company receives from its normal business activities, usually from the sale of goods and services to customers. Some companies also receive _____ from interest, dividends or royalties paid to them by other companies. _____ may refer to business income in general, or it may refer to the amount, in a monetary unit, received during a period of time, as in 'Last year, Company X had _____ of $32 million.'

In many countries, including the UK, _____ is referred to as turnover.

- a. Bottom line
- b. Furniture, Fixtures and Equipment
- c. Revenue
- d. Matching principle

21. In economic models, the _____ time frame assumes no fixed factors of production. Firms can enter or leave the marketplace, and the cost (and availability) of land, labor, raw materials, and capital goods can be assumed to vary. In contrast, in the short-run time frame, certain factors are assumed to be fixed, because there is not sufficient time for them to change.
- a. 529 plan
- b. 4-4-5 Calendar
- c. Short-run
- d. Long-run

22. The _____, interest yield, income yield, flat yield or running yield is a financial term used in reference to bonds and other fixed-interest securities such as gilts. It is the ratio of the annual interest payment and the bond's current price.

The _____ only therefore refers to the yield of the bond at the current moment. It does not reflect the total return over the life of the bond. In particular, it takes no account of reinvestment risk (the uncertainty about the rate at which future cashflows can be reinvested) or the fact that bonds usually mature at par value, which can be an important component of a bond's return.

- a. Perpetuity
- b. Stochastic volatility
- c. Modified Internal Rate of Return
- d. Current yield

23. In finance, the _____ is the relation between the interest rate (or cost of borrowing) and the time to maturity of the debt for a given borrower in a given currency. For example, the current U.S. dollar interest rates paid on U.S. Treasury securities for various maturities are closely watched by many traders, and are commonly plotted on a graph such as the one on the right which is informally called 'the _____.' More formal mathematical descriptions of this relation are often called the term structure of interest rates.

The yield of a debt instrument is the annualized percentage increase in the value of the investment.

- a. 7-Eleven
- b. 529 plan
- c. 4-4-5 Calendar
- d. Yield curve

Chapter 6. Interest Rates and Bond Valuation

24. _____ is the process of decreasing an amount over a period of time. The word comes from Middle English amortisen to kill, alienate in mortmain, from Anglo-French amorteser, alteration of amortir, from Vulgar Latin admortire to kill, from Latin ad- + mort-, mors death. Particular instances of the term include:

- _____ (business), the allocation of a lump sum amount to different time periods, particularly for loans and other forms of finance, including related interest or other finance charges.
    - _____ schedule, a table detailing each periodic payment on a loan (typically a mortgage), as generated by an _____ calculator.
    - Negative _____, an _____ schedule where the loan amount actually increases through not paying the full interest
- Amortized analysis, analyzing the execution cost of algorithms over a sequence of operations.
- _____ of capital expenditures of certain assets under accounting rules, particularly intangible assets, in a manner analogous to depreciation.
- _____ (tax law)

_____ is also used in the context of zoning regulations and describes the time in which a property owner has to relocate when the property's use constitutes a preexisting nonconforming use under zoning regulations.

- Depreciation

a. Amortization
c. AT'T Inc.
b. Intrinsic value
d. Option

25. In finance, a _____ is the party in a loan agreement which receives money or other instrument from a lender and promises to repay the lender in a specified time.
    a. Line of credit
    b. Debt management plan
    c. Cash credit
    d. Borrower

26. A _____ is a party (e.g. person, organization, company, or government) that has a claim to the services of a second party. The first party, in general, has provided some property or service to the second party under the assumption (usually enforced by contract) that the second party will return an equivalent property or service. The second party is frequently called a debtor or borrower.
    a. False billing
    b. NOPLAT
    c. Redemption value
    d. Creditor

27. In economics a _____ is simply an entity that owes a debt to someone else, the entity could be an individual, a firm, a government, or an organization. The counterparty of this arrangement is called a creditor. When the counterparty of this debt arrangement is a bank, the _____ is more often referred to as a borrower.
    a. Financial rand
    b. Tick size
    c. Debtor
    d. Biweekly Mortgage

28. A _____ is a fungible, negotiable instrument representing financial value. They are broadly categorized into debt securities (such as banknotes, bonds and debentures), and equity securities; e.g., common stocks. The company or other entity issuing the _____ is called the issuer.

a. Securities lending
b. Book entry
c. Tracking stock
d. Security

29. In political science and economics, the _____ or agency dilemma treats the difficulties that arise under conditions of incomplete and asymmetric information when a principal hires an agent. Various mechanisms may be used to try to align the interests of the agent with those of the principal, such as piece rates/commissions, profit sharing, efficiency wages, performance measurement (including financial statements), the agent posting a bond, or fear of firing. The _____ is found in most employer/employee relationships, for example, when stockholders hire top executives of corporations.

a. 7-Eleven
b. 4-4-5 Calendar
c. 529 plan
d. Principal-agent problem

30. _____ or financing is to provide capital (funds), which means money for a project, a person, a business or any other private or public institutions.

Those funds can be allocated for either short term or long term purposes. The health fund is a new way of _____ private healthcare centers.

a. Funding
b. Proxy fight
c. Product life cycle
d. Synthetic CDO

31. In economics, business, and accounting, a _____ is the value of money that has been used up to produce something, and hence is not available for use anymore. In business, the _____ may be one of acquisition, in which case the amount of money expended to acquire it is counted as _____. In this case, money is the input that is gone in order to acquire the thing.

a. Sliding scale fees
b. Fixed costs
c. Cost
d. Marginal cost

32. In finance, the _____ is the minimum rate of return a firm must offer shareholders to compensate for waiting for their returns, and for bearing some risk.

The _____ capital for a particular company is the rate of return on investment that is required by the company's ordinary shareholders. The return consists both of dividend and capital gains, e.g. increases in the share price.

a. Cost of equity
b. Residual value
c. Net pay
d. Round-tripping

33. A _____ is defined as a certificate of agreement of loans which is given under the company's stamp and carries an undertaking that the _____ holder will get a fixed return (fixed on the basis of interest rates) and the principal amount whenever the _____ matures.

In finance, a _____ is a long-term debt instrument used by governments and large companies to obtain funds. It is defined as 'a debt secured only by the debtor's earning power, not by a lien on any specific asset.' It is similar to a bond except the securitization conditions are different.

Chapter 6. Interest Rates and Bond Valuation

a. Collection agency
b. Collateral Management
c. Partial Payment
d. Debenture

34. _____ is a legally declared inability or impairment of ability of an individual or organization to pay their creditors. Creditors may file a _____ petition against a debtor ('involuntary _____') in an effort to recoup a portion of what they are owed or initiate a restructuring. In the majority of cases, however, _____ is initiated by the debtor (a 'voluntary _____' that is filed by the bankrupt individual or organization.)
   a. 529 plan
   b. Debt settlement
   c. 4-4-5 Calendar
   d. Bankruptcy

35. In lending agreements, _____ is a borrower's pledge of specific property to a lender, to secure repayment of a loan. The _____ serves as protection for a lender against a borrower's risk of default - that is, a borrower failing to pay the principal and interest under the terms of a loan obligation. If a borrower does default on a loan (due to insolvency or other event), that borrower forfeits (gives up) the property pledged as _____ *ollateral* - and the lender then becomes the owner of the _____.
   a. Future-oriented
   b. Collateral
   c. Refinancing risk
   d. Nominal value

36. The _____ is an expected return that the provider of capital plans to earn on their investment.

Capital (money) used for funding a business should earn returns for the capital providers who risk their capital. For an investment to be worthwhile, the expected return on capital must be greater than the _____.

   a. Capital intensity
   b. Weighted average cost of capital
   c. 4-4-5 Calendar
   d. Cost of capital

37. _____ (also trust indenture or deed of trust) is a legal document issued to lenders and describes key terms such as the interest rate, maturity date, convertibility, pledge, promises, representations, covenants, and other terms of the bond offering. When the Offering Memorandum is prepared in advance of marketing a Bond, the indenture will typically be summarised in the 'Description of Notes' section.
   a. Fair Labor Standards Act
   b. Court of Audit of Belgium
   c. McFadden Act
   d. Bond indenture

38. A _____ is a corporation, especially a commercial bank, organized to perform the fiduciary functions of trusts and agencies. It is normally owned by one of three types of structures: an independent partnership, a bank, or a law firm, each of which specializes in being a trustee of various kinds of trusts and in managing estates.
   a. Savings and loan association
   b. Mutual fund
   c. Person-to-person lending
   d. Trust company

39. In financial accounting, _____s are precautions for which the amount or probability of occurrence are not known. Typical examples are _____s for warranty costs and _____ for taxes the term reserve is used instead of term _____; such a use, however, is inconsistent with the terminology suggested by International Accounting Standards Board.

a. Money measurement concept
b. Petty cash
c. Momentum Accounting and Triple-Entry Bookkeeping
d. Provision

40. In economics, the concept of the _____ refers to the decision-making time frame of a firm in which at least one factor of production is fixed. Costs which are fixed in the _____ have no impact on a firms decisions. For example a firm can raise output by increasing the amount of labour through overtime.
 a. Long-run
 b. 529 plan
 c. Short-run
 d. 4-4-5 Calendar

41. A _____ is a document that indicates that the bearer of the document has title to property, such as shares or bonds. They differ from normal registered instruments, in that no records are kept of who owns the underlying property, or of the transactions involving transfer of ownership. Whoever physically holds the bearer bond papers owns the property.
 a. Securities lending
 b. Book entry
 c. Marketable
 d. Bearer instrument

42. A _____ is a single mortgage that covers more than one parcel of real estate.
 a. Blanket mortgage
 b. Construction loan
 c. Commercial mortgage
 d. Reverse mortgage

43. A _____ is a bond issued by a corporation. The term is usually applied to longer-term debt instruments, generally with a maturity date falling at least a year after their issue date. (The term 'commercial paper' is sometimes used for instruments with a shorter maturity.)
 a. Government bond
 b. Serial bond
 c. Brady bonds
 d. Corporate bond

44. _____, in accrual accounting, is any account where the asset or liability is not realized until a future date, e.g. annuities, charges, taxes, income, etc. The _____ item may be carried, dependent on type of deferral, as either an asset or liability.See also: accrual

_____ is also used in the university admissions process. It is the action by which a school rejects a student for early admission but still opts to review that student in the general admissions pool.

 a. Net profit
 b. Deferred
 c. Revenue
 d. Current asset

45. The _____ is an interest rate a central bank charges depository institutions that borrow reserves from it.

Chapter 6. Interest Rates and Bond Valuation

The term _____ has two meanings:

- the same as interest rate; the term 'discount' does not refer to the meaning of the word, but to the purpose of using the quantity, such as computations of present value, e.g. net present value / discounted cash flow

- the annual effective _____, which is the annual interest divided by the capital including that interest; this rate is lower than the interest rate; it corresponds to using the value after a year as the nominal value, and seeing the initial value as the nominal value minus a discount; it is used for Treasury Bills and similar financial instruments

The annual effective _____ is the annual interest divided by the capital including that interest, which is the interest rate divided by 100% plus the interest rate. It is the annual discount factor to be applied to the future cash flow, to find the discount, subtracted from a future value to find the value one year earlier.

For example, suppose there is a government bond that sells for $95 and pays $100 in a year's time.

a. Fisher equation
b. Stochastic volatility
c. Black-Scholes
d. Discount rate

46. A _____ is a fund established by a government agency or business for the purpose of reducing debt.

The _____ was first used in Great Britain in the 18th century to reduce national debt. While used by Robert Walpole in 1716 and effectively in the 1720s and early 1730s, it originated in the commercial tax syndicates of the Italian peninsula of the 14th century to retire redeemable public debt of those cities.

a. Modern portfolio theory
b. Debtor
c. Security interest
d. Sinking fund

47. In finance, _____ is debt which ranks after other debts should a company fall into receivership or be closed.

Such debt is referred to as subordinate, because the debt providers have subordinate status in relationship to the normal debt. A typical example for this would be when a promoter of a company invests money in the form of debt, rather than in the form of stock.

a. Credit rating
b. Participation loan
c. Cross-collateralization
d. Subordinated Debt

48. The institution most often referenced by the word '_____' is a public or publicly traded _____, the shares of which are traded on a public stock exchange (e.g., the New York Stock Exchange or Nasdaq in the United States) where shares of stock of _____s are bought and sold by and to the general public. Most of the largest businesses in the world are publicly traded _____s. However, the majority of _____s are said to be closely held, privately held or close _____s, meaning that no ready market exists for the trading of shares.

a. Protect	b. Federal Home Loan Mortgage Corporation
c. Corporation	d. Depository Trust Company

49. _____ is the provision of resources (such as granting a loan) by one party to another party where that second party does not reimburse the first party immediately, thereby generating a debt, and instead arranges either to repay or return those resources (or material(s) of equal value) at a later date. The first party is called a creditor, also known as a lender, while the second party is called a debtor, also known as a borrower.

Movements of financial capital are normally dependent on either _____ or equity transfers.

a. Credit	b. Comparable
c. Warrant	d. Clearing house

50. A _____ assesses the credit worthiness of an individual, corporation, or even a country. _____s are calculated from financial history and current assets and liabilities. Typically, a _____ tells a lender or investor the probability of the subject being able to pay back a loan.

a. Debenture	b. Credit report monitoring
c. Credit cycle	d. Credit rating

51. In finance, _____ occurs when a debtor has not met its legal obligations according to the debt contract, e.g. it has not made a scheduled payment, or has violated a loan covenant (condition) of the debt contract. _____ may occur if the debtor is either unwilling or unable to pay their debt. This can occur with all debt obligations including bonds, mortgages, loans, and promissory notes.

a. Credit crunch	b. Debt validation
c. Vendor finance	d. Default

52. A _____, in its most general sense, is a solemn promise to engage in or refrain from a specified action.

More specifically, a _____, in contrast to a contract, is a one-way agreement whereby the _____er is the only party bound by the promise. A _____ may have conditions and prerequisites that qualify the undertaking, including the actions of second or third parties, but there is no inherent agreement by such other parties to fulfill those requirements.

a. Federal Trade Commission Act	b. Partnership
c. Covenant	d. Clayton Antitrust Act

53. The value of speculative bonds is affected to a higher degree than investment grade bonds by the possibility of default. For example, in a recession interest rates may drop, and the drop in interest rates tends to increase the value of investment grade bonds; however, a recession tends to increase the possibility of default in speculative-grade bonds.

The original speculative grade bonds were bonds that once had been investment grade at time of issue, but where the credit rating of the issuer had slipped and the possibility of default increased significantly. These bonds are called '_____'.

Chapter 6. Interest Rates and Bond Valuation

a. Sharpe ratio
b. Return on capital employed
c. Fallen angels
d. Seed round

54. In finance, a _____ (non-investment grade bond, speculative grade bond or junk bond) is a bond that is rated below investment grade at the time of purchase. These bonds have a higher risk of default or other adverse credit events, but typically pay higher yields than better quality bonds in order to make them attractive to investors.
   a. Sharpe ratio
   b. Volatility
   c. Private equity
   d. High yield bond

55. A _____ or stock divide increases or decreases the number of shares in a public company. The price is adjusted such that the before and after market capitalization of the company remains the same and dilution does not occur. Options and warrants are included.
   a. Stock split
   b. Contract for difference
   c. Stop order
   d. Stop price

56. _____ is the risk of loss due to a debtor's non-payment of a loan or other line of credit (either the principal or interest (coupon) or both)

Most lenders employ their own models (credit scorecards) to rank potential and existing customers according to risk, and then apply appropriate strategies. With products such as unsecured personal loans or mortgages, lenders charge a higher price for higher risk customers and vice versa. With revolving products such as credit cards and overdrafts, risk is controlled through careful setting of credit limits.

   a. Liquidity risk
   b. Transaction risk
   c. Market risk
   d. Credit risk

57. A _____ is a bond issued by a national government denominated in the country's own currency. Bonds issued by national governments in foreign currencies are normally referred to as sovereign bonds. The first ever _____ was issued by the British government in 1693 to raise money to fund a war against France.
   a. Government bond
   b. Zero-coupon bond
   c. Municipal bond
   d. Collateralized debt obligations

58. In the United States, a _____ is a bond issued by a city or other local government, or their agencies. Potential issuers of these bonds include cities, counties, redevelopment agencies, school districts, publicly owned airports and seaports, and any other governmental entity (or group of governments) below the state level. They may be general obligations of the issuer or secured by specified revenues.
   a. Premium bond
   b. Puttable bond
   c. Senior debt
   d. Municipal bond

59. _____ are government bonds issued by the United States Department of the Treasury through the Bureau of the Public Debt. They are the debt financing instruments of the U.S. Federal government, and they are often referred to simply as Treasuries or Treasurys. There are four types of marketable _____: Treasury bills, Treasury notes, Treasury bonds, and Treasury Inflation Protected Securities (TIPS.)
   a. Treasury Inflation Protected Securities
   b. Treasury Inflation-Protected Securities
   c. 4-4-5 Calendar
   d. Treasury securities

60. In economics, the _____ is the proposition by Irving Fisher that the real interest rate is independent of monetary measures, especially the nominal interest rate. The Fisher equation is

$r_r = r_n >- >\pi^e$.

This means, the real interest rate (r_r) equals the nominal interest rate (r_n) minus expected rate of inflation ($>\pi^e$.) Here all the rates are continuously compounded.

a. Fisher hypothesis
b. 529 plan
c. 4-4-5 Calendar
d. 7-Eleven

61. _____ relates to the cost of borrowing money. It is the price that a lender charges a borrower for the use of the lender's money. _____ is different from OPEX and CAPEX, for it relates to the capital structure of a company.

a. A Random Walk Down Wall Street
b. ABN Amro
c. AAB
d. Interest expense

62. _____ is a form of corporation equity ownership represented in the securities. It is dangerous in comparison to preferred shares and some other investment options, in that in the event of bankruptcy, _____ investors receive their funds after preferred stockholders, bondholders, creditors, etc. On the other hand, common shares on average perform better than preferred shares or bonds over time.

a. Common stock
b. Stock market bubble
c. Stop-limit order
d. Stock split

63. In finance, a _____ is a type of bond that can be converted into shares of stock in the issuing company, usually at some pre-announced ratio. It is a hybrid security with debt- and equity-like features. Although it typically has a low coupon rate, the holder is compensated with the ability to convert the bond to common stock, usually at a substantial discount to the stock's market value.

a. Gilts
b. Corporate bond
c. Bond fund
d. Convertible bond

64. _____, refers to consumption opportunity gained by an entity within a specified time frame, which is generally expressed in monetary terms. However, for households and individuals, '_____ is the sum of all the wages, salaries, profits, interests payments, rents and other forms of earnings received... in a given period of time.' For firms, _____ generally refers to net-profit: what remains of revenue after expenses have been subtracted.

a. Annual report
b. Accrual
c. OIBDA
d. Income

65. In economics, _____ is a rise in the general level of prices of goods and services in an economy over a period of time. The term '_____' once referred to increases in the money supply (monetary _____); however, economic debates about the relationship between money supply and price levels have led to its primary use today in describing price _____. _____ can also be described as a decline in the real value of money--a loss of purchasing power in the medium of exchange which is also the monetary unit of account.

a. ABN Amro
b. AAB
c. A Random Walk Down Wall Street
d. Inflation

Chapter 6. Interest Rates and Bond Valuation

66. _____ are bonds where the principal is indexed to inflation. They are thus designed to cut out the inflation risk of an investment. _____ pay a periodic coupon that is equal to the product of the inflation index and the nominal coupon rate. The relationship between coupon payments, breakeven inflation and real interest rates is given by the Fisher equation.

a. ABN Amro
b. AAB
c. A Random Walk Down Wall Street
d. Inflation-indexed bonds

67. _____ is typically a higher ranking stock than voting shares, and its terms are negotiated between the corporation and the investor.

_____ usually carry no voting rights, but may carry superior priority over common stock in the payment of dividends and upon liquidation. _____ may carry a dividend that is paid out prior to any dividends to common stock holders.

a. Trade-off theory
b. Follow-on offering
c. Preferred stock
d. Second lien loan

68. _____ is a combination of straight bond and embedded put option. The holder of the _____ has the right, but not the obligation, to demand early repayment of the principal. The put option is usually exercisable on specified dates.

a. Callable bond
b. Puttable bond
c. Convertible bond
d. Brady bonds

69. The _____, in terms of finance and investing, describes how the expected return of a stock or portfolio is correlated to the return of the financial market as a whole.

An asset with a beta of 0 means that its price is not at all correlated with the market; that asset is independent. A positive beta means that the asset generally follows the market.

a. Beta coefficient
b. Perpetuity
c. Current yield
d. LIBOR market model

70. A _____, securities exchange or (in Europe) bourse is a corporation or mutual organization which provides 'trading' facilities for stock brokers and traders, to trade stocks and other securities. _____s also provide facilities for the issue and redemption of securities as well as other financial instruments and capital events including the payment of income and dividends. The securities traded on a _____ include: shares issued by companies, unit trusts and other pooled investment products and bonds.

a. Stock exchange
b. 7-Eleven
c. 4-4-5 Calendar
d. 529 plan

71. The _____ is a financial market where participants buy and sell debt securities, usually in the form of bonds. As of 2006, the size of the international _____ is an estimated $45 trillion, of which the size of the outstanding U.S. _____ debt was $25.2 trillion.

Nearly all of the $923 billion average daily trading volume in the U.S. _____ takes place between broker-dealers and large institutions in a decentralized, over-the-counter market.

a. 529 plan	b. 4-4-5 Calendar
c. Fixed income	d. Bond market

72. _____ are risk-linked securities that transfer a specified set of risks from a sponsor to investors. They are often structured as floating rate corporate bonds whose principal is forgiven if specified trigger conditions are met. They are typically used by insurers as an alternative to traditional catastrophe reinsurance.

a. Brady bonds	b. Catastrophe bonds
c. Callable bond	d. Clean price

73. In economics, a _____ is a mechanism that allows people to easily buy and sell (trade) financial securities (such as stocks and bonds), commodities (such as precious metals or agricultural goods), and other fungible items of value at low transaction costs and at prices that reflect the efficient-market hypothesis.

_____s have evolved significantly over several hundred years and are undergoing constant innovation to improve liquidity.

Both general markets (where many commodities are traded) and specialized markets (where only one commodity is traded) exist.

a. Cost of carry	b. Delta hedging
c. Financial market	d. Secondary market

74. The _____ is a stock exchange based in New York City, New York. It is the largest stock exchange in the world by dollar value of its listed companies securities. As of October 2008, the combined capitalization of all domestic _____ listed companies was $10.1 trillion.

a. 529 plan	b. New York Stock Exchange
c. 4-4-5 Calendar	d. 7-Eleven

75. _____ is an economic concept with commonplace familiarity. It is the price that a good or service is offered at, or will fetch, in the marketplace. It is of interest mainly in the study of microeconomics.

a. Convertible arbitrage	b. Central Securities Depository
c. Market price	d. Delta hedging

76. In finance, the _____ is the difference between the quoted rates of return on two different investments, usually of different credit quality.

It is a compound of yield and spread.

The '_____ of X over Y' is simply the percentage return on investment (ROI) from financial instrument X minus the percentage return on investment from financial instrument Y (per annum.)

a. Portfolio insurance	b. Yield spread
c. Debtor-in-possession financing	d. Duty of loyalty

77. A _____ is the highest price that a buyer (i.e., bidder) is willing to pay for a good. It is usually referred to simply as the 'bid.'

Chapter 6. Interest Rates and Bond Valuation 71

In bid and ask, the _____ stands in contrast to the ask price or 'offer', and the difference between the two is called the bid/ask spread.

An unsolicited bid or offer is when a person or company receives a bid even though they are not looking to sell.

a. Bid price
b. Settlement date
c. Political risk
d. Mid price

78. A _____ or market-based mechanism is any of a wide variety of ways to match up buyers and sellers.

An example of a _____ uses announced bid and ask prices. Generally speaking, when two parties wish to engage in a trade, the purchaser will announce a price he is willing to pay (the bid price) and seller will announce a price he is willing to accept (the ask price).

a. 4-4-5 Calendar
b. 7-Eleven
c. Price mechanism
d. 529 plan

79. The _____ for securities is the difference between the price quoted by a market maker for an immediate sale and an immediate purchase The size of the bid-offer spread in a given commodity is a measure of the liquidity of the market.

The trader initiating the transaction is said to demand liquidity, and the other party to the transaction supplies liquidity.

a. Trade-off
b. Capital outflow
c. Defined contribution plan
d. Bid/offer spread

80. In financial markets, a _____ is the smallest increment in which prices for a futures contract can move.
a. Credit card balance transfer
b. Collateralized loan obligation
c. CFA Institute
d. Tick size

81. In the stock market, a _____ is the stock of a company that is regarded as a leader in its given industry. The performance of the stock is said to reflect the performance of the industry in general. These stocks are used as barometers for the rest of the market. General Motors is an example of a _____ stock. As the major auto maker in the US, it sets the tone for the rest of the industry. General Motors also has contracts with companies in other industries so its performance is reflected in other sectors of the market.
a. 4-4-5 Calendar
b. 529 plan
c. 7-Eleven
d. Bellwether

82. In finance, _____ is the interest that has accumulated since the principal investment, or since the previous interest payment if there has been one already. For a financial instrument such as a bond, interest is calculated and paid in set intervals.

The primary formula for calculating the interest accrued in a given period is:

$$I_A = T \times P \times R$$

where I_A is the _____, T is the fraction of the year, P is the principal, and R is the annualized interest rate.

a. AAB
b. A Random Walk Down Wall Street
c. ABN Amro
d. Accrued interest

83. In finance, the _____ is the price of a bond excluding any interest that has accrued since issue or the most recent coupon payment. This is to be compared with the dirty price, which is the price of a bond including the accrued interest.

When bond prices are quoted on a Bloomberg Terminal or Reuters they are quoted using the _____.

a. Gilts
b. Clean price
c. Bowie bonds
d. Bond valuation

84. The _____ of a bond represents the value of a bond, exclusive of any commissions or fees. The _____ is also called the 'full price.'

Bonds, as well as a variety of other fixed income securities, provide for coupon payments to be made to bond holders on a fixed schedule. The _____ of a bond will decrease on the days coupons are paid, resulting in a saw-tooth pattern for the bond value.

a. Collateralized debt obligations
b. Premium bond
c. Serial bond
d. Dirty price

85. _____ in economics is a persistent decrease in the general price level of goods and services - a negative inflation rate. When the inflation rate slows down (decreases, but remains positive), this is known as disinflation.

Inflation destroys real value in money.

a. Mercantilism
b. Fixed exchange rate
c. Recession
d. Deflation

86. In finance, the yield curve is the relation between the interest rate (or cost of borrowing) and the time to maturity of the debt for a given borrower in a given currency. For example, the current U.S. dollar interest rates paid on U.S. Treasury securities for various maturities are closely watched by many traders, and are commonly plotted on a graph such as the one on the right which is informally called 'the yield curve.' More formal mathematical descriptions of this relation are often called the _____.

The yield of a debt instrument is the annualized percentage increase in the value of the investment.

a. Term structure of interest rates
b. 4-4-5 Calendar
c. 7-Eleven
d. 529 plan

Chapter 6. Interest Rates and Bond Valuation

87.

In finance, the _____ can be the expected rate of return above the risk-free interest rate. When measuring risk, a common sense approach is to compare the risk-free return on T-bills and the very risky return on other investments. The difference between these two returns can be interpreted as a measure of the excess return on the average risky asset. This excess return is known as the _____.

a. Risk adjusted return on capital
c. Risk modeling
b. Risk aversion
d. Risk premium

88. _____ is a measure of the ability of a debtor to pay their debts as and when they fall due. It is usually expressed as a ratio or a percentage of current liabilities.

For a corporation with a published balance sheet there are various ratios used to calculate a measure of liquidity.

a. Operating leverage
c. Invested capital
b. Accounting liquidity
d. Operating profit margin

89. _____ is a term used to explain a difference between two types of financial securities (e.g. stocks), that have all the same qualities except liquidity. For example:

_____ is a segment of a three-part theory that works to explain the behavior of yield curves for interest rates. The upwards-curving component of the interest yield can be explained by the _____.

a. 4-4-5 Calendar
c. 7-Eleven
b. Liquidity premium
d. 529 plan

90. In financial accounting, the term _____ is most commonly used to describe any part of shareholders' equity, except for basic share capital. Sometimes, the term is used instead of the term provision; such a use, however, is inconsistent with the terminology suggested by International Accounting Standards Board. For more information about provisions, see provision (accounting.)

a. Closing entries
c. Treasury stock
b. FIFO and LIFO accounting
d. Reserve

Chapter 7. Equity Markets and Stock Valuation

1. A _____ is the price of a single share of a no. of saleable stocks of the company. Once the stock is purchased, the owner becomes a shareholder of the company that issued the share.
    a. Trading curb
    b. Whisper numbers
    c. Stock split
    d. Share price

2. In finance, a _____ is a debt security, in which the authorized issuer owes the holders a debt and, depending on the terms of the _____, is obliged to pay interest (the coupon) and/or to repay the principal at a later date, termed maturity.

    Thus a _____ is a loan: the issuer is the borrower, the _____ holder is the lender, and the coupon is the interest. _____s provide the borrower with external funds to finance long-term investments, or, in the case of government _____s, to finance current expenditure.

    a. Convertible bond
    b. Puttable bond
    c. Catastrophe bonds
    d. Bond

3. _____ is a form of corporation equity ownership represented in the securities. It is dangerous in comparison to preferred shares and some other investment options, in that in the event of bankruptcy, _____ investors receive their funds after preferred stockholders, bondholders, creditors, etc. On the other hand, common shares on average perform better than preferred shares or bonds over time.
    a. Stock split
    b. Common stock
    c. Stock market bubble
    d. Stop-limit order

4. _____ is the balance of the amounts of cash being received and paid by a business during a defined period of time, sometimes tied to a specific project. Measurement of _____ can be used

    - to evaluate the state or performance of a business or project.
    - to determine problems with liquidity. Being profitable does not necessarily mean being liquid. A company can fail because of a shortage of cash, even while profitable.
    - to generate project rate of returns. The time of _____s into and out of projects are used as inputs to financial models such as internal rate of return, and net present value.
    - to examine income or growth of a business when it is believed that accrual accounting concepts do not represent economic realities. Alternately, _____ can be used to 'validate' the net income generated by accrual accounting.

    _____ as a generic term may be used differently depending on context, and certain _____ definitions may be adapted by analysts and users for their own uses. Common terms include operating _____ and free _____.

    _____s can be classified into:

    1. Operational _____s: Cash received or expended as a result of the company's core business activities.
    2. Investment _____s: Cash received or expended through capital expenditure, investments or acquisitions.
    3. Financing _____s: Cash received or expended as a result of financial activities, such as interests and dividends.

Chapter 7. Equity Markets and Stock Valuation

All three together - the net _____ - are necessary to reconcile the beginning cash balance to the ending cash balance. Loan draw downs or equity injections, that is just shifting of capital but no expenditure as such, are not considered in the net _____.

a. Real option
b. Corporate finance
c. Shareholder value
d. Cash flow

5. A _____ is a payment made by a corporation to its shareholder members. When a corporation earns a profit or surplus, that money can be put to two uses: it can either be re-invested in the business (called retained earnings), or it can be paid to the shareholders as a _____. Many corporations retain a portion of their earnings and pay the remainder as a _____.

a. Dividend yield
b. Special dividend
c. Dividend
d. Dividend puzzle

6. _____ is an estimate of the fair value of corporations and their stocks, by using fundamental economic criteria. This theoretical valuation has to be perfected with market criteria, as the final purpose is to determine potential market prices.

a. Stock valuation
b. 4-4-5 Calendar
c. Security Analysis
d. Growth stocks

7. In finance, _____ is the process of estimating the potential market value of a financial asset or liability. they can be done on assets (for example, investments in marketable securities such as stocks, options, business enterprises, or intangible assets such as patents and trademarks) or on liabilities (e.g., Bonds issued by a company.) _____ s are required in many contexts including investment analysis, capital budgeting, merger and acquisition transactions, financial reporting, taxable events to determine the proper tax liability, and in litigation.

a. Procter ' Gamble
b. Share
c. Margin
d. Valuation

8. In finance, _____ are stocks that appreciate in value and yield a high return on equity (ROE.) Analysts compute ROE by taking the company's net income and dividing it by the company's equity. To be classified as a growth stock, analysts expect to see at least 15 percent return on equity.

a. Security Analysis
b. Stock valuation
c. 4-4-5 Calendar
d. Growth stocks

9. _____ are those dividends paid out in form of additional stock shares of the issuing corporation or other corporation They are usually issued in proportion to shares owned (for example for every 100 shares of stock owned, 5% stock dividend will yield 5 extra shares). If this payment involves the issue of new shares, this is very similar to a stock split in that it increases the total number of shares while lowering the price of each share and does not change the market capitalization or the total value of the shares held

a. Database auditing
b. Time-based currency
c. The Hong Kong Securities Institute
d. Stock or scrip dividends

10. In business and finance, a _____ (also referred to as equity _____) of stock means a _____ of ownership in a corporation (company.) In the plural, stocks is often used as a synonym for _____ s especially in the United States, but it is less commonly used that way outside of North America.

Chapter 7. Equity Markets and Stock Valuation

In the United Kingdom, South Africa, and Australia, stock can also refer to completely different financial instruments such as government bonds or, less commonly, to all kinds of marketable securities.

a. Bucket shop
b. Procter ' Gamble
c. Margin
d. Share

11. A _____ is an annuity in which the periodic payments begin on a fixed date and continue indefinitely. It is sometimes referred to as a perpetual annuity. Fixed coupon payments on permanently invested (irredeemable) sums of money are prime examples of these. Scholarships paid perpetually from an endowment fit the definition of _____.
a. Current yield
b. Perpetuity
c. LIBOR market model
d. Stochastic volatility

12. _____ is a theory that all economic activities and policies should be oriented towards achieving a state of equilibrium, a steady state.

The theory asserts that the continuous growth model is inherently unstable resulting in a 'boom/bust' cycle, and that continuous growth in the context of finite resources is unlikely to support current levels of prosperity indefinitely.

Proponents of this theory also explicitly challenge the popular equation of economic growth with progress - an equation they have labelled Growth Fetish - and posit that sustainability has inherent value.

a. 7-Eleven
b. 4-4-5 Calendar
c. 529 plan
d. Zero growth

13. A _____, is a mathematical formalization of a trajectory that consists of taking successive random steps. The results of _____ analysis have been applied to computer science, physics, ecology, economics and a number of other fields as a fundamental model for random processes in time. For example, the path traced by a molecule as it travels in a liquid or a gas, the search path of a foraging animal, the price of a fluctuating stock and the financial status of a gambler can all be modeled as _____s.
a. 529 plan
b. Random Walk
c. 4-4-5 Calendar
d. 7-Eleven

14. _____ is the value on a given date of a future payment or series of future payments, discounted to reflect the time value of money and other factors such as investment risk. _____ calculations are widely used in business and economics to provide a means to compare cash flows at different times on a meaningful 'like to like' basis.

The most commonly applied model of the time value of money is compound interest.

a. Negative gearing
b. Present value
c. Present value of benefits
d. Net present value

Chapter 7. Equity Markets and Stock Valuation

15. A _____ is a profit that results from investments into a capital asset, such as stocks, bonds or real estate, which exceeds the purchase price. It is the difference between a higher selling price and a lower purchase price, resulting in a financial gain for the seller. Conversely, a capital loss arises if the proceeds from the sale of a capital asset are less than the purchase price.

   a. Capital gains tax
   b. Tax brackets
   c. Payroll tax
   d. Capital gain

16. The _____ on a company stock is the company's annual dividend payments divided by its market cap, or the dividend per share divided by the price per share. It is often expressed as a percentage.

   Dividend payments on preferred shares are stipulated by the prospectus.

   a. Dividend reinvestment plan
   b. Dividend yield
   c. Special dividend
   d. Dividend imputation

17. In finance, the term _____ describes the amount in cash that returns to the owners of a security. Normally it does not include the price variations, at the difference of the total return. _____ applies to various stated rates of return on stocks (common and preferred, and convertible), fixed income instruments (bonds, notes, bills, strips, zero coupon), and some other investment type insurance products (e.g. annuities.)

   a. 4-4-5 Calendar
   b. Macaulay duration
   c. Yield to maturity
   d. Yield

18. _____ is a multiple-winner voting system intended to promote proportional representation while also being simple to understand.

   _____ is used frequently in corporate governance, where it is mandated by many U.S. states, and it was used to elect the Illinois House of Representatives from 1870 until its repeal in 1980. It was used in England in the late 19th century to elect school boards.

   a. 7-Eleven
   b. 4-4-5 Calendar
   c. Cumulative voting
   d. 529 plan

19. _____, is when a company issues common stock or shares to the public for the first time. They are often issued by smaller, younger companies seeking capital to expand, but can also be done by large privately-owned companies looking to become publicly traded.

   In an _____ the issuer may obtain the assistance of an underwriting firm, which helps it determine what type of security to issue (common or preferred), best offering price and time to bring it to market.

   a. Asian Financial Crisis
   b. Insolvency
   c. Initial public offering
   d. Interest

Chapter 7. Equity Markets and Stock Valuation

20. In political science and economics, the _____ or agency dilemma treats the difficulties that arise under conditions of incomplete and asymmetric information when a principal hires an agent. Various mechanisms may be used to try to align the interests of the agent with those of the principal, such as piece rates/commissions, profit sharing, efficiency wages, performance measurement (including financial statements), the agent posting a bond, or fear of firing. The _____ is found in most employer/employee relationships, for example, when stockholders hire top executives of corporations.
   - a. 7-Eleven
   - b. 529 plan
   - c. 4-4-5 Calendar
   - d. Principal-agent problem

21. The phrase _____ refers to the aspect of corporate strategy, corporate finance and management dealing with the buying, selling and combining of different companies that can aid, finance, or help a growing company in a given industry grow rapidly without having to create another business entity.

   An acquisition, also known as a takeover, is the buying of one company (the 'target') by another. An acquisition may be friendly or hostile.

   - a. 7-Eleven
   - b. 4-4-5 Calendar
   - c. Mergers and acquisitions
   - d. 529 plan

22. A _____ is an event that may occur when a corporation's stockholders develop opposition to some aspect of the corporate governance, often focusing on directorial and management positions. Corporate activists may attempt to persuade shareholders to use their proxy votes (i.e. votes by one individual or institution as the authorized representative of another) to install new management for any of a variety of reasons.

   In a _____, incumbent directors and management have the odds stacked in their favor over those trying to force the corporate change.

   - a. Proxy fight
   - b. Trade finance
   - c. Procurement
   - d. Forfaiting

23. _____ is commonly used in corporations for voting by members or shareholders, because it allows members who have confidence in the judgment of other members to vote for them and allows the assembly to have a quorum of votes when it is difficult for all members to attend, or there are too many members for all of them to conveniently meet and deliberate.
   - a. 529 plan
   - b. 4-4-5 Calendar
   - c. 7-Eleven
   - d. Proxy voting

24. The _____ is one of several stock market indices, created by nineteenth-century Wall Street Journal editor and Dow Jones ' Company co-founder Charles Dow. Dow compiled the index to gauge the performance of the industrial sector of the American stock market. It is the second-oldest U.S. market index, after the Dow Jones Transportation Average, which Dow also created.
   - a. 4-4-5 Calendar
   - b. 529 plan
   - c. 7-Eleven
   - d. Dow Jones Industrial Average

Chapter 7. Equity Markets and Stock Valuation

25. The _____ is a stock exchange based in New York City, New York. It is the largest stock exchange in the world by dollar value of its listed companies securities. As of October 2008, the combined capitalization of all domestic _____ listed companies was $10.1 trillion.

 a. 4-4-5 Calendar
 b. 7-Eleven
 c. New York Stock Exchange
 d. 529 plan

26. A _____ is a right to acquire certain property in preference to any other person. It usually refers to property newly coming into existence. A right to acquire existing property in preference to any other person is usually referred to as a right of first refusal.

In practice, the most common form of _____ is the right of existing shareholders to acquire newly issued shares issued by a company in a rights issue, a usually but not always public offering.

 a. Pre-emption right
 b. Fraud deterrence
 c. Down payment
 d. Court of Audit of Belgium

27. A _____, securities exchange or (in Europe) bourse is a corporation or mutual organization which provides 'trading' facilities for stock brokers and traders, to trade stocks and other securities. _____s also provide facilities for the issue and redemption of securities as well as other financial instruments and capital events including the payment of income and dividends. The securities traded on a _____ include: shares issued by companies, unit trusts and other pooled investment products and bonds.

 a. 7-Eleven
 b. 529 plan
 c. 4-4-5 Calendar
 d. Stock Exchange

28. The _____ is the market for securities, where companies and governments can raise longterm funds. The _____ includes the stock market and the bond market. Financial regulators, such as the U.S. Securities and Exchange Commission, oversee the _____s in their designated countries to ensure that investors are protected against fraud.

 a. Spot rate
 b. Delta neutral
 c. Forward market
 d. Capital market

29. In economics, business, and accounting, a _____ is the value of money that has been used up to produce something, and hence is not available for use anymore. In business, the _____ may be one of acquisition, in which case the amount of money expended to acquire it is counted as _____. In this case, money is the input that is gone in order to acquire the thing.

 a. Cost
 b. Sliding scale fees
 c. Marginal cost
 d. Fixed costs

30. _____ is typically a higher ranking stock than voting shares, and its terms are negotiated between the corporation and the investor.

_____ usually carry no voting rights, but may carry superior priority over common stock in the payment of dividends and upon liquidation. _____ may carry a dividend that is paid out prior to any dividends to common stock holders.

Chapter 7. Equity Markets and Stock Valuation

a. Trade-off theory
b. Preferred stock
c. Follow-on offering
d. Second lien loan

31. In business, _____ is income that a company receives from its normal business activities, usually from the sale of goods and services to customers. Some companies also receive _____ from interest, dividends or royalties paid to them by other companies. _____ may refer to business income in general, or it may refer to the amount, in a monetary unit, received during a period of time, as in 'Last year, Company X had _____ of $32 million.'

In many countries, including the UK, _____ is referred to as turnover.

a. Revenue
b. Furniture, Fixtures and Equipment
c. Matching principle
d. Bottom line

32. A _____ is a fund established by a government agency or business for the purpose of reducing debt.

The _____ was first used in Great Britain in the 18th century to reduce national debt. While used by Robert Walpole in 1716 and effectively in the 1720s and early 1730s, it originated in the commercial tax syndicates of the Italian peninsula of the 14th century to retire redeemable public debt of those cities.

a. Sinking fund
b. Security interest
c. Modern portfolio theory
d. Debtor

33. _____ is a legally declared inability or impairment of ability of an individual or organization to pay their creditors. Creditors may file a _____ petition against a debtor ('involuntary _____') in an effort to recoup a portion of what they are owed or initiate a restructuring. In the majority of cases, however, _____ is initiated by the debtor (a 'voluntary _____' that is filed by the bankrupt individual or organization.)

a. 529 plan
b. Bankruptcy
c. 4-4-5 Calendar
d. Debt settlement

34. _____ is that which is owed; usually referencing assets owed, but the term can cover other obligations. In the case of assets, _____ is a means of using future purchasing power in the present before a summation has been earned. Some companies and corporations use _____ as a part of their overall corporate finance strategy.

a. Cross-collateralization
b. Partial Payment
c. Credit cycle
d. Debt

35. A _____ is the highest price that a buyer (i.e., bidder) is willing to pay for a good. It is usually referred to simply as the 'bid.'

In bid and ask, the _____ stands in contrast to the ask price or 'offer', and the difference between the two is called the bid/ask spread.

An unsolicited bid or offer is when a person or company receives a bid even though they are not looking to sell.

a. Political risk
b. Mid price
c. Bid price
d. Settlement date

Chapter 7. Equity Markets and Stock Valuation

36. The _____ is an American stock exchange. It is the largest electronic screen-based equity securities trading market in the United States. With approximately 3,200 companies, it has more trading volume per day than any other stock exchange in the world.

   a. 4-4-5 Calendar
   b. NASDAQ
   c. 7-Eleven
   d. 529 plan

37. The _____ is that part of the capital markets that deals with the issuance of new securities. Companies, governments or public sector institutions can obtain funding through the sale of a new stock or bond issue. This is typically done through a syndicate of securities dealers.

   a. Primary market
   b. Peer group analysis
   c. Sector rotation
   d. Volatility clustering

38. The _____ is the financial market where previously issued securities and financial instruments such as stock, bonds, options, and futures are bought and sold. The term '_____' is also used refer to the market for any used goods or assets, or an alternative use for an existing product or asset where the customer base is the second market

   With primary issuances of securities or financial instruments, or the primary market, investors purchase these securities directly from issuers such as corporations issuing shares in an IPO or private placement, or directly from the federal government in the case of treasuries.

   a. Performance attribution
   b. Delta neutral
   c. Financial market
   d. Secondary market

39. A _____ is a fungible, negotiable instrument representing financial value. They are broadly categorized into debt securities (such as banknotes, bonds and debentures), and equity securities; e.g., common stocks. The company or other entity issuing the _____ is called the issuer.

   a. Tracking stock
   b. Security
   c. Book entry
   d. Securities lending

40. A _____ is a private or public market for the trading of company stock and derivatives of company stock at an agreed price; these are securities listed on a stock exchange as well as those only traded privately.

   The size of the world _____ is estimated at about $36.6 trillion US at the beginning of October 2008 . The world derivatives market has been estimated at about $480 trillion face or nominal value, 12 times the size of the entire world economy.

   a. Adolph Coors
   b. Andrew Tobias
   c. Anton Gelonkin
   d. Stock market

41. _____ offer, asking price is a price a seller of a good is willing to accept for that particular good.

   In bid and ask, the term _____ is used in contrast to the term bid price. The difference between the _____ and the bid price is called the spread.

Chapter 7. Equity Markets and Stock Valuation

   a. A Random Walk Down Wall Street
   b. AAB
   c. Interest rate parity
   d. Ask price

42. A _____ is a member of an exchange who is an employee of a member firm and executes orders, as agent, on the floor of the exchange for clients. The _____ receives an order via teletype machine from his firm's trading department and then proceeds to the appropriate trading post on the exchange floor. There he joins other brokers and the specialist in the security being bought or sold and executes the trade at the best competitive price available.
   a. Business valuation standards
   b. Floor broker
   c. Case-Shiller Home Price Indices
   d. Multivariate normal distribution

43. A _____ is a firm that quotes both a buy and a sell price in a financial instrument or commodity, hoping to make a profit on the bid/offer spread, or turn.

In foreign exchange trading, where most deals are conducted over-the-counter and are, therefore, completely virtual, the _____ sells to and buys from its clients. Hence, the client's loss and the spread is the _____ firm's profit, which gets thus compensated for the effort of providing liquidity in a competitive market.

   a. 7-Eleven
   b. 529 plan
   c. 4-4-5 Calendar
   d. Market maker

44. The institution most often referenced by the word '_____' is a public or publicly traded _____, the shares of which are traded on a public stock exchange (e.g., the New York Stock Exchange or Nasdaq in the United States) where shares of stock of _____s are bought and sold by and to the general public. Most of the largest businesses in the world are publicly traded _____s. However, the majority of _____s are said to be closely held, privately held or close _____s, meaning that no ready market exists for the trading of shares.
   a. Corporation
   b. Federal Home Loan Mortgage Corporation
   c. Depository Trust Company
   d. Protect

45. An _____ is the term used in financial circles for a type of computer system that facilitates trading of financial products outside of stock exchanges. The primary products that are traded on an _____ are stocks and currencies. They came into existence in 1998 when the SEC authorized their creation.
   a. Intellidex
   b. Insider trading
   c. Open outcry
   d. Electronic communication network

46. A _____ is an order to buy a security at no more (or sell at no less) than a specific price. This gives the customer some control over the price at which the trade is executed, but may prevent the order from being executed ('filled'.)

A buy _____ can only be executed by the broker at the limit price or lower.

   a. Commercial mortgage-backed securities
   b. Block premium
   c. Limit order
   d. Common stock

47. _____ is a risk-adjusted measure of the so-called active return on an investment. It is the return in excess of the compensation for the risk borne, and thus commonly used to assess active managers' performances. Often, the return of a benchmark is subtracted in order to consider relative performance, which yields Jensen's _____.

Chapter 7. Equity Markets and Stock Valuation

a. Amortization
b. Annuity
c. Option
d. Alpha

48. The _____ is an electronic quotation system in the United States that displays real-time quotes, last-sale prices, and volume information for many over-the-counter (OTC) equity securities that are not listed on the NASDAQ stock exchange or a national securities exchange. Broker-dealers who subscribe to the system can use the _____ to look up prices or enter quotes for OTC securities.

a. AT'T Inc.
b. Insolvency
c. Internal control
d. OTC Bulletin Board

49. In the United States, a _____ is a common stock that trades for less than two cents a share and are traded over the counter (OTC) through quotation services such as the OTC Bulletin Board or the Pink Sheets. Although a _____ is said to be 'thinly traded,' share volumes traded daily can be in the hundreds of millions for a sub-_____. Legitimate information on _____ companies can be difficult to find and a stock can be easily manipulated.

a. Penny stock
b. Risk management
c. 4-4-5 Calendar
d. FIFO

50. The _____, in terms of finance and investing, describes how the expected return of a stock or portfolio is correlated to the return of the financial market as a whole.

An asset with a beta of 0 means that its price is not at all correlated with the market; that asset is independent. A positive beta means that the asset generally follows the market.

a. Current yield
b. Beta coefficient
c. LIBOR market model
d. Perpetuity

51. _____ or financing is to provide capital (funds), which means money for a project, a person, a business or any other private or public institutions.

Those funds can be allocated for either short term or long term purposes. The health fund is a new way of _____ private healthcare centers.

a. Product life cycle
b. Proxy fight
c. Funding
d. Synthetic CDO

Chapter 8. Net Present Value and Other Investment Criteria

1. _____ is the planning process used to determine whether a firm's long term investments such as new machinery, replacement machinery, new plants, new products, and research development projects are worth pursuing. It is budget for major capital, or investment, expenditures.

Many formal methods are used in _____, including the techniques such as

- Net present value
- Profitability index
- Internal rate of return
- Modified Internal Rate of Return
- Equivalent annuity

These methods use the incremental cash flows from each potential investment, or project. Techniques based on accounting earnings and accounting rules are sometimes used - though economists consider this to be improper - such as the accounting rate of return, and 'return on investment.' Simplified and hybrid methods are used as well, such as payback period and discounted payback period.

a. Preferred stock
b. Capital budgeting
c. Financial distress
d. Shareholder value

2. The institution most often referenced by the word '_____' is a public or publicly traded _____, the shares of which are traded on a public stock exchange (e.g., the New York Stock Exchange or Nasdaq in the United States) where shares of stock of _____s are bought and sold by and to the general public. Most of the largest businesses in the world are publicly traded _____s. However, the majority of _____s are said to be closely held, privately held or close _____s, meaning that no ready market exists for the trading of shares.

a. Federal Home Loan Mortgage Corporation
b. Protect
c. Corporation
d. Depository Trust Company

3. In finance, _____ refers to the way a corporation finances its assets through some combination of equity, debt, or hybrid securities. A firm's _____ is then the composition or 'structure' of its liabilities. For example, a firm that sells $20 billion in equity and $80 billion in debt is said to be 20% equity-financed and 80% debt-financed.

a. Rights issue
b. Book building
c. Capital structure
d. Market for corporate control

4. _____ or financing is to provide capital (funds), which means money for a project, a person, a business or any other private or public institutions.

Those funds can be allocated for either short term or long term purposes. The health fund is a new way of _____ private healthcare centers.

a. Product life cycle
b. Synthetic CDO
c. Proxy fight
d. Funding

5. _____ or net present worth (NPW) is defined as the total present value (PV) of a time series of cash flows. It is a standard method for using the time value of money to appraise long-term projects. Used for capital budgeting, and widely throughout economics, it measures the excess or shortfall of cash flows, in present value terms, once financing charges are met.

Chapter 8. Net Present Value and Other Investment Criteria

a. Negative gearing
c. Tax shield
b. Net present value
d. Present value of costs

6. _____ is a financial metric which represents operating liquidity available to a business. Along with fixed assets such as plant and equipment, _____ is considered a part of operating capital. It is calculated as current assets minus current liabilities.
   a. 529 plan
   c. 4-4-5 Calendar
   b. Working capital management
   d. Working capital

7. An _____ is an economic concept that relates to the cost incurred by an entity (such as organizations) associated with problems such as divergent management-shareholder objectives and information asymmetry. The costs consist of two main sources:

   1. The costs inherently associated with using an agent (e.g., the risk that agents will use organizational resource for their own benefit) and
   2. The costs of techniques used to mitigate the problems associated with using an agent (e.g., the costs of producing financial statements or the use of stock options to align executive interests to shareholder interests.)

Though effects of _____ are present in any agency relationship, the term is most used in business contexts.

The information asymmetry that exists between shareholders and the Chief Executive Officer is generally considered to be a classic example of a principal-agent problem. The agent (the manager) is working on behalf of the principal (the shareholders), who does not observe the actions of the agent.

   a. ABN Amro
   c. AAB
   b. A Random Walk Down Wall Street
   d. Agency cost

8. In political science and economics, the _____ or agency dilemma treats the difficulties that arise under conditions of incomplete and asymmetric information when a principal hires an agent. Various mechanisms may be used to try to align the interests of the agent with those of the principal, such as piece rates/commissions, profit sharing, efficiency wages, performance measurement (including financial statements), the agent posting a bond, or fear of firing. The _____ is found in most employer/employee relationships, for example, when stockholders hire top executives of corporations.
   a. 529 plan
   c. 7-Eleven
   b. 4-4-5 Calendar
   d. Principal-agent problem

9. In finance, a _____ is a debt security, in which the authorized issuer owes the holders a debt and, depending on the terms of the _____, is obliged to pay interest (the coupon) and/or to repay the principal at a later date, termed maturity.

Thus a _____ is a loan: the issuer is the borrower, the _____ holder is the lender, and the coupon is the interest. _____s provide the borrower with external funds to finance long-term investments, or, in the case of government _____s, to finance current expenditure.

   a. Convertible bond
   c. Puttable bond
   b. Catastrophe bonds
   d. Bond

Chapter 8. Net Present Value and Other Investment Criteria

10. In economics, business, and accounting, a _____ is the value of money that has been used up to produce something, and hence is not available for use anymore. In business, the _____ may be one of acquisition, in which case the amount of money expended to acquire it is counted as _____. In this case, money is the input that is gone in order to acquire the thing.
    a. Marginal cost
    b. Cost
    c. Sliding scale fees
    d. Fixed costs

11. _____ is the value on a given date of a future payment or series of future payments, discounted to reflect the time value of money and other factors such as investment risk. _____ calculations are widely used in business and economics to provide a means to compare cash flows at different times on a meaningful 'like to like' basis.

    The most commonly applied model of the time value of money is compound interest.

    a. Negative gearing
    b. Present value of benefits
    c. Net present value
    d. Present value

12. In finance, the _____ approach describes a method of valuing a project, company, or asset using the concepts of the time value of money. All future cash flows are estimated and discounted to give their present values. The discount rate used is generally the appropriate cost of capital and may incorporate judgments of the uncertainty (riskiness) of the future cash flows.
    a. Discounted cash flow
    b. Net present value
    c. Present value of benefits
    d. Future-oriented

13. _____ is the balance of the amounts of cash being received and paid by a business during a defined period of time, sometimes tied to a specific project. Measurement of _____ can be used

    - to evaluate the state or performance of a business or project.
    - to determine problems with liquidity. Being profitable does not necessarily mean being liquid. A company can fail because of a shortage of cash, even while profitable.
    - to generate project rate of returns. The time of _____s into and out of projects are used as inputs to financial models such as internal rate of return, and net present value.
    - to examine income or growth of a business when it is believed that accrual accounting concepts do not represent economic realities. Alternately, _____ can be used to 'validate' the net income generated by accrual accounting.

    _____ as a generic term may be used differently depending on context, and certain _____ definitions may be adapted by analysts and users for their own uses. Common terms include operating _____ and free _____.

    _____s can be classified into:

    1. Operational _____s: Cash received or expended as a result of the company's core business activities.
    2. Investment _____s: Cash received or expended through capital expenditure, investments or acquisitions.
    3. Financing _____s: Cash received or expended as a result of financial activities, such as interests and dividends.

Chapter 8. Net Present Value and Other Investment Criteria

All three together - the net _____ - are necessary to reconcile the beginning cash balance to the ending cash balance. Loan draw downs or equity injections, that is just shifting of capital but no expenditure as such, are not considered in the net _____.

a. Shareholder value
c. Real option
b. Corporate finance
d. Cash flow

14. In finance, _____ is the process of estimating the potential market value of a financial asset or liability. they can be done on assets (for example, investments in marketable securities such as stocks, options, business enterprises, or intangible assets such as patents and trademarks) or on liabilities (e.g., Bonds issued by a company.) _____s are required in many contexts including investment analysis, capital budgeting, merger and acquisition transactions, financial reporting, taxable events to determine the proper tax liability, and in litigation.

a. Share
c. Margin
b. Procter ' Gamble
d. Valuation

15. _____ is the process of decreasing an amount over a period of time. The word comes from Middle English amortisen to kill, alienate in mortmain, from Anglo-French amorteser, alteration of amortir, from Vulgar Latin admortire to kill, from Latin ad- + mort-, mors death. Particular instances of the term include:

- _____ (business), the allocation of a lump sum amount to different time periods, particularly for loans and other forms of finance, including related interest or other finance charges.
    - _____ schedule, a table detailing each periodic payment on a loan (typically a mortgage), as generated by an _____ calculator.
    - Negative _____, an _____ schedule where the loan amount actually increases through not paying the full interest
- Amortized analysis, analyzing the execution cost of algorithms over a sequence of operations.
- _____ of capital expenditures of certain assets under accounting rules, particularly intangible assets, in a manner analogous to depreciation.
- _____ (tax law)

_____ is also used in the context of zoning regulations and describes the time in which a property owner has to relocate when the property's use constitutes a preexisting nonconforming use under zoning regulations.

- Depreciation

a. AT'T Inc.
c. Option
b. Intrinsic value
d. Amortization

16. _____ in business and economics refers to the period of time required for the return on an investment to 'repay' the sum of the original investment. For example, a $1000 investment which returned $500 per year would have a two year _____. It intuitively measures how long something takes to 'pay for itself.' _____ is widely used due to its ease of use despite recognized limitations.

a. Financial Gerontology
c. Payback period
b. Seasoned equity offering
d. Consignment stock

17. _____ is a measure of the ability of a debtor to pay their debts as and when they fall due. It is usually expressed as a ratio or a percentage of current liabilities.

For a corporation with a published balance sheet there are various ratios used to calculate a measure of liquidity.

a. Accounting liquidity
c. Operating leverage
b. Operating profit margin
d. Invested capital

18. In economics and business, specifically cost accounting, the _____ is the point at which cost or expenses and revenue are equal: there is no net loss or gain, and one has 'broken even'. A profit or a loss has not been made, although opportunity costs have been paid, and capital has received the risk-adjusted, expected return.

For example, if the business sells less than 200 tables each month, it will make a loss, if it sells more, it will be a profit.

a. Fixed asset turnover
c. Market microstructure
b. Defined contribution plan
d. Break-even point

19. The _____ is the average project earnings after taxes and depreciation, divided by the average book value of the investment during its life.

There are three steps to calculating the _____.

First, determine the average net income of each year of the project's life. Second, determine the average investment, taking depreciation into account. Third, determine the _____ by dividing the average net income by the average investment.

a. Assets turnover
c. Operating leverage
b. Information ratio
d. Average accounting return

20. The _____ is a capital budgeting metric used by firms to decide whether they should make investments. It is an indicator of the efficiency or quality of an investment, as opposed to net present value (NPV), which indicates value or magnitude.

The IRR is the annualized effective compounded return rate which can be earned on the invested capital, i.e., the yield on the investment.

a. AAB
c. ABN Amro
b. A Random Walk Down Wall Street
d. Internal rate of return

Chapter 8. Net Present Value and Other Investment Criteria

21. In finance, _____, also known as return on investment is the ratio of money gained or lost on an investment relative to the amount of money invested. The amount of money gained or lost may be referred to as interest, profit/loss, gain/loss, or net income/loss. The money invested may be referred to as the asset, capital, principal, or the cost basis of the investment.

    a. Doctrine of the Proper Law
    b. Rate of return
    c. Composiition of Creditors
    d. Stock or scrip dividends

22. An _____ can be defined as a contract which provides an income stream in return for an initial payment.

    An immediate _____ is an _____ for which the time between the contract date and the date of the first payment is not longer than the time interval between payments. A common use for an immediate _____ is to provide a pension to a retired person or persons.

    a. AT'T Inc.
    b. Intrinsic value
    c. Annuity
    d. Amortization

23. A '_____' is a 'Charge' that is paid to obtain the right to delay a payment. Essentially, the payer purchases the right to make a given payment in the future instead of in the Present. The '_____', or 'Charge' that must be paid to delay the payment, is simply the difference between what the payment amount would be if it were paid in the present and what the payment amount would be paid if it were paid in the future.

    a. Risk modeling
    b. Risk aversion
    c. Value at risk
    d. Discount

24. The _____ is an interest rate a central bank charges depository institutions that borrow reserves from it.

    The term _____ has two meanings:

    - the same as interest rate; the term 'discount' does not refer to the meaning of the word, but to the purpose of using the quantity, such as computations of present value, e.g. net present value / discounted cash flow

    - the annual effective _____, which is the annual interest divided by the capital including that interest; this rate is lower than the interest rate; it corresponds to using the value after a year as the nominal value, and seeing the initial value as the nominal value minus a discount; it is used for Treasury Bills and similar financial instruments

    The annual effective _____ is the annual interest divided by the capital including that interest, which is the interest rate divided by 100% plus the interest rate. It is the annual discount factor to be applied to the future cash flow, to find the discount, subtracted from a future value to find the value one year earlier.

    For example, suppose there is a government bond that sells for $95 and pays $100 in a year's time.

    a. Black-Scholes
    b. Discount rate
    c. Fisher equation
    d. Stochastic volatility

25. _____ are made by investors and investment managers.

Investors commonly perform investment analysis by making use of fundamental analysis, technical analysis and gut feel.

_____ are often supported by decision tools.

a. Investment performance
b. Asset allocation
c. Investing online
d. Investment decisions

26. A _____ is an indicator, used in the formal discipline of cost-benefit analysis, that attempts to summarize the overall value for money of a project or proposal. A _____ is the ratio of the benefits of a project or proposal, expressed in monetary terms, relative to its costs, also expressed in monetary terms. All benefits and costs should be expressed in discounted present values.

a. 4-4-5 Calendar
b. Benefit-cost ratio
c. 7-Eleven
d. 529 plan

27. _____ identifies the relationship of investment to payoff of a proposed project. The ratio is calculated as follows:

- >

_____ is also known as Profit Investment Ratio, abbreviated to P.I. and Value Investment Ratio (V.I.R.). _____ is a good tool for ranking projects because it allows you to clearly identify the amount of value created per unit of investment, thus if you are capital constrained you wish to invest in those projects which create value most efficiently first.

a. Total return
b. Conditional prepayment rate
c. Capitalization rate
d. Profitability index

Chapter 9. Making Capital Investment Decisions

1. In economics, the concept of the _____ refers to the decision-making time frame of a firm in which at least one factor of production is fixed. Costs which are fixed in the _____ have no impact on a firms decisions. For example a firm can raise output by increasing the amount of labour through overtime.

   a. 529 plan
   b. Long-run
   c. Short-run
   d. 4-4-5 Calendar

2. _____ are made by investors and investment managers.

   Investors commonly perform investment analysis by making use of fundamental analysis, technical analysis and gut feel.

   _____ are often supported by decision tools.

   a. Investment performance
   b. Investing online
   c. Asset allocation
   d. Investment decisions

3. In finance, _____ is the ability of an entity to pay its debts with available cash. _____ can also be described as the ability of a corporation to meet its long-term fixed expenses and to accomplish long-term expansion and growth. The better a company's _____, the better it is financially.

   a. Capital asset
   b. Mid price
   c. Political risk
   d. Solvency

4. _____ is the planning process used to determine whether a firm's long term investments such as new machinery, replacement machinery, new plants, new products, and research development projects are worth pursuing. It is budget for major capital, or investment, expenditures.

   Many formal methods are used in _____, including the techniques such as

   - Net present value
   - Profitability index
   - Internal rate of return
   - Modified Internal Rate of Return
   - Equivalent annuity

   These methods use the incremental cash flows from each potential investment, or project. Techniques based on accounting earnings and accounting rules are sometimes used - though economists consider this to be improper - such as the accounting rate of return, and 'return on investment.' Simplified and hybrid methods are used as well, such as payback period and discounted payback period.

   a. Preferred stock
   b. Shareholder value
   c. Capital budgeting
   d. Financial distress

Chapter 9. Making Capital Investment Decisions

5. _____ is the balance of the amounts of cash being received and paid by a business during a defined period of time, sometimes tied to a specific project. Measurement of _____ can be used

- to evaluate the state or performance of a business or project.
- to determine problems with liquidity. Being profitable does not necessarily mean being liquid. A company can fail because of a shortage of cash, even while profitable.
- to generate project rate of returns. The time of _____s into and out of projects are used as inputs to financial models such as internal rate of return, and net present value.
- to examine income or growth of a business when it is believed that accrual accounting concepts do not represent economic realities. Alternately, _____ can be used to 'validate' the net income generated by accrual accounting.

_____ as a generic term may be used differently depending on context, and certain _____ definitions may be adapted by analysts and users for their own uses. Common terms include operating _____ and free _____.

_____s can be classified into:

1. Operational _____s: Cash received or expended as a result of the company's core business activities.
2. Investment _____s: Cash received or expended through capital expenditure, investments or acquisitions.
3. Financing _____s: Cash received or expended as a result of financial activities, such as interests and dividends.

All three together - the net _____ - are necessary to reconcile the beginning cash balance to the ending cash balance. Loan draw downs or equity injections, that is just shifting of capital but no expenditure as such, are not considered in the net _____.

a. Corporate finance
b. Shareholder value
c. Real option
d. Cash flow

6. _____ or economic opportunity loss is the value of the next best alternative foregone as the result of making a decision. _____ analysis is an important part of a company's decision-making processes but is not treated as an actual cost in any financial statement. The next best thing that a person can engage in is referred to as the _____ of doing the best thing and ignoring the next best thing to be done.
   a. AAB
   b. ABN Amro
   c. A Random Walk Down Wall Street
   d. Opportunity cost

7. In economics, business, and accounting, a _____ is the value of money that has been used up to produce something, and hence is not available for use anymore. In business, the _____ may be one of acquisition, in which case the amount of money expended to acquire it is counted as _____. In this case, money is the input that is gone in order to acquire the thing.
   a. Sliding scale fees
   b. Marginal cost
   c. Fixed costs
   d. Cost

Chapter 9. Making Capital Investment Decisions

8. In economics and business decision-making, _____ are costs that cannot be recovered once they have been incurred. _____ are sometimes contrasted with variable costs, which are the costs that will change due to the proposed course of action, and prospective costs which are costs that will be incurred if an action is taken. In microeconomic theory, only variable costs are relevant to a decision.
   a. Hyperbolic discounting
   b. 4-4-5 Calendar
   c. Sunk costs
   d. Hindsight bias

9. _____ is a term used in accounting, economics and finance to spread the cost of an asset over the span of several years.

   In simple words we can say that _____ is the reduction in the value of an asset due to usage, passage of time, wear and tear, technological outdating or obsolescence, depletion or other such factors.

   In accounting, _____ is a term used to describe any method of attributing the historical or purchase cost of an asset across its useful life, roughly corresponding to normal wear and tear.

   a. Deferred financing costs
   b. Bottom line
   c. Matching principle
   d. Depreciation

10. _____ or financing is to provide capital (funds), which means money for a project, a person, a business or any other private or public institutions.

    Those funds can be allocated for either short term or long term purposes. The health fund is a new way of _____ private healthcare centers.

    a. Synthetic CDO
    b. Product life cycle
    c. Funding
    d. Proxy fight

11. _____ or net present worth (NPW) is defined as the total present value (PV) of a time series of cash flows. It is a standard method for using the time value of money to appraise long-term projects. Used for capital budgeting, and widely throughout economics, it measures the excess or shortfall of cash flows, in present value terms, once financing charges are met.
    a. Tax shield
    b. Present value of costs
    c. Negative gearing
    d. Net present value

12. _____ is a financial metric which represents operating liquidity available to a business. Along with fixed assets such as plant and equipment, _____ is considered a part of operating capital. It is calculated as current assets minus current liabilities.
    a. Working capital
    b. 529 plan
    c. 4-4-5 Calendar
    d. Working capital management

13. _____ is the value on a given date of a future payment or series of future payments, discounted to reflect the time value of money and other factors such as investment risk. _____ calculations are widely used in business and economics to provide a means to compare cash flows at different times on a meaningful 'like to like' basis.

    The most commonly applied model of the time value of money is compound interest.

a. Present value
c. Net present value
b. Negative gearing
d. Present value of benefits

14. _____ are business expenses that are not dependent on the level of production or sales. They tend to be time-related, such as salaries or rents being paid per month. This is in contrast to Variable costs, which are volume-related (and are paid per quantity.)

a. Fixed costs
c. Transaction cost
b. Marginal cost
d. Sliding scale fees

15. In financial accounting, _____ , cash flow provided by operations or cash flow from operating activities, refers to the amount of cash a company generates from the revenues it brings in, excluding costs associated with long-term investment on capital items or investment in securities.

_____ = Cash generated from operations less taxation and interest paid, investment income received and less dividends paid gives rise to _____s per International Financial Reporting Standards.

To calculate cash generated from operations, one must calculate cash generated from customers and cash paid to suppliers.

a. Other Comprehensive Basis of Accounting
c. A Random Walk Down Wall Street
b. Appreciation
d. Operating cash flow

16. The term _____ is a term applied to practices that are perfunctory, or seek to satisfy the minimum requirements or to conform to a convention or doctrine. It has different meanings in different fields.

In accounting, _____ earnings are those earnings of companies in addition to actual earnings calculated under the Generally Accepted Accounting Principles (GAAP) in their quarterly and yearly financial reports.

a. Deferred financing costs
c. Deferred income
b. Long-term liabilities
d. Pro forma

17. _____ are formal records of a business' financial activities.

_____ provide an overview of a business' financial condition in both short and long term. There are four basic _____:

1. **Balance sheet**: also referred to as statement of financial position or condition, reports on a company's assets, liabilities, and net equity as of a given point in time.
2. **Income statement**: also referred to as Profit and Loss statement (or a 'P'L'), reports on a company's income, expenses, and profits over a period of time.
3. **Statement of retained earnings**: explains the changes in a company's retained earnings over the reporting period.
4. **Statement of cash flows**: reports on a company's cash flow activities, particularly its operating, investing and financing activities.

Chapter 9. Making Capital Investment Decisions

a. Statement on Auditing Standards No. 70: Service Organizations
b. Statement of retained earnings
c. Notes to the Financial Statements
d. Financial statements

18. _____ is the corporate management term for the act of reorganizing the legal, ownership, operational, or other structures of a company for the purpose of making it more profitable or better organized for its present needs. Alternate reasons for restructing include a change of ownership or ownership structure, demerger repositioning debt _____ and financial _____.

a. Day trading
b. Cross-border leasing
c. Restructuring
d. Concentrated stock

19. The _____ is a capital budgeting metric used by firms to decide whether they should make investments. It is an indicator of the efficiency or quality of an investment, as opposed to net present value (NPV), which indicates value or magnitude.

The IRR is the annualized effective compounded return rate which can be earned on the invested capital, i.e., the yield on the investment.

a. ABN Amro
b. AAB
c. A Random Walk Down Wall Street
d. Internal rate of return

20. A _____ is the reduction in income taxes that results from taking an allowable deduction from taxable income. For example, because interest on debt is a tax-deductible expense, taking on debt creates a _____. Since a _____ is a way to save cash flows, it increases the value of the business, and it is an important aspect of business valuation.

a. Tax shield
b. Present value of benefits
c. Present value of costs
d. Refinancing risk

21. In finance, _____, also known as return on investment is the ratio of money gained or lost on an investment relative to the amount of money invested. The amount of money gained or lost may be referred to as interest, profit/loss, gain/loss, or net income/loss. The money invested may be referred to as the asset, capital, principal, or the cost basis of the investment.

a. Composiition of Creditors
b. Stock or scrip dividends
c. Doctrine of the Proper Law
d. Rate of return

22. The _____ is the current method of accelerated asset depreciation required by the United States income tax code. Under _____, all assets are divided into classes which dictate the number of years over which an asset's cost will be recovered.

Prior to the Accelerated Cost Recovery System (ACRS), most capital purchases were depreciated using a straight line technique, that allowed for the depreciation of the asset over its useful life.

a. 529 plan
b. 7-Eleven
c. Modified Accelerated Cost Recovery System
d. 4-4-5 Calendar

Chapter 9. Making Capital Investment Decisions

23. In business and accounting, _____s are everything of value that is owned by a person or company. The balance sheet of a firm records the monetary value of the _____s owned by the firm. The two major _____ classes are tangible _____s and intangible _____s.
   a. Income
   b. Asset
   c. EBITDA
   d. Accounts payable

24. _____ is the price at which an asset would trade in a competitive Walrasian auction setting. _____ is often used interchangeably with open _____, fair value or fair _____, although these terms have distinct definitions in different standards, and may differ in some circumstances.

   International Valuation Standards defines _____ as 'the estimated amount for which a property should exchange on the date of valuation between a willing buyer and a willing seller in an arm'e;s-length transaction after proper marketing wherein the parties had each acted knowledgeably, prudently, and without compulsion.'

   _____ is a concept distinct from market price, which is 'e;the price at which one can transact'e;, while _____ is 'e;the true underlying value'e; according to theoretical standards.

   a. Wrap account
   b. T-Model
   c. Debt restructuring
   d. Market value

25. In accounting, _____ or *Carrying value* is the value of an asset according to its balance sheet account balance. For assets, the value is based on the original cost of the asset less any depreciation, amortization or impairment costs made against the asset. A company's _____ is its total assets minus intangible assets and liabilities.
   a. Book value
   b. Current liabilities
   c. Retained earnings
   d. Pro forma

26. A _____ is a profit that results from investments into a capital asset, such as stocks, bonds or real estate, which exceeds the purchase price. It is the difference between a higher selling price and a lower purchase price, resulting in a financial gain for the seller. Conversely, a capital loss arises if the proceeds from the sale of a capital asset are less than the purchase price.
   a. Capital gain
   b. Payroll tax
   c. Tax brackets
   d. Capital gains tax

27. In finance, the _____ approach describes a method of valuing a project, company, or asset using the concepts of the time value of money. All future cash flows are estimated and discounted to give their present values. The discount rate used is generally the appropriate cost of capital and may incorporate judgments of the uncertainty (riskiness) of the future cash flows.
   a. Discounted cash flow
   b. Present value of benefits
   c. Net present value
   d. Future-oriented

28. In finance, _____ is the process of estimating the potential market value of a financial asset or liability. they can be done on assets (for example, investments in marketable securities such as stocks, options, business enterprises, or intangible assets such as patents and trademarks) or on liabilities (e.g., Bonds issued by a company.) _____s are required in many contexts including investment analysis, capital budgeting, merger and acquisition transactions, financial reporting, taxable events to determine the proper tax liability, and in litigation.

Chapter 9. Making Capital Investment Decisions

a. Valuation
b. Procter ' Gamble
c. Share
d. Margin

29. The _____ is an expected return that the provider of capital plans to earn on their investment.

Capital (money) used for funding a business should earn returns for the capital providers who risk their capital. For an investment to be worthwhile, the expected return on capital must be greater than the _____.

a. 4-4-5 Calendar
b. Weighted average cost of capital
c. Capital intensity
d. Cost of capital

30. The phrase _____ refers to the aspect of corporate strategy, corporate finance and management dealing with the buying, selling and combining of different companies that can aid, finance, or help a growing company in a given industry grow rapidly without having to create another business entity.

An acquisition, also known as a takeover, is the buying of one company (the 'target') by another. An acquisition may be friendly or hostile.

a. 7-Eleven
b. Mergers and acquisitions
c. 4-4-5 Calendar
d. 529 plan

31. _____ is a process of analyzing possible future events by considering alternative possible outcomes (scenarios.) The analysis is designed to allow improved decision-making by allowing consideration of outcomes and their implications.

For example, in economics and finance, a financial institution might attempt to forecast several possible scenarios for the economy (e.g. rapid growth, moderate growth, slow growth) and it might also attempt to forecast financial market returns (for bonds, stocks and cash) in each of those scenarios.

a. 4-4-5 Calendar
b. Detection Risk
c. 529 plan
d. Scenario analysis

32. _____ is the study of how the variation (uncertainty) in the output of a mathematical model can be apportioned, qualitatively or quantitatively, to different sources of variation in the input of a model.

In more general terms uncertainty and sensitivity analyses investigate the robustness of a study when the study includes some form of mathematical modelling. While uncertainty analysis studies the overall uncertainty in the conclusions of the study, _____ tries to identify what source of uncertainty weights more on the study's conclusions.

a. Sensitivity analysis
b. Golden parachute
c. Proxy fight
d. Synthetic CDO

33. An _____ is a contract written by a seller that conveys to the buyer the right -- but not the obligation -- to buy (in the case of a call _____) or to sell (in the case of a put _____) a particular asset, such as a piece of property such as, among others, a futures contract. In return for granting the _____, the seller collects a payment (the premium) from the buyer.

For example, buying a call _____ provides the right to buy a specified quantity of a security at a set strike price at some time on or before expiration, while buying a put _____ provides the right to sell.

a. AT'T Mobility LLC
b. Annuity
c. Amortization
d. Option

Chapter 10. Some Lessons from Capital Market History

1. The _____ is the market for securities, where companies and governments can raise longterm funds. The _____ includes the stock market and the bond market. Financial regulators, such as the U.S. Securities and Exchange Commission, oversee the _____s in their designated countries to ensure that investors are protected against fraud.
   a. Forward market
   b. Delta neutral
   c. Spot rate
   d. Capital market

2. In finance, _____, also known as return on investment is the ratio of money gained or lost on an investment relative to the amount of money invested. The amount of money gained or lost may be referred to as interest, profit/loss, gain/loss, or net income/loss. The money invested may be referred to as the asset, capital, principal, or the cost basis of the investment.
   a. Doctrine of the Proper Law
   b. Composiition of Creditors
   c. Stock or scrip dividends
   d. Rate of return

3. A _____ is a private or public market for the trading of company stock and derivatives of company stock at an agreed price; these are securities listed on a stock exchange as well as those only traded privately.

   The size of the world _____ is estimated at about $36.6 trillion US at the beginning of October 2008 . The world derivatives market has been estimated at about $480 trillion face or nominal value, 12 times the size of the entire world economy.

   a. Stock market
   b. Adolph Coors
   c. Anton Gelonkin
   d. Andrew Tobias

4. An _____ is an economic concept that relates to the cost incurred by an entity (such as organizations) associated with problems such as divergent management-shareholder objectives and information asymmetry. The costs consist of two main sources:

   1. The costs inherently associated with using an agent (e.g., the risk that agents will use organizational resource for their own benefit) and
   2. The costs of techniques used to mitigate the problems associated with using an agent (e.g., the costs of producing financial statements or the use of stock options to align executive interests to shareholder interests.)

   Though effects of _____ are present in any agency relationship, the term is most used in business contexts.

   The information asymmetry that exists between shareholders and the Chief Executive Officer is generally considered to be a classic example of a principal-agent problem. The agent (the manager) is working on behalf of the principal (the shareholders), who does not observe the actions of the agent.

   a. ABN Amro
   b. AAB
   c. Agency cost
   d. A Random Walk Down Wall Street

5. In economics, business, and accounting, a _____ is the value of money that has been used up to produce something, and hence is not available for use anymore. In business, the _____ may be one of acquisition, in which case the amount of money expended to acquire it is counted as _____. In this case, money is the input that is gone in order to acquire the thing.
   a. Fixed costs
   b. Sliding scale fees
   c. Marginal cost
   d. Cost

6. In finance, _____ refers to Monday, October 19, 1987, when stock markets around the world crashed, shedding a huge value in a very short time. The crash began in Hong Kong, spread west through international time zones to Europe, hitting the United States after other markets had already declined by a significant margin. The Dow Jones Industrial Average (DJIA) dropped by 508 points to 1738.74 (22.61%).

   a. 7-Eleven
   b. 529 plan
   c. Black Monday
   d. 4-4-5 Calendar

7. A _____ is a profit that results from investments into a capital asset, such as stocks, bonds or real estate, which exceeds the purchase price. It is the difference between a higher selling price and a lower purchase price, resulting in a financial gain for the seller. Conversely, a capital loss arises if the proceeds from the sale of a capital asset are less than the purchase price.

   a. Capital gain
   b. Payroll tax
   c. Tax brackets
   d. Capital gains tax

8. _____ is the difference between a lower selling price and a higher purchase price, resulting in a financial loss for the seller. Pursuant to IRS TAX TIP 2009-35 'If your _____ exceeds your capital gain, the excess can be deducted on your tax return, up to an annual limit of $3,000 ($1,500 if you are married filing separately.)'.

   a. 4-4-5 Calendar
   b. 529 plan
   c. Capital loss
   d. 7-Eleven

9. _____ is a form of corporation equity ownership represented in the securities. It is dangerous in comparison to preferred shares and some other investment options, in that in the event of bankruptcy, _____ investors receive their funds after preferred stockholders, bondholders, creditors, etc. On the other hand, common shares on average perform better than preferred shares or bonds over time.

   a. Stock split
   b. Common stock
   c. Stock market bubble
   d. Stop-limit order

10. A _____ is a payment made by a corporation to its shareholder members. When a corporation earns a profit or surplus, that money can be put to two uses: it can either be re-invested in the business (called retained earnings), or it can be paid to the shareholders as a _____. Many corporations retain a portion of their earnings and pay the remainder as a _____.

    a. Special dividend
    b. Dividend puzzle
    c. Dividend yield
    d. Dividend

11. _____ is typically a higher ranking stock than voting shares, and its terms are negotiated between the corporation and the investor.

    _____ usually carry no voting rights, but may carry superior priority over common stock in the payment of dividends and upon liquidation. _____ may carry a dividend that is paid out prior to any dividends to common stock holders.

    a. Second lien loan
    b. Follow-on offering
    c. Trade-off theory
    d. Preferred stock

Chapter 10. Some Lessons from Capital Market History

12. A _____ is a fungible, negotiable instrument representing financial value. They are broadly categorized into debt securities (such as banknotes, bonds and debentures), and equity securities; e.g., common stocks. The company or other entity issuing the _____ is called the issuer.

   a. Tracking stock
   b. Securities lending
   c. Book entry
   d. Security

13. The _____, in terms of finance and investing, describes how the expected return of a stock or portfolio is correlated to the return of the financial market as a whole.

   An asset with a beta of 0 means that its price is not at all correlated with the market; that asset is independent. A positive beta means that the asset generally follows the market.

   a. LIBOR market model
   b. Beta coefficient
   c. Current yield
   d. Perpetuity

14. _____ are cash, evidence of an ownership interest in an entity or deliver, cash or another financial instrument.

   _____ can be categorized by form depending on whether they are cash instruments or derivative instruments:

   - Cash instruments are _____ whose value is determined directly by markets. They can be divided into securities, which are readily transferable, and other cash instruments such as loans and deposits, where both borrower and lender have to agree on a transfer.
   - Derivative instruments are _____ which derive their value from the value and characteristics of one or more underlying assets. They can be divided into exchange-traded derivatives and over-the-counter (OTC) derivatives.

   Alternatively, _____ can be categorized by 'asset class' depending on whether they are equity based (reflecting ownership of the issuing entity) or debt based (reflecting a loan the investor has made to the issuing entity.) If it is debt, it can be further categorised into short term (less than one year) or long term.

   Foreign Exchange instruments and transactions are neither debt nor equity based and belong in their own category.

   a. Financial instruments
   b. Financial services
   c. Cost of carry
   d. Secondary market

15. The _____ is a capital budgeting metric used by firms to decide whether they should make investments. It is an indicator of the efficiency or quality of an investment, as opposed to net present value (NPV), which indicates value or magnitude.

   The IRR is the annualized effective compounded return rate which can be earned on the invested capital, i.e., the yield on the investment.

a. A Random Walk Down Wall Street
b. Internal rate of return
c. ABN Amro
d. AAB

16. The _____ is the average project earnings after taxes and depreciation, divided by the average book value of the investment during its life.

There are three steps to calculating the _____.

First, determine the average net income of each year of the project's life. Second, determine the average investment, taking depreciation into account. Third, determine the _____ by dividing the average net income by the average investment.

a. Information ratio
b. Operating leverage
c. Average accounting return
d. Assets turnover

17. In business and finance, a _____ (also referred to as equity _____) of stock means a _____ of ownership in a corporation (company.) In the plural, stocks is often used as a synonym for _____s especially in the United States, but it is less commonly used that way outside of North America.

In the United Kingdom, South Africa, and Australia, stock can also refer to completely different financial instruments such as government bonds or, less commonly, to all kinds of marketable securities.

a. Bucket shop
b. Procter ' Gamble
c. Margin
d. Share

18. A _____ is a measure of the average price of consumer goods and services purchased by households. The _____ can be used to index (i.e., adjust for the effects of inflation) wages, salaries, pensions, or regulated or contracted prices. The _____ is, along with the population census and the National Income and Product Accounts, one of the most closely watched national economic statistics.

a. Consumer price index
b. 529 plan
c. 4-4-5 Calendar
d. Divisia index

19. A _____ is a bond issued by a corporation. The term is usually applied to longer-term debt instruments, generally with a maturity date falling at least a year after their issue date. (The term 'commercial paper' is sometimes used for instruments with a shorter maturity.)

a. Corporate bond
b. Government bond
c. Brady bonds
d. Serial bond

20. A _____ is a bond issued by a national government denominated in the country's own currency. Bonds issued by national governments in foreign currencies are normally referred to as sovereign bonds. The first ever _____ was issued by the British government in 1693 to raise money to fund a war against France.

a. Collateralized debt obligations
b. Government bond
c. Municipal bond
d. Zero-coupon bond

Chapter 10. Some Lessons from Capital Market History

21. In economic models, the _____ time frame assumes no fixed factors of production. Firms can enter or leave the marketplace, and the cost (and availability) of land, labor, raw materials, and capital goods can be assumed to vary. In contrast, in the short-run time frame, certain factors are assumed to be fixed, because there is not sufficient time for them to change.
   a. Short-run
   b. 4-4-5 Calendar
   c. Long-run
   d. 529 plan

22. The _____ is a stock exchange based in New York City, New York. It is the largest stock exchange in the world by dollar value of its listed companies securities. As of October 2008, the combined capitalization of all domestic _____ listed companies was $10.1 trillion.
   a. 529 plan
   b. 4-4-5 Calendar
   c. 7-Eleven
   d. New York Stock Exchange

23. A _____, securities exchange or (in Europe) bourse is a corporation or mutual organization which provides 'trading' facilities for stock brokers and traders, to trade stocks and other securities. _____s also provide facilities for the issue and redemption of securities as well as other financial instruments and capital events including the payment of income and dividends. The securities traded on a _____ include: shares issued by companies, unit trusts and other pooled investment products and bonds.
   a. 4-4-5 Calendar
   b. 529 plan
   c. 7-Eleven
   d. Stock Exchange

24. _____ mature in one year or less. Like zero-coupon bonds, they do not pay interest prior to maturity; instead they are sold at a discount of the par value to create a positive yield to maturity. Many regard _____ as the least risky investment available to U.S. investors.
   a. Treasury bills
   b. 4-4-5 Calendar
   c. Treasury securities
   d. Treasury Inflation Protected Securities

25. A _____ is a document that indicates that the bearer of the document has title to property, such as shares or bonds. They differ from normal registered instruments, in that no records are kept of who owns the underlying property, or of the transactions involving transfer of ownership. Whoever physically holds the bearer bond papers owns the property.
   a. Marketable
   b. Book entry
   c. Securities lending
   d. Bearer instrument

26. The coupon or _____ of a bond is the amount of interest paid per year expressed as a percentage of the face value of the bond.

For example if you hold $10,000 nominal of a bond described as a 4.5% loan stock, you will receive $450 in interest each year (probably in two installments of $225 each.)

Not all bonds have coupons.

   a. Revenue bonds
   b. Zero-coupon bond
   c. Puttable bond
   d. Coupon rate

27. In finance, a _____ is a debt security, in which the authorized issuer owes the holders a debt and, depending on the terms of the _____, is obliged to pay interest (the coupon) and/or to repay the principal at a later date, termed maturity.

Thus a _____ is a loan: the issuer is the borrower, the _____ holder is the lender, and the coupon is the interest. _____s provide the borrower with external funds to finance long-term investments, or, in the case of government _____s, to finance current expenditure.

a. Convertible bond
c. Puttable bond
b. Catastrophe bonds
d. Bond

28. A _____ is a normalized average (typically a weighted average) of prices for a given class of goods or services in a given region, during a given interval of time. It is a statistic designed to help to compare how these prices, taken as a whole, differ between time periods or geographical locations.

a. Price index
c. Price discrimination
b. Discounts and allowances
d. Transfer pricing

29. _____ is a risk-adjusted measure of the so-called active return on an investment. It is the return in excess of the compensation for the risk borne, and thus commonly used to assess active managers' performances. Often, the return of a benchmark is subtracted in order to consider relative performance, which yields Jensen's _____.

a. Amortization
c. Option
b. Annuity
d. Alpha

30.

In finance, the _____ can be the expected rate of return above the risk-free interest rate. When measuring risk, a common sense approach is to compare the risk-free return on T-bills and the very risky return on other investments. The difference between these two returns can be interpreted as a measure of the excess return on the average risky asset. This excess return is known as the _____.

a. Risk aversion
c. Risk modeling
b. Risk adjusted return on capital
d. Risk premium

31. In statistics, a _____ is a tabulation of the values that one or more variables take in a sample.

Univariate _____s are often presented as lists ordered by quantity showing the number of times each value appears. For example, if 100 people rate a five-point Likert scale assessing their agreement with a statement on a scale on which 1 denotes strong agreement and 5 strong disagreement, the _____ of their responses might look like:

This simple tabulation has two drawbacks.

a. Frequency distribution
c. Random variables
b. Variance
d. Covariance

32. _____, is when a company issues common stock or shares to the public for the first time. They are often issued by smaller, younger companies seeking capital to expand, but can also be done by large privately-owned companies looking to become publicly traded.

In an _____ the issuer may obtain the assistance of an underwriting firm, which helps it determine what type of security to issue (common or preferred), best offering price and time to bring it to market.

a. Asian Financial Crisis
c. Initial public offering
b. Insolvency
d. Interest

33. In probability and statistics, the _____ of a collection of numbers is a measure of the dispersion of the numbers from their expected (mean) value. It can apply to a probability distribution, a random variable, a population or a data set. The _____ is usually denoted with the letter σ (lowercase sigma.)

a. Standard deviation
c. Kurtosis
b. Sample size
d. Mean

34. In probability theory and statistics, the _____ of a random variable, probability distribution averaging the squared distance of its possible values from the expected value (mean.) Whereas the mean is a way to describe the location of a distribution, the _____ is a way to capture its scale or degree of being spread out. The unit of _____ is the square of the unit of the original variable.

a. Semivariance
c. Harmonic mean
b. Variance
d. Monte Carlo methods

35. A _____ is a professionally managed type of collective investment scheme that pools money from many investors and invests it in stocks, bonds, short-term money market instruments, and/or other securities. The _____ will have a fund manager that trades the pooled money on a regular basis. Currently, the worldwide value of all _____s totals more than $26 trillion.

Since 1940, there have been three basic types of investment companies in the United States: open-end funds, also known in the US as _____s; unit investment trusts (UITs); and closed-end funds.

a. Trust company
c. Financial intermediary
b. Net asset value
d. Mutual fund

36. The _____ is an important family of continuous probability distributions, applicable in many fields. Each member of the family may be defined by two parameters, location and scale: the mean and variance respectively. The standard _____ is the _____ with a mean of zero and a variance of one

a. Correlation
c. Random variables
b. Probability distribution
d. Normal distribution

37. In finance, _____ are stocks that appreciate in value and yield a high return on equity (ROE.) Analysts compute ROE by taking the company's net income and dividing it by the company's equity. To be classified as a growth stock, analysts expect to see at least 15 percent return on equity.

a. Stock valuation
c. Security Analysis
b. 4-4-5 Calendar
d. Growth stocks

38. _____ or net present worth (NPW) is defined as the total present value (PV) of a time series of cash flows. It is a standard method for using the time value of money to appraise long-term projects. Used for capital budgeting, and widely throughout economics, it measures the excess or shortfall of cash flows, in present value terms, once financing charges are met.
- a. Present value of costs
- b. Negative gearing
- c. Tax shield
- d. Net present value

39. A _____ is the price of a single share of a no. of saleable stocks of the company. Once the stock is purchased, the owner becomes a shareholder of the company that issued the share.
- a. Whisper numbers
- b. Stock split
- c. Trading curb
- d. Share price

40. _____ in finance is a risk management technique, related to hedging, that mixes a wide variety of investments within a portfolio. Because the fluctuations of a single security have less impact on a diverse portfolio, _____ minimizes the risk from any one investment.

A simple example of _____ is the following: On a particular island the entire economy consists of two companies: one that sells umbrellas and another that sells sunscreen.

- a. 4-4-5 Calendar
- b. 529 plan
- c. 7-Eleven
- d. Diversification

41. _____ is an economic concept with commonplace familiarity. It is the price that a good or service is offered at, or will fetch, in the marketplace. It is of interest mainly in the study of microeconomics.
- a. Central Securities Depository
- b. Delta hedging
- c. Market price
- d. Convertible arbitrage

42. _____ is the value on a given date of a future payment or series of future payments, discounted to reflect the time value of money and other factors such as investment risk. _____ calculations are widely used in business and economics to provide a means to compare cash flows at different times on a meaningful 'like to like' basis.

The most commonly applied model of the time value of money is compound interest.

- a. Negative gearing
- b. Net present value
- c. Present value of benefits
- d. Present value

43. A _____ or equity fund is a fund that invests in Equities more commonly known as stocks. Such funds are typically held either in stock or cash, as opposed to Bonds, notes, or other securities. This may be a mutual fund or exchange-traded fund.
- a. Money market funds
- b. Closed-end fund
- c. Stock fund
- d. Mutual fund fees and expenses

Chapter 10. Some Lessons from Capital Market History

44. In economics, _____ describes the state of a market with respect to competition.

- Perfect competition, in which the market consists of a very large number of firms producing a homogeneous product.
- Monopolistic competition where there are a large number of independent firms which have a very small proportion of the market share.
- Oligopoly, in which a market is dominated by a small number of firms which own more than 40% of the market share.
- Oligopsony, a market dominated by many sellers and a few buyers.
- Monopoly, where there is only one provider of a product or service.
- Natural monopoly, a monopoly in which economies of scale cause efficiency to increase continuously with the size of the firm. A firm is a natural monopoly if it is able to serve the entire market demand at a lower cost than any combination of two or more smaller, more specialized firms.
- Monopsony, when there is only one buyer in a market.

The imperfectly competitive structure is quite identical to the realistic market conditions where some monopolistic competitors, monopolists, oligopolists, and duopolists exist and dominate the market conditions. The elements of _____ include the number and size distribution of firms, entry conditions, and the extent of differentiation.

These somewhat abstract concerns tend to determine some but not all details of a specific concrete market system where buyers and sellers actually meet and commit to trade.

a. Fixed exchange rate
c. Human capital
b. Gross domestic product
d. Market structure

Chapter 11. Risk and Return

1. _____ is equal to the income that a firm has after subtracting costs and expenses from the total revenue. _____ can be distributed among holders of common stock as a dividend or held by the firm as retained earnings. _____ is an accounting term; in some countries (such as the UK) profit is the usual term.

   a. Historical cost
   b. Write-off
   c. Net income
   d. Furniture, Fixtures and Equipment

2. A _____ is the price of a single share of a no. of saleable stocks of the company. Once the stock is purchased, the owner becomes a shareholder of the company that issued the share.

   a. Whisper numbers
   b. Stock split
   c. Trading curb
   d. Share price

3. _____, refers to consumption opportunity gained by an entity within a specified time frame, which is generally expressed in monetary terms. However, for households and individuals, '_____ is the sum of all the wages, salaries, profits, interests payments, rents and other forms of earnings received... in a given period of time.' For firms, _____ generally refers to net-profit: what remains of revenue after expenses have been subtracted.

   a. Income
   b. Accrual
   c. OIBDA
   d. Annual report

4. The _____, in terms of finance and investing, describes how the expected return of a stock or portfolio is correlated to the return of the financial market as a whole.

   An asset with a beta of 0 means that its price is not at all correlated with the market; that asset is independent. A positive beta means that the asset generally follows the market.

   a. Beta coefficient
   b. Current yield
   c. LIBOR market model
   d. Perpetuity

5. _____ is a form of corporation equity ownership represented in the securities. It is dangerous in comparison to preferred shares and some other investment options, in that in the event of bankruptcy, _____ investors receive their funds after preferred stockholders, bondholders, creditors, etc. On the other hand, common shares on average perform better than preferred shares or bonds over time.

   a. Common stock
   b. Stop-limit order
   c. Stock market bubble
   d. Stock split

6. _____ in finance is a risk management technique, related to hedging, that mixes a wide variety of investments within a portfolio. Because the fluctuations of a single security have less impact on a diverse portfolio, _____ minimizes the risk from any one investment.

   A simple example of _____ is the following: On a particular island the entire economy consists of two companies: one that sells umbrellas and another that sells sunscreen.

   a. 4-4-5 Calendar
   b. 7-Eleven
   c. 529 plan
   d. Diversification

7. The _____ is the weighted-average most likely outcome in gambling, probability theory, economics or finance.

Chapter 11. Risk and Return

In gambling and probability theory, there is usually a discrete set of possible outcomes. In this case, _____ is a measure of the relative balance of win or loss weighted by their chances of occurring.

a. Expected return
c. ABN Amro
b. A Random Walk Down Wall Street
d. AAB

8. _____ is typically a higher ranking stock than voting shares, and its terms are negotiated between the corporation and the investor.

_____ usually carry no voting rights, but may carry superior priority over common stock in the payment of dividends and upon liquidation. _____ may carry a dividend that is paid out prior to any dividends to common stock holders.

a. Second lien loan
c. Follow-on offering
b. Trade-off theory
d. Preferred stock

9. In finance, _____, also known as return on investment is the ratio of money gained or lost on an investment relative to the amount of money invested. The amount of money gained or lost may be referred to as interest, profit/loss, gain/loss, or net income/loss. The money invested may be referred to as the asset, capital, principal, or the cost basis of the investment.

a. Doctrine of the Proper Law
c. Composiition of Creditors
b. Stock or scrip dividends
d. Rate of return

10.

In finance, the _____ can be the expected rate of return above the risk-free interest rate. When measuring risk, a common sense approach is to compare the risk-free return on T-bills and the very risky return on other investments. The difference between these two returns can be interpreted as a measure of the excess return on the average risky asset. This excess return is known as the _____.

a. Risk modeling
c. Risk aversion
b. Risk adjusted return on capital
d. Risk premium

11. A _____ is a fungible, negotiable instrument representing financial value. They are broadly categorized into debt securities (such as banknotes, bonds and debentures), and equity securities; e.g., common stocks. The company or other entity issuing the _____ is called the issuer.

a. Book entry
c. Securities lending
b. Tracking stock
d. Security

12. In Modern Portfolio Theory, the _____ is the graphical representation of the Capital Asset Pricing Model. It displays the expected rate of return for an overall market as a function of systematic (non-diversifiable) risk (beta.)

The Y-Intercept (beta=0) of the _____ is equal to the risk-free interest rate.

a. Security market line
c. Rebalancing
b. Divestment
d. Certificate in Investment Performance Measurement

13. In finance, _____ is that risk which is common to an entire market and not to any individual entity or component thereof. It should be distinguished from systemic risk which is the risk that the entire financial system will collapse as a result of some catastrophic event.

Risks can be reduced in four main ways: Avoidance, Reduction, Retention and Transfer.

a. Conglomerate merger
c. Systematic risk
b. Primary market
d. Capital surplus

14. In economics, business, and accounting, a _____ is the value of money that has been used up to produce something, and hence is not available for use anymore. In business, the _____ may be one of acquisition, in which case the amount of money expended to acquire it is counted as _____. In this case, money is the input that is gone in order to acquire the thing.

a. Marginal cost
c. Fixed costs
b. Sliding scale fees
d. Cost

15. The _____ is an expected return that the provider of capital plans to earn on their investment.

Capital (money) used for funding a business should earn returns for the capital providers who risk their capital. For an investment to be worthwhile, the expected return on capital must be greater than the _____.

a. Weighted average cost of capital
c. Cost of capital
b. 4-4-5 Calendar
d. Capital intensity

16. The _____ is one of the measures of national income and input for a given country's economy. _____ is defined as the total cost of all finished goods and services produced within the country in a stipulated period of time (usually a 365-day year.) It is sometimes regarded as the sum of profits added at every level of production (the intermediate stages) of all final goods and services produced within a country in a stipulated timeframe, and it is rarely given a monetary value.

a. Behavioral finance
c. Recession
b. Macroeconomics
d. Gross domestic product

17. An _____ is an economic concept that relates to the cost incurred by an entity (such as organizations) associated with problems such as divergent management-shareholder objectives and information asymmetry. The costs consist of two main sources:

1. The costs inherently associated with using an agent (e.g., the risk that agents will use organizational resource for their own benefit) and
2. The costs of techniques used to mitigate the problems associated with using an agent (e.g., the costs of producing financial statements or the use of stock options to align executive interests to shareholder interests.)

Though effects of _____ are present in any agency relationship, the term is most used in business contexts.

Chapter 11. Risk and Return

The information asymmetry that exists between shareholders and the Chief Executive Officer is generally considered to be a classic example of a principal-agent problem. The agent (the manager) is working on behalf of the principal (the shareholders), who does not observe the actions of the agent.

a. AAB
b. ABN Amro
c. A Random Walk Down Wall Street
d. Agency cost

18. In probability theory and statistics, the _____ of a random variable, probability distribution averaging the squared distance of its possible values from the expected value (mean.) Whereas the mean is a way to describe the location of a distribution, the _____ is a way to capture its scale or degree of being spread out. The unit of _____ is the square of the unit of the original variable.

a. Harmonic mean
b. Semivariance
c. Monte Carlo methods
d. Variance

19. In probability and statistics, the _____ of a collection of numbers is a measure of the dispersion of the numbers from their expected (mean) value. It can apply to a probability distribution, a random variable, a population or a data set. The _____ is usually denoted with the letter σ (lowercase sigma.)

a. Sample size
b. Standard deviation
c. Kurtosis
d. Mean

20. In economics, a _____ is a general slowdown in economic activity in a country over a sustained period of time, or a business cycle contraction. During _____s, many macroeconomic indicators vary in a similar way. Production as measured by Gross Domestic Product (GDP), employment, investment spending, capacity utilization, household incomes and business profits all fall during _____s.

a. Behavioral finance
b. Recession
c. Mercantilism
d. Fixed exchange rate

21. In business, _____ is the total assets minus total outside liabilities of an individual or a company. For a company, this is called shareholders' equity and may be referred to as book value. _____ is stated as at a particular point in time.

a. Certified International Investment Analyst
b. Moneylender
c. Restructuring
d. Net worth

22. _____ is the risk that the value of an investment will decrease due to moves in market factors. The five standard _____ factors are:

- Equity risk, the risk that stock prices will change.
- Interest rate risk, the risk that interest rates will change.
- Currency risk, the risk that foreign exchange rates will change.
- Commodity risk, the risk that commodity prices (e.g. grains, metals) will change.

As with other forms of risk, _____ may be measured in a number of ways. Traditionally, this is done using a Value at Risk methodology. Value at risk is well established as a risk management technique, but it contains a number of limiting assumptions that constrain its accuracy.

Chapter 11. Risk and Return

a. Tracking error
b. Market risk
c. Currency risk
d. Transaction risk

23. The _____ is the market for securities, where companies and governments can raise longterm funds. The _____ includes the stock market and the bond market. Financial regulators, such as the U.S. Securities and Exchange Commission, oversee the _____s in their designated countries to ensure that investors are protected against fraud.
   a. Capital market
   b. Delta neutral
   c. Spot rate
   d. Forward market

24. The _____ is a stock exchange based in New York City, New York. It is the largest stock exchange in the world by dollar value of its listed companies securities. As of October 2008, the combined capitalization of all domestic _____ listed companies was $10.1 trillion.
   a. 529 plan
   b. 7-Eleven
   c. 4-4-5 Calendar
   d. New York Stock Exchange

25. A _____, securities exchange or (in Europe) bourse is a corporation or mutual organization which provides 'trading' facilities for stock brokers and traders, to trade stocks and other securities. _____s also provide facilities for the issue and redemption of securities as well as other financial instruments and capital events including the payment of income and dividends. The securities traded on a _____ include: shares issued by companies, unit trusts and other pooled investment products and bonds.
   a. 7-Eleven
   b. 529 plan
   c. Stock Exchange
   d. 4-4-5 Calendar

26. The _____ on a portfolio of investments takes into account not only the capital appreciation on the portfolio, but also the income received on the portfolio. The income typically consists of interest, dividends, and securities lending fees. This contrasts with the price return, which takes into account only the capital gain on an investment.
   a. Global tactical asset allocation
   b. Capitalization rate
   c. Profitability index
   d. Total return

27. _____ was formed in 1971 and today operates a chain of domestic merchandise retail stores across United States and Canada. They feature mostly medium-ranged, but also a limited selection of high quality, domestic merchandise: items for the bedroom, bathroom, kitchen, and dining room.
   a. Loan participation
   b. Comanity
   c. Global depository receipt
   d. Bed Bath ' Beyond Inc.

28. The institution most often referenced by the word '_____' is a public or publicly traded _____, the shares of which are traded on a public stock exchange (e.g., the New York Stock Exchange or Nasdaq in the United States) where shares of stock of _____s are bought and sold by and to the general public. Most of the largest businesses in the world are publicly traded _____s. However, the majority of _____s are said to be closely held, privately held or close _____s, meaning that no ready market exists for the trading of shares.
   a. Federal Home Loan Mortgage Corporation
   b. Depository Trust Company
   c. Protect
   d. Corporation

29. In finance, a _____ is a debt security, in which the authorized issuer owes the holders a debt and, depending on the terms of the _____, is obliged to pay interest (the coupon) and/or to repay the principal at a later date, termed maturity.

Chapter 11. Risk and Return

Thus a _____ is a loan: the issuer is the borrower, the _____ holder is the lender, and the coupon is the interest. _____s provide the borrower with external funds to finance long-term investments, or, in the case of government _____s, to finance current expenditure.

a. Puttable bond
c. Catastrophe bonds

b. Convertible bond
d. Bond

30. A '_____' is a 'Charge' that is paid to obtain the right to delay a payment. Essentially, the payer purchases the right to make a given payment in the future instead of in the Present. The '_____', or 'Charge' that must be paid to delay the payment, is simply the difference between what the payment amount would be if it were paid in the present and what the payment amount would be paid if it were paid in the future.

a. Risk aversion
c. Value at risk

b. Risk modeling
d. Discount

31. A _____ is a bond bought at a price lower than its face value, with the face value repaid at the time of maturity. It does not make periodic interest payments, or so-called 'coupons,' hence the term zero-coupon bond. Investors earn return from the compounded interest all paid at maturity plus the difference between the discounted price of the bond and its par value.

a. Callable bond
c. Zero coupon bond

b. Municipal bond
d. Bowie bonds

32. The term _____ has three unrelated technical definitions, and is also used in a variety of non-technical ways.

- In financial economics, it refers to any asset used to make money, as opposed to assets used for personal enjoyment or consumption. This is an important distinction because two people can disagree sharply about the value of personal assets, one person might think a sports car is more valuable than a pickup truck, another person might have the opposite taste. But if an asset is held for the purpose of making money, taste has nothing to do with it, only differences of opinion about how much money the asset will produce. With the further assumption that people agree on the probability distribution of future cash flows, it is possible to have an objective _____ pricing model. Even without the assumption of agreement, it is possible to set rational limits on _____ value.
- In governmental accounting, it is defined as any asset used in operations with an initial useful life extending beyond one reporting period. Generally, government managers have a 'stewardship' duty to maintain _____s under their control. See International Public Sector Accounting Standards for details.
- In US tax accounting, it is defined as any property other than a list of exceptions. The main exceptions are anything held for sale, and any real estate or depreciable property used in business. Almost everything you own and use for personal purposes, pleasure or investment is a _____. If something is a _____ for tax purposes, gains or losses on sale or disposition are capital gains or capital losses. For individuals, however, capital losses on property held for personal use are generally not deductible. See the IRS publication Tax Facts about Capital Gains and Losses for details.

A well-known financial accounting textbook advises that the term be avoided except in tax accounting because it is used in so many different senses, not all of them well-defined. For example it is often used as a synonym for fixed assets or for investments in securities.

A common non-technical usage occurs when people ask that employees or the environment or something else be treated as a _____.

a. Capital asset
b. Settlement date
c. Political risk
d. Solvency

33. In finance, the _____ is used to determine a theoretically appropriate required rate of return of an asset, if that asset is to be added to an already well-diversified portfolio, given that asset's non-diversifiable risk. The model takes into account the asset's sensitivity to non-diversifiable risk (also known as systemic risk or market risk), often represented by the quantity beta (β) in the financial industry, as well as the expected return of the market and the expected return of a theoretical risk-free asset.

The model was introduced by Jack Treynor (1961, 1962), William Sharpe (1964), John Lintner (1965a,b) and Jan Mossin (1966) independently, building on the earlier work of Harry Markowitz on diversification and modern portfolio theory.

a. Hull-White model
b. Cox-Ingersoll-Ross model
c. Capital asset pricing model
d. Random walk hypothesis

34. A _____ is a portfolio consisting of a weighted sum of every asset in the market, with weights in the proportions that they exist in the market (with the necessary assumption that these assets are infinitely divisible.)

Neha Tyagi's critique (1977) states that this is only a theoretical concept, as to create a _____ for investment purposes in practice would necessarily include every single possible available asset, including real estate, precious metals, stamp collections, jewelry, and anything with any worth, as the theoretical market being referred to would be the world market. As a result, proxies for the market are used in practice by investors.

a. Central Securities Depository
b. Market price
c. Delta neutral
d. Market portfolio

35. In business and accounting, _____s are everything of value that is owned by a person or company. The balance sheet of a firm records the monetary value of the _____s owned by the firm. The two major _____ classes are tangible _____s and intangible _____s.
a. Asset
b. Income
c. Accounts payable
d. EBITDA

36. In finance, _____ is the process of estimating the potential market value of a financial asset or liability. they can be done on assets (for example, investments in marketable securities such as stocks, options, business enterprises, or intangible assets such as patents and trademarks) or on liabilities (e.g., Bonds issued by a company.) _____s are required in many contexts including investment analysis, capital budgeting, merger and acquisition transactions, financial reporting, taxable events to determine the proper tax liability, and in litigation.
a. Margin
b. Procter ' Gamble
c. Valuation
d. Share

Chapter 11. Risk and Return

37. In finance, the value of an option consists of two components, its intrinsic value and its _____. Time value is simply the difference between option value and intrinsic value. _____ is also known as theta, extrinsic value, or instrumental value.
    a. Debt buyer
    b. Conservatism
    c. Time value
    d. Global Squeeze

38. Simply put, _____ is the value of money figuring in a given amount of interest for a given amount of time. For example 100 dollars of todays money held for a year at 5 percent interest is worth 105 dollars, therefore 100 dollars paid now or 105 dollars paid exactly one year from now is the same amount of payment of money with that given intersest at that given amount of time. This notion dates at least to Martín de Azpilcueta of the School of Salamanca.

    All of the standard calculations for _____ derive from the most basic algebraic expression for the present value of a future sum, 'discounted' to the present by an amount equal to the _____. For example, a sum of FV to be received in one year is discounted (at the rate of interest r) to give a sum of PV at present: PV = FV -- rÂ·PV = FV/(1+r).

    a. Coefficient of variation
    b. Current account
    c. Zero-coupon bond
    d. Time value of money

39. The _____ is a capital budgeting metric used by firms to decide whether they should make investments. It is an indicator of the efficiency or quality of an investment, as opposed to net present value (NPV), which indicates value or magnitude.

    The IRR is the annualized effective compounded return rate which can be earned on the invested capital, i.e., the yield on the investment.

    a. ABN Amro
    b. A Random Walk Down Wall Street
    c. AAB
    d. Internal rate of return

40. _____ or net present worth (NPW) is defined as the total present value (PV) of a time series of cash flows. It is a standard method for using the time value of money to appraise long-term projects. Used for capital budgeting, and widely throughout economics, it measures the excess or shortfall of cash flows, in present value terms, once financing charges are met.
    a. Negative gearing
    b. Net present value
    c. Tax shield
    d. Present value of costs

41. An _____ can be defined as a contract which provides an income stream in return for an initial payment.

    An immediate _____ is an _____ for which the time between the contract date and the date of the first payment is not longer than the time interval between payments. A common use for an immediate _____ is to provide a pension to a retired person or persons.

    a. Intrinsic value
    b. AT'T Inc.
    c. Annuity
    d. Amortization

Chapter 11. Risk and Return

42. _____ is the value on a given date of a future payment or series of future payments, discounted to reflect the time value of money and other factors such as investment risk. _____ calculations are widely used in business and economics to provide a means to compare cash flows at different times on a meaningful 'like to like' basis.

The most commonly applied model of the time value of money is compound interest.

   a. Net present value
   b. Present value
   c. Negative gearing
   d. Present value of benefits

43. _____ is a Fortune 500, American multinational corporation headquartered in Cincinnati, Ohio, that manufactures a wide range of consumer goods. As of 2008, P'G is the 8th largest corporation in the world by market capitalization and 14th largest US company by profit.

   a. 7-Eleven
   b. 4-4-5 Calendar
   c. 529 plan
   d. Procter ' Gamble Co.

44. A _____ is a collective investment scheme that invests in bonds and other debt securities. _____s yield monthly dividends that include interest payments on the fund's underlying securities plus any capital appreciation in the prices of the portfolio's bonds. _____s tend to pay higher dividends than CDs and money market accounts, and they generally pay out dividends more frequently and regularly than individual bonds.

   a. Premium bond
   b. Gilts
   c. Private activity bond
   d. Bond fund

45. _____ refer to services provided by the finance industry.

The finance industry encompasses a broad range of organizations that deal with the management of money. Among these organizations are banks, credit card companies, insurance companies, consumer finance companies, stock brokerages, investment funds and some government sponsored enterprises.

   a. Financial Services
   b. Delta hedging
   c. Financial instruments
   d. Cost of carry

46. In finance, the _____ is the global financial market for short-term borrowing and lending. It provides short-term liquidity funding for the global financial system. The _____ is where short-term obligations such as Treasury bills, commercial paper and bankers' acceptances are bought and sold.

   a. Consumer debt
   b. Debt-for-equity swap
   c. Cramdown
   d. Money market

47. An _____ is a contract written by a seller that conveys to the buyer the right -- but not the obligation -- to buy (in the case of a call _____) or to sell (in the case of a put _____) a particular asset, such as a piece of property such as, among others, a futures contract. In return for granting the _____, the seller collects a payment (the premium) from the buyer.

For example, buying a call _____ provides the right to buy a specified quantity of a security at a set strike price at some time on or before expiration, while buying a put _____ provides the right to sell.

Chapter 11. Risk and Return

a. AT'T Mobility LLC
b. Option
c. Amortization
d. Annuity

48. A _____ or equity fund is a fund that invests in Equities more commonly known as stocks. Such funds are typically held either in stock or cash, as opposed to Bonds, notes, or other securities. This may be a mutual fund or exchange-traded fund.

a. Mutual fund fees and expenses
b. Money market funds
c. Stock fund
d. Closed-end fund

Chapter 12. Cost of Capital

1. The institution most often referenced by the word '_____' is a public or publicly traded _____, the shares of which are traded on a public stock exchange (e.g., the New York Stock Exchange or Nasdaq in the United States) where shares of stock of _____s are bought and sold by and to the general public. Most of the largest businesses in the world are publicly traded _____s. However, the majority of _____s are said to be closely held, privately held or close _____s, meaning that no ready market exists for the trading of shares.

   a. Protect
   b. Federal Home Loan Mortgage Corporation
   c. Depository Trust Company
   d. Corporation

2. In economics, business, and accounting, a _____ is the value of money that has been used up to produce something, and hence is not available for use anymore. In business, the _____ may be one of acquisition, in which case the amount of money expended to acquire it is counted as _____. In this case, money is the input that is gone in order to acquire the thing.

   a. Sliding scale fees
   b. Cost
   c. Marginal cost
   d. Fixed costs

3. The _____ is an expected return that the provider of capital plans to earn on their investment.

   Capital (money) used for funding a business should earn returns for the capital providers who risk their capital. For an investment to be worthwhile, the expected return on capital must be greater than the _____.

   a. Weighted average cost of capital
   b. 4-4-5 Calendar
   c. Capital intensity
   d. Cost of capital

4. _____ is the planning process used to determine whether a firm's long term investments such as new machinery, replacement machinery, new plants, new products, and research development projects are worth pursuing. It is budget for major capital, or investment, expenditures.

   Many formal methods are used in _____, including the techniques such as

   - Net present value
   - Profitability index
   - Internal rate of return
   - Modified Internal Rate of Return
   - Equivalent annuity

   These methods use the incremental cash flows from each potential investment, or project. Techniques based on accounting earnings and accounting rules are sometimes used - though economists consider this to be improper - such as the accounting rate of return, and 'return on investment.' Simplified and hybrid methods are used as well, such as payback period and discounted payback period.

   a. Financial distress
   b. Preferred stock
   c. Shareholder value
   d. Capital budgeting

5. A _____ is a fungible, negotiable instrument representing financial value. They are broadly categorized into debt securities (such as banknotes, bonds and debentures), and equity securities; e.g., common stocks. The company or other entity issuing the _____ is called the issuer.

Chapter 12. Cost of Capital

a. Securities lending
b. Book entry
c. Tracking stock
d. Security

6. In Modern Portfolio Theory, the _____ is the graphical representation of the Capital Asset Pricing Model. It displays the expected rate of return for an overall market as a function of systematic (non-diversifiable) risk (beta.)

The Y-Intercept (beta=0) of the _____ is equal to the risk-free interest rate.

a. Rebalancing
b. Certificate in Investment Performance Measurement
c. Divestment
d. Security market line

7. The _____ is the rate that a company is expected to pay to finance its assets. WACC is the minimum return that a company must earn on existing asset base to satisfy its creditors, owners, and other providers of capital.

Companies raise money from a number of sources: common equity, preferred equity, straight debt, convertible debt, exchangeable debt, warrants, options, pension liabilities, executive stock options, governmental subsidies, and so on.

a. Capital intensity
b. Cost of capital
c. 4-4-5 Calendar
d. Weighted average cost of capital

8. An _____ can be defined as a contract which provides an income stream in return for an initial payment.

An immediate _____ is an _____ for which the time between the contract date and the date of the first payment is not longer than the time interval between payments. A common use for an immediate _____ is to provide a pension to a retired person or persons.

a. AT'T Inc.
b. Intrinsic value
c. Amortization
d. Annuity

9. A '_____' is a 'Charge' that is paid to obtain the right to delay a payment. Essentially, the payer purchases the right to make a given payment in the future instead of in the Present. The '_____', or 'Charge' that must be paid to delay the payment, is simply the difference between what the payment amount would be if it were paid in the present and what the payment amount would be paid if it were paid in the future.

a. Risk aversion
b. Discount
c. Risk modeling
d. Value at risk

10. The _____ is an interest rate a central bank charges depository institutions that borrow reserves from it.

The term _____ has two meanings:

- the same as interest rate; the term 'discount' does not refer to the meaning of the word, but to the purpose of using the quantity, such as computations of present value, e.g. net present value / discounted cash flow

- the annual effective _____, which is the annual interest divided by the capital including that interest; this rate is lower than the interest rate; it corresponds to using the value after a year as the nominal value, and seeing the initial value as the nominal value minus a discount; it is used for Treasury Bills and similar financial instruments

The annual effective _____ is the annual interest divided by the capital including that interest, which is the interest rate divided by 100% plus the interest rate. It is the annual discount factor to be applied to the future cash flow, to find the discount, subtracted from a future value to find the value one year earlier.

For example, suppose there is a government bond that sells for $95 and pays $100 in a year's time.

a. Black-Scholes
b. Fisher equation
c. Stochastic volatility
d. Discount rate

11. In finance, _____ refers to the way a corporation finances its assets through some combination of equity, debt, or hybrid securities. A firm's _____ is then the composition or 'structure' of its liabilities. For example, a firm that sells $20 billion in equity and $80 billion in debt is said to be 20% equity-financed and 80% debt-financed.

a. Book building
b. Market for corporate control
c. Rights issue
d. Capital structure

12. _____ or net present worth (NPW) is defined as the total present value (PV) of a time series of cash flows. It is a standard method for using the time value of money to appraise long-term projects. Used for capital budgeting, and widely throughout economics, it measures the excess or shortfall of cash flows, in present value terms, once financing charges are met.

a. Tax shield
b. Negative gearing
c. Present value of costs
d. Net present value

13. An _____ is an economic concept that relates to the cost incurred by an entity (such as organizations) associated with problems such as divergent management-shareholder objectives and information asymmetry. The costs consist of two main sources:

1. The costs inherently associated with using an agent (e.g., the risk that agents will use organizational resource for their own benefit) and
2. The costs of techniques used to mitigate the problems associated with using an agent (e.g., the costs of producing financial statements or the use of stock options to align executive interests to shareholder interests.)

Though effects of _____ are present in any agency relationship, the term is most used in business contexts.

Chapter 12. Cost of Capital

The information asymmetry that exists between shareholders and the Chief Executive Officer is generally considered to be a classic example of a principal-agent problem. The agent (the manager) is working on behalf of the principal (the shareholders), who does not observe the actions of the agent.

a. A Random Walk Down Wall Street
b. ABN Amro
c. AAB
d. Agency cost

14. _____ is the value on a given date of a future payment or series of future payments, discounted to reflect the time value of money and other factors such as investment risk. _____ calculations are widely used in business and economics to provide a means to compare cash flows at different times on a meaningful 'like to like' basis.

The most commonly applied model of the time value of money is compound interest.

a. Present value of benefits
b. Negative gearing
c. Net present value
d. Present value

15. In finance, the _____ is the minimum rate of return a firm must offer shareholders to compensate for waiting for their returns, and for bearing some risk.

The _____ capital for a particular company is the rate of return on investment that is required by the company's ordinary shareholders. The return consists both of dividend and capital gains, e.g. increases in the share price.

a. Cost of equity
b. Residual value
c. Round-tripping
d. Net pay

16. A _____ is a payment made by a corporation to its shareholder members. When a corporation earns a profit or surplus, that money can be put to two uses: it can either be re-invested in the business (called retained earnings), or it can be paid to the shareholders as a _____. Many corporations retain a portion of their earnings and pay the remainder as a _____.

a. Dividend puzzle
b. Special dividend
c. Dividend yield
d. Dividend

17. A _____ is the price of a single share of a no. of saleable stocks of the company. Once the stock is purchased, the owner becomes a shareholder of the company that issued the share.

a. Trading curb
b. Stock split
c. Whisper numbers
d. Share price

18. The _____, in terms of finance and investing, describes how the expected return of a stock or portfolio is correlated to the return of the financial market as a whole.

An asset with a beta of 0 means that its price is not at all correlated with the market; that asset is independent. A positive beta means that the asset generally follows the market.

Chapter 12. Cost of Capital

a. Beta coefficient
c. LIBOR market model
b. Current yield
d. Perpetuity

19. The _____ on a company stock is the company's annual dividend payments divided by its market cap, or the dividend per share divided by the price per share. It is often expressed as a percentage.

Dividend payments on preferred shares are stipulated by the prospectus.

a. Special dividend
c. Dividend reinvestment plan
b. Dividend imputation
d. Dividend yield

20. The _____ is the weighted-average most likely outcome in gambling, probability theory, economics or finance.

In gambling and probability theory, there is usually a discrete set of possible outcomes. In this case, _____ is a measure of the relative balance of win or loss weighted by their chances of occurring.

a. A Random Walk Down Wall Street
c. ABN Amro
b. AAB
d. Expected return

21.

In finance, the _____ can be the expected rate of return above the risk-free interest rate. When measuring risk, a common sense approach is to compare the risk-free return on T-bills and the very risky return on other investments. The difference between these two returns can be interpreted as a measure of the excess return on the average risky asset. This excess return is known as the _____.

a. Risk modeling
c. Risk adjusted return on capital
b. Risk aversion
d. Risk premium

22. In finance, the term _____ describes the amount in cash that returns to the owners of a security. Normally it does not include the price variations, at the difference of the total return. _____ applies to various stated rates of return on stocks (common and preferred, and convertible), fixed income instruments (bonds, notes, bills, strips, zero coupon), and some other investment type insurance products (e.g. annuities.)

a. 4-4-5 Calendar
c. Yield
b. Macaulay duration
d. Yield to maturity

23. _____ is that which is owed; usually referencing assets owed, but the term can cover other obligations. In the case of assets, _____ is a means of using future purchasing power in the present before a summation has been earned. Some companies and corporations use _____ as a part of their overall corporate finance strategy.

a. Debt
c. Credit cycle
b. Partial Payment
d. Cross-collateralization

24. _____ is typically a higher ranking stock than voting shares, and its terms are negotiated between the corporation and the investor.

Chapter 12. Cost of Capital 123

_____ usually carry no voting rights, but may carry superior priority over common stock in the payment of dividends and upon liquidation. _____ may carry a dividend that is paid out prior to any dividends to common stock holders.

a. Follow-on offering
b. Second lien loan
c. Trade-off theory
d. Preferred stock

25. _____ is the price at which an asset would trade in a competitive Walrasian auction setting. _____ is often used interchangeably with open _____, fair value or fair _____, although these terms have distinct definitions in different standards, and may differ in some circumstances.

International Valuation Standards defines _____ as 'the estimated amount for which a property should exchange on the date of valuation between a willing buyer and a willing seller in an arm'e;s-length transaction after proper marketing wherein the parties had each acted knowledgeably, prudently, and without compulsion.'

_____ is a concept distinct from market price, which is 'e;the price at which one can transact'e;, while _____ is 'e;the true underlying value'e; according to theoretical standards.

a. T-Model
b. Debt restructuring
c. Wrap account
d. Market value

26. _____ is a legally declared inability or impairment of ability of an individual or organization to pay their creditors. Creditors may file a _____ petition against a debtor ('involuntary _____') in an effort to recoup a portion of what they are owed or initiate a restructuring. In the majority of cases, however, _____ is initiated by the debtor (a 'voluntary _____' that is filed by the bankrupt individual or organization.)

a. Debt settlement
b. 4-4-5 Calendar
c. 529 plan
d. Bankruptcy

27. In accounting, _____ or *Carrying value* is the value of an asset according to its balance sheet account balance. For assets, the value is based on the original cost of the asset less any depreciation, amortization or impairment costs made against the asset. A company's _____ is its total assets minus intangible assets and liabilities.

a. Book value
b. Current liabilities
c. Retained earnings
d. Pro forma

28. A _____ is a private or public market for the trading of company stock and derivatives of company stock at an agreed price; these are securities listed on a stock exchange as well as those only traded privately.

The size of the world _____ is estimated at about $36.6 trillion US at the beginning of October 2008. The world derivatives market has been estimated at about $480 trillion face or nominal value, 12 times the size of the entire world economy.

a. Adolph Coors
b. Stock market
c. Anton Gelonkin
d. Andrew Tobias

29. In economics, the _____ is the proposition by Irving Fisher that the real interest rate is independent of monetary measures, especially the nominal interest rate. The Fisher equation is

$$r_r = r_n - \pi^e.$$

This means, the real interest rate (r_r) equals the nominal interest rate (r_n) minus expected rate of inflation (π^e.) Here all the rates are continuously compounded.

a. 7-Eleven
b. 529 plan
c. 4-4-5 Calendar
d. Fisher hypothesis

30. _____ is a fee paid on borrowed assets. It is the price paid for the use of borrowed money , or, money earned by deposited funds . Assets that are sometimes lent with _____ include money, shares, consumer goods through hire purchase, major assets such as aircraft, and even entire factories in finance lease arrangements.

a. Insolvency
b. AAB
c. A Random Walk Down Wall Street
d. Interest

31. Briggs could refer to:

- Briggs cliff, a fictional place in Fullmetal Alchemist manga
- Briggs (crater), a lunar crater
- Briggs Initiative, either of two pieces of Californian legislation sponsored by John Briggs
- Briggs Islet, Tasmania, Australia
- Briggs, Oklahoma, USA
- Briggs, Texas, USA
- _____, a manufacturer of air-cooled gasoline engines
- The Briggs - a punk rock band
- Myers-Briggs Type Indicator

- Anne Briggs, English folk singer
- Ansel Briggs, American politician
- Arthur E. Briggs, California politician
- Asa Briggs, British historian
- Barbara Briggs, American dramatist
- Barbara G. Briggs, Australian botanist
- Barry Briggs, New Zealand World Motorcycle speedway champion
- Barry Bruce-Briggs, public policy writer
- Benjamin Briggs, captain of the Mary Celeste
- Bill Briggs, American skier
- Billy Briggs, American musician
- Bobby Briggs, fictional character from Twin Peaks
- Charles Augustus Briggs, American theologian
- Charles Frederick Briggs, American journalist
- Clare Briggs, American comics artist
- David Briggs:
    - David Briggs (producer) (1944-1995), American record producer
    - David Briggs (composer) English organist and composer
    - David Briggs (Australian musician) , guitarist with Little River Band and Australian record producer
- Derek Briggs, Irish paleontologist
- Everett Francis Briggs, (1908-2006), American Catholic priest
- Frank A. Briggs, American politician
- Frank O. Briggs, American politician
- Frank P. Briggs, American politician
- Gary Briggs (musician), British guitarist
- Gary Briggs (footballer), British footballer
- George N. Briggs, American politician
- Major Garland Briggs, fictional character from Twin Peaks
- Harold Briggs
    - Harold Briggs (General), British general
    - Harold Briggs (politician), British Conservative MP
- Henry Briggs (politician)
- Henry Briggs (mathematician), English mathematician
- Hortense Briggs, fictional character from An American Tragedy by Theodore Dreiser
- Ian Briggs, television writer
- Jack Briggs, American instrument maker
- James Briggs, any of several people
- Jason W. Briggs, American Latter Day Saint leader
- Jeff Briggs, American composer and former computer games executive
- Joe Bob Briggs, pseudonym of John Irving Bloom, film critic and actor
- John Briggs (politician), a California politician
- John Briggs (author)
- Johnny Briggs:

- - Johnny Briggs (cricketer)
  - Johnny Briggs (actor), actor who played Mike Baldwin on the British soap opera Coronation Street
  - Johnny Briggs (baseball), a former Major League Baseball outfielder
- Jon Briggs, British radio personality
- Jonny Briggs, BBC children's television programme first broadcast in 1985.
- Karen Briggs, American violinist
- Katharine Cook Briggs, co-inventor of the Myers-Briggs Type Indicator personality test
- Katharine Mary Briggs, British author
- Kevin 'She'kspere' Briggs, American record producer
- Lance Briggs, American football player
- LeBaron Russell Briggs, American educator
- Luke Briggs, British Steward
- Lyman James Briggs, American physicist and civil servant
- Matilda Briggs, passenger on the Marie Celeste
- Matthew Briggs, English footballer
- Nicholas Briggs, British actor
- Nigel Briggs, Singer/Song writer
- Patricia Briggs, American fantasy writer
- Paul Briggs, Australian boxer
- Raymond Briggs, British illustrator and author
- Sandra Briggs, fictional character from Emmerdale
- Shannon Briggs, American boxer
- Stephen Briggs, British Discworld adapter
- Stephen Foster Briggs, American engineer, co-founder of The _____ Company
- Ted Briggs, British seaman
- Tom Briggs, American football player
- Walter Briggs, Major League Baseball owner

a. 7-Eleven
c. 529 plan
b. 4-4-5 Calendar
d. Briggs ' Stratton

32. In corporate finance, _____ is an estimate of true economic profit after making corrective adjustments to GAAP accounting, including deducting the opportunity cost of equity capital. GAAP is estimated to ignore US$300 billion in shareholder opportunity costs. _____ can be measured as Net Operating Profit After Taxes(or NOPAT) less the money cost of capital.
   a. ABN Amro
   c. A Random Walk Down Wall Street
   b. AAB
   d. Economic value added

33. _____ was founded in 1898 by Frank Seiberling. Today it is the third largest tire company in the world after Bridgestone and Michelin. Goodyear manufactures tires for automobiles, commercial trucks, light trucks, SUVs, race cars, airplanes, and heavy earth-mover machinery.
   a. Selling short
   c. Composiition of Creditors
   b. Loan participation
   d. The Goodyear Tire ' Rubber Company

34. _____ is the largest provider of local, long distance telephone services in the United States, and also serves digital subscriber line Internet access. AT'T is the second largest provider of wireless service in the United States, with over 77 million wireless customers, and more than 150 million total customers.
   a. Alpha
   c. Option
   b. Intrinsic value
   d. AT'T Inc.

35. A mutual shareholder or _____ is an individual or company (including a corporation) that legally owns one or more shares of stock in a joint stock company. A company's shareholders collectively own that company. Thus, the typical goal of such companies is to enhance shareholder value.
   a. Trading curb
   c. Limit order
   b. Stockholder
   d. Stock market bubble

36. _____ refers to the additional value of a commodity over the cost of commodities used to produce it from the previous stage of production. An example is the price of gasoline at the pump over the price of the oil in it. In national accounts used in macroeconomics, it refers to the contribution of the factors of production, i.e., land, labor, and capital goods, to raising the value of a product and corresponds to the incomes received by the owners of these factors.
   a. Supply shock
   c. Demand shock
   b. Deregulation
   d. Value added

37. _____, in bookkeeping, refers to assets, liabilities, income, and expenses recorded on individual pages of the so called book of final entry or ledger. Changes in _____ value are made by chronologically posting debit (DR) and credit (CR) entries to its page. Examples of _____s are cash, _____s receivable, mortgages, loans, land and buildings, common stock, sales, services provided, wages, and payroll overhead.
   a. Alpha
   c. Accretion
   b. Option
   d. Account

38. The U.S. _____ is an independent agency of the United States government which holds primary responsibility for enforcing the federal securities laws and regulating the securities industry, the nation's stock and options exchanges, and other electronic securities markets. The SEC was created by section 4 of the SEC of 1934 (now codified as 15 U.S.C. Â§ 78d and commonly referred to as the 1934 Act.)

a. 4-4-5 Calendar
c. 529 plan
b. 7-Eleven
d. Securities and Exchange Commission

39. In e-business terms, a _____ is an organization that originated and does business purely through the internet, they have no physical store (brick and mortar) where customers can shop. Examples of large _____ companies include Amazon.com and Netflix.com. There are also many smaller, niche oriented _____ mail order companies such as women's travel accessories company Christine Columbus and fashion jewelry merchant Jewels of Denial.
   a. 4-4-5 Calendar
   c. The Dogs of the Dow
   b. 529 plan
   d. Pure play

40. In political science and economics, the _____ or agency dilemma treats the difficulties that arise under conditions of incomplete and asymmetric information when a principal hires an agent. Various mechanisms may be used to try to align the interests of the agent with those of the principal, such as piece rates/commissions, profit sharing, efficiency wages, performance measurement (including financial statements), the agent posting a bond, or fear of firing. The _____ is found in most employer/employee relationships, for example, when stockholders hire top executives of corporations.
   a. 7-Eleven
   c. Principal-agent problem
   b. 529 plan
   d. 4-4-5 Calendar

Chapter 13. Leverage and Capital Structure

1. In finance, _____ refers to the way a corporation finances its assets through some combination of equity, debt, or hybrid securities. A firm's _____ is then the composition or 'structure' of its liabilities. For example, a firm that sells $20 billion in equity and $80 billion in debt is said to be 20% equity-financed and 80% debt-financed.
   a. Book building
   b. Rights issue
   c. Market for corporate control
   d. Capital structure

2. The institution most often referenced by the word '_____' is a public or publicly traded _____, the shares of which are traded on a public stock exchange (e.g., the New York Stock Exchange or Nasdaq in the United States) where shares of stock of _____s are bought and sold by and to the general public. Most of the largest businesses in the world are publicly traded _____s. However, the majority of _____s are said to be closely held, privately held or close _____s, meaning that no ready market exists for the trading of shares.
   a. Depository Trust Company
   b. Corporation
   c. Federal Home Loan Mortgage Corporation
   d. Protect

3. In a _____, a company's creditors generally agree to cancel some or all of the debt in exchange for equity in the company.

   These deals often occur when large companies run into serious financial trouble, and often result in these companies being taken over by their principal creditors. This is because both the debt and the remaining assets in these companies are so large that there is no advantage for the creditors to drive the company into bankruptcy.

   a. Debt restructuring
   b. Covestor
   c. Financial Gerontology
   d. Debt-for-equity swap

4. A _____ is an international bond that is denominated in a currency not native to the country where it is issued. It can be categorised according to the currency in which it is issued. London is one of the centers of the _____ market, but _____s may be traded throughout the world - for example in Singapore or Tokyo.
   a. Economic entity
   b. Education production function
   c. Eurobond
   d. Interest rate option

5. In finance, a _____ (non-investment grade bond, speculative grade bond or junk bond) is a bond that is rated below investment grade at the time of purchase. These bonds have a higher risk of default or other adverse credit events, but typically pay higher yields than better quality bonds in order to make them attractive to investors.
   a. High yield bond
   b. Private equity
   c. Volatility
   d. Sharpe ratio

6. In some countries, including the United States and the United Kingdom, corporations can buy back their own stock in a share repurchase, also known as a _____ or share buyback. There has been a meteoric rise in the use of share repurchases in the U.S. in the past twenty years, from $5b in 1980 to $349b in 2005. A share repurchase distributes cash to existing shareholders in exchange for a fraction of the firm's outstanding equity.
   a. Stock repurchase
   b. Common stock
   c. Stockholder
   d. Trading curb

7. In finance, a _____ is a debt security, in which the authorized issuer owes the holders a debt and, depending on the terms of the _____, is obliged to pay interest (the coupon) and/or to repay the principal at a later date, termed maturity.

Chapter 13. Leverage and Capital Structure

Thus a _____ is a loan: the issuer is the borrower, the _____ holder is the lender, and the coupon is the interest. _____s provide the borrower with external funds to finance long-term investments, or, in the case of government _____s, to finance current expenditure.

a. Puttable bond
b. Convertible bond
c. Catastrophe bonds
d. Bond

8. In finance, a _____ is a derivative in which two counterparties agree to exchange one stream of cash flows against another stream. These streams are called the legs of the _____.

The cash flows are calculated over a notional principal amount, which is usually not exchanged between counterparties.

a. Local volatility
b. Volatility arbitrage
c. Volatility swap
d. Swap

9. In economics, business, and accounting, a _____ is the value of money that has been used up to produce something, and hence is not available for use anymore. In business, the _____ may be one of acquisition, in which case the amount of money expended to acquire it is counted as _____. In this case, money is the input that is gone in order to acquire the thing.

a. Marginal cost
b. Sliding scale fees
c. Fixed costs
d. Cost

10. _____ is the corporate management term for the act of reorganizing the legal, ownership, operational, or other structures of a company for the purpose of making it more profitable or better organized for its present needs. Alternate reasons for restructing include a change of ownership or ownership structure, demerger repositioning debt _____ and financial _____.

a. Concentrated stock
b. Day trading
c. Restructuring
d. Cross-border leasing

11. The _____ is the rate that a company is expected to pay to finance its assets. WACC is the minimum return that a company must earn on existing asset base to satisfy its creditors, owners, and other providers of capital.

Companies raise money from a number of sources: common equity, preferred equity, straight debt, convertible debt, exchangeable debt, warrants, options, pension liabilities, executive stock options, governmental subsidies, and so on.

a. Capital intensity
b. Weighted average cost of capital
c. 4-4-5 Calendar
d. Cost of capital

12. _____ is a legally declared inability or impairment of ability of an individual or organization to pay their creditors. Creditors may file a _____ petition against a debtor ('involuntary _____') in an effort to recoup a portion of what they are owed or initiate a restructuring. In the majority of cases, however, _____ is initiated by the debtor (a 'voluntary _____' that is filed by the bankrupt individual or organization.)

Chapter 13. Leverage and Capital Structure

a. 4-4-5 Calendar
b. 529 plan
c. Debt settlement
d. Bankruptcy

13. The _____ is an expected return that the provider of capital plans to earn on their investment.

Capital (money) used for funding a business should earn returns for the capital providers who risk their capital. For an investment to be worthwhile, the expected return on capital must be greater than the _____.

a. Cost of capital
b. 4-4-5 Calendar
c. Capital intensity
d. Weighted average cost of capital

14. _____ is that which is owed; usually referencing assets owed, but the term can cover other obligations. In the case of assets, _____ is a means of using future purchasing power in the present before a summation has been earned. Some companies and corporations use _____ as a part of their overall corporate finance strategy.

a. Credit cycle
b. Cross-collateralization
c. Partial Payment
d. Debt

15. In financial and business accounting, _____ is a measure of a firm's profitability that excludes interest and income tax expenses.

EBIT = Operating Revenue - Operating Expenses (OPEX) + Non-operating Income

Operating Income = Operating Revenue - Operating Expenses

Operating income is the difference between operating revenues and operating expenses, but it is also sometimes used as a synonym for EBIT and operating profit. This is true if the firm has no non-operating income.

a. AAB
b. A Random Walk Down Wall Street
c. ABN Amro
d. Earnings before interest and taxes

16. _____ are the earnings returned on the initial investment amount.

In the US, the Financial Accounting Standards Board (FASB) requires companies' income statements to report _____ for each of the major categories of the income statement: continuing operations, discontinued operations, extraordinary items, and net income.

The _____ formula does not include preferred dividends for categories outside of continued operations and net income.

a. Average accounting return
b. Assets turnover
c. Inventory turnover
d. Earnings per share

17. _____ measures the rate of return on the ownership interest (shareholders' equity) of the common stock owners. _____ is viewed as one of the most important financial ratios. It measures a firm's efficiency at generating profits from every dollar of shareholders' equity (also known as net assets or assets minus liabilities.)

a. Return of capital
b. Diluted Earnings Per Share
c. Return on sales
d. Return on equity

18. In political science and economics, the _____ or agency dilemma treats the difficulties that arise under conditions of incomplete and asymmetric information when a principal hires an agent. Various mechanisms may be used to try to align the interests of the agent with those of the principal, such as piece rates/commissions, profit sharing, efficiency wages, performance measurement (including financial statements), the agent posting a bond, or fear of firing. The _____ is found in most employer/employee relationships, for example, when stockholders hire top executives of corporations.
   a. 7-Eleven
   b. 4-4-5 Calendar
   c. 529 plan
   d. Principal-agent problem

19. _____ or financing is to provide capital (funds), which means money for a project, a person, a business or any other private or public institutions.

Those funds can be allocated for either short term or long term purposes. The health fund is a new way of _____ private healthcare centers.

   a. Proxy fight
   b. Product life cycle
   c. Synthetic CDO
   d. Funding

20. In finance, _____ (or gearing) is borrowing money to supplement existing funds for investment in such a way that the potential positive or negative outcome is magnified and/or enhanced. It generally refers to using borrowed funds, or debt, so as to attempt to increase the returns to equity. Deleveraging is the action of reducing borrowings.
   a. Limited partnership
   b. Financial endowment
   c. Pension fund
   d. Leverage

21. In business and finance, a _____ (also referred to as equity _____) of stock means a _____ of ownership in a corporation (company.) In the plural, stocks is often used as a synonym for _____s especially in the United States, but it is less commonly used that way outside of North America.

In the United Kingdom, South Africa, and Australia, stock can also refer to completely different financial instruments such as government bonds or, less commonly, to all kinds of marketable securities.

   a. Share
   b. Procter ' Gamble
   c. Bucket shop
   d. Margin

22. A mutual shareholder or _____ is an individual or company (including a corporation) that legally owns one or more shares of stock in a joint stock company. A company's shareholders collectively own that company. Thus, the typical goal of such companies is to enhance shareholder value.
   a. Stock market bubble
   b. Limit order
   c. Stockholder
   d. Trading curb

23. _____ is a fee paid on borrowed assets. It is the price paid for the use of borrowed money , or, money earned by deposited funds . Assets that are sometimes lent with _____ include money, shares, consumer goods through hire purchase, major assets such as aircraft, and even entire factories in finance lease arrangements.

a. AAB
b. Insolvency
c. A Random Walk Down Wall Street
d. Interest

24. In economics and business, specifically cost accounting, the _____ is the point at which cost or expenses and revenue are equal: there is no net loss or gain, and one has 'broken even'. A profit or a loss has not been made, although opportunity costs have been paid, and capital has received the risk-adjusted, expected return.

For example, if the business sells less than 200 tables each month, it will make a loss, if it sells more, it will be a profit.

a. Defined contribution plan
b. Fixed asset turnover
c. Market microstructure
d. Break-even point

25. _____ is a term in Corporate Finance used to indicate a condition when promises to creditors of a company are broken or honored with difficulty. Sometimes _____ can lead to bankruptcy. _____ is usually associated with some costs to the company and these are known as Costs of _____.

a. Commercial paper
b. Cashflow matching
c. Capital structure
d. Financial distress

26. _____ is a form of corporation equity ownership represented in the securities. It is dangerous in comparison to preferred shares and some other investment options, in that in the event of bankruptcy, _____ investors receive their funds after preferred stockholders, bondholders, creditors, etc. On the other hand, common shares on average perform better than preferred shares or bonds over time.

a. Stock split
b. Stop-limit order
c. Stock market bubble
d. Common stock

27. _____ is typically a higher ranking stock than voting shares, and its terms are negotiated between the corporation and the investor.

_____ usually carry no voting rights, but may carry superior priority over common stock in the payment of dividends and upon liquidation. _____ may carry a dividend that is paid out prior to any dividends to common stock holders.

a. Follow-on offering
b. Trade-off theory
c. Second lien loan
d. Preferred stock

28. A _____ is a fungible, negotiable instrument representing financial value. They are broadly categorized into debt securities (such as banknotes, bonds and debentures), and equity securities; e.g., common stocks. The company or other entity issuing the _____ is called the issuer.

a. Book entry
b. Securities lending
c. Tracking stock
d. Security

29. The _____, in terms of finance and investing, describes how the expected return of a stock or portfolio is correlated to the return of the financial market as a whole.

An asset with a beta of 0 means that its price is not at all correlated with the market; that asset is independent. A positive beta means that the asset generally follows the market.

a. Current yield
b. LIBOR market model
c. Perpetuity
d. Beta coefficient

30. In finance, the _____ is the minimum rate of return a firm must offer shareholders to compensate for waiting for their returns, and for bearing some risk.

The _____ capital for a particular company is the rate of return on investment that is required by the company's ordinary shareholders. The return consists both of dividend and capital gains, e.g. increases in the share price.

a. Round-tripping
b. Net pay
c. Residual value
d. Cost of equity

31. _____ refers to a tax levied by various jurisdictions on the profits made by companies or associations. It is a tax on the value of the corporation's profits.

The measure of taxable profits varies from country to country.

a. First-mover advantage
b. Proxy fight
c. Trade finance
d. Corporate tax

32. _____ is normally any risk associated with any form of financing.

Depending on the nature of the investment, the type of 'investment' risk will vary. High risk investments have greater potential rewards, but you may lose your money instead by taking the risk for more money.

a. Liquidating dividend
b. Revaluation
c. Financial risk
d. Stock market index option

33. In finance, _____ is that risk which is common to an entire market and not to any individual entity or component thereof. It should be distinguished from systemic risk which is the risk that the entire financial system will collapse as a result of some catastrophic event.

Risks can be reduced in four main ways: Avoidance, Reduction, Retention and Transfer.

a. Capital surplus
b. Conglomerate merger
c. Systematic risk
d. Primary market

34. A _____ is the reduction in income taxes that results from taking an allowable deduction from taxable income. For example, because interest on debt is a tax-deductible expense, taking on debt creates a _____. Since a _____ is a way to save cash flows, it increases the value of the business, and it is an important aspect of business valuation.

Chapter 13. Leverage and Capital Structure

a. Refinancing risk
c. Present value of benefits
b. Present value of costs
d. Tax shield

35. _____ is the largest provider of local, long distance telephone services in the United States, and also serves digital subscriber line Internet access. AT'T is the second largest provider of wireless service in the United States, with over 77 million wireless customers, and more than 150 million total customers.
a. Option
c. Intrinsic value
b. Alpha
d. AT'T Inc.

36. The _____ is a United States government system for classifying industries by a four-digit code. Established in 1937, it is being supplanted by the six-digit North American Industry Classification System, which was released in 1997; however certain government departments and agencies, such as the U.S. Securities and Exchange Commission (SEC), still use the _____ codes.

The following table is from the SEC's site, which allows searching for companies by _____ code in its database of filings.

a. Standard Industrial Classification
c. 4-4-5 Calendar
b. 529 plan
d. 7-Eleven

37. _____ is the process of decreasing an amount over a period of time. The word comes from Middle English amortisen to kill, alienate in mortmain, from Anglo-French amorteser, alteration of amortir, from Vulgar Latin admortire to kill, from Latin ad- + mort-, mors death. Particular instances of the term include:

- _____ (business), the allocation of a lump sum amount to different time periods, particularly for loans and other forms of finance, including related interest or other finance charges.
    - _____ schedule, a table detailing each periodic payment on a loan (typically a mortgage), as generated by an _____ calculator.
    - Negative _____, an _____ schedule where the loan amount actually increases through not paying the full interest
- Amortized analysis, analyzing the execution cost of algorithms over a sequence of operations.
- _____ of capital expenditures of certain assets under accounting rules, particularly intangible assets, in a manner analogous to depreciation.
- _____ (tax law)

_____ is also used in the context of zoning regulations and describes the time in which a property owner has to relocate when the property's use constitutes a preexisting nonconforming use under zoning regulations.

- Depreciation

a. Intrinsic value
c. AT'T Inc.
b. Option
d. Amortization

Chapter 13. Leverage and Capital Structure

38. The _____, was a law enacting several significant changes to the U.S. Bankruptcy Code. Referred to colloquially as the 'New Bankruptcy Law', the Act of Congress attempts to, among other things, make it more difficult for some consumers to file bankruptcy under Chapter 7; some of these consumers may instead utilize Chapter 13.

    a. Personal property
    b. Foreclosure
    c. Covenant
    d. Bankruptcy Abuse Prevention and Consumer Protection Act of 2005

39. A _____ is a party (e.g. person, organization, company, or government) that has a claim to the services of a second party. The first party, in general, has provided some property or service to the second party under the assumption (usually enforced by contract) that the second party will return an equivalent property or service. The second party is frequently called a debtor or borrower.

    a. NOPLAT
    b. False billing
    c. Redemption value
    d. Creditor

40. _____ means the inability to pay one's debts as they fall due. Usually used in Business terms, _____ refers to the inability for a 'limited liability' company to pay off debts.

This is defined in two different ways:

Cash flow _____ -
    Unable to pay debts as they fall due.

Balance sheet _____ -
    Having negative net assets: liabilities exceed assets; or net liabilities.

    a. Insolvency
    b. Interest
    c. A Random Walk Down Wall Street
    d. AAB

41. In law, _____ refers to the process by which a company (or part of a company) is brought to an end, and the assets and property of the company redistributed. _____ can also be referred to as winding-up or dissolution, although dissolution technically refers to the last stage of _____. The process of _____ also arises when customs, an authority or agency in a country responsible for collecting and safeguarding customs duties, determines the final computation or ascertainment of the duties or drawback accruing on an entry.

    a. 4-4-5 Calendar
    b. Liquidation
    c. 529 plan
    d. Debt settlement

42. A _____ is the involuntary imposition by a court of a reorganization plan over the objection of some classes of creditors.

While typically used in a corporate context, the phrase has gained currency in a personal context the financial crisis of 2007-2009.

Under current United States law, bankruptcy courts are not allowed to perform a _____ on mortgages of bankruptcy filers' primary residences. The term has also gained currency to denote informally any transaction where existing investors (debt or equity) are forced by circumstance to accept an unappealing transaction, such as an expensive financing, a debt transaction that subordinates them, a dilutive equity raising, or an acquisition at an unappealingly low price.

a. Netting
b. Dow Jones Indexes
c. Security interest
d. Cramdown

43. _____ is the lengthening the time of debt repayment and forgiving part of the loan for a date. .
a. Synthetic lease
b. 4-4-5 Calendar
c. 529 plan
d. Debt rescheduling

Chapter 14. Dividends and Dividend Policy

1. The institution most often referenced by the word '_____' is a public or publicly traded _____, the shares of which are traded on a public stock exchange (e.g., the New York Stock Exchange or Nasdaq in the United States) where shares of stock of _____s are bought and sold by and to the general public. Most of the largest businesses in the world are publicly traded _____s. However, the majority of _____s are said to be closely held, privately held or close _____s, meaning that no ready market exists for the trading of shares.
   a. Corporation
   b. Depository Trust Company
   c. Federal Home Loan Mortgage Corporation
   d. Protect

2. A _____ is a payment made by a corporation to its shareholder members. When a corporation earns a profit or surplus, that money can be put to two uses: it can either be re-invested in the business (called retained earnings), or it can be paid to the shareholders as a _____. Many corporations retain a portion of their earnings and pay the remainder as a _____.
   a. Special dividend
   b. Dividend puzzle
   c. Dividend yield
   d. Dividend

3. A _____ is the price of a single share of a no. of saleable stocks of the company. Once the stock is purchased, the owner becomes a shareholder of the company that issued the share.
   a. Stock split
   b. Share price
   c. Whisper numbers
   d. Trading curb

4. _____, refers to consumption opportunity gained by an entity within a specified time frame, which is generally expressed in monetary terms. However, for households and individuals, '_____ is the sum of all the wages, salaries, profits, interests payments, rents and other forms of earnings received... in a given period of time.' For firms, _____ generally refers to net-profit: what remains of revenue after expenses have been subtracted.
   a. Accrual
   b. Income
   c. OIBDA
   d. Annual report

5. In accounting, _____ refers to the portion of net income which is retained by the corporation rather than distributed to its owners as dividends. Similarly, if the corporation makes a loss, then that loss is retained and called variously retained losses, accumulated losses or accumulated deficit. _____ and losses are cumulative from year to year with losses offsetting earnings.
   a. Historical cost
   b. Generally Accepted Accounting Principles
   c. Matching principle
   d. Retained earnings

6. _____ represents the impact on the stock price that investors would cause in reaction to a change in policy of a company.
   a. Volatility clustering
   b. Trade date
   c. Bonus share
   d. Clientele effect

7. An _____ is a contract written by a seller that conveys to the buyer the right -- but not the obligation -- to buy (in the case of a call _____) or to sell (in the case of a put _____) a particular asset, such as a piece of property such as, among others, a futures contract. In return for granting the _____, the seller collects a payment (the premium) from the buyer.

For example, buying a call _____ provides the right to buy a specified quantity of a security at a set strike price at some time on or before expiration, while buying a put _____ provides the right to sell.

a. Amortization
c. AT'T Mobility LLC
b. Annuity
d. Option

8. The _____ on a company stock is the company's annual dividend payments divided by its market cap, or the dividend per share divided by the price per share. It is often expressed as a percentage.

Dividend payments on preferred shares are stipulated by the prospectus.

a. Dividend reinvestment plan
c. Dividend imputation
b. Dividend yield
d. Special dividend

9. The key date to remember for dividend paying stocks is the _____. The _____ is different from the record date. The _____ is typically two trading days before the record date.

In order to receive the upcoming dividend payment payout, you must already own or you must purchase the stock prior to the _____. It is important to note that in most countries, when you buy or sell any stock, there is a three trading-day settlement period on your order.

a. Insolvency
c. Index number
b. Ex-dividend date
d. Asian Financial Crisis

10. _____ is a payment of a dividend to stockholders that exceeds the company's retained earnings. Once retained earnings is depleted, capital accounts such as additional paid-in capital are decreased to make up for the remaining dividend to be paid to stockholders. When a _____ occurs, it is considered to be a return of investment instead of profits.

a. Liquidating dividend
c. Securities offering
b. Stock market index option
d. Revolving credit

11. A _____ is a payment made by a company to its shareholders that is separate from the typical recurring dividend cycle, if any, for the company. The difference may be the result of the date of issue, the amount, the type of payment, or a combination of these factors.

The amount of the dividend is declared special or significant in relation to the stock price. For this reason, the ex-dividend date is set one stock trading day after the payment date. The stock will trade on an ex-distribution basis, adjusted for the amount of the dividend paid one trading day after the payment date.

a. Dividend decision
c. Special dividend
b. Dividend puzzle
d. Dividend imputation

12. _____ are those dividends paid out in form of additional stock shares of the issuing corporation or other corporation They are usually issued in proportion to shares owned (for example for every 100 shares of stock owned, 5% stock dividend will yield 5 extra shares). If this payment involves the issue of new shares, this is very similar to a stock split in that it increases the total number of shares while lowering the price of each share and does not change the market capitalization or the total value of the shares held

Chapter 14. Dividends and Dividend Policy

a. Database auditing
b. Stock or scrip dividends
c. The Hong Kong Securities Institute
d. Time-based currency

13. In business and finance, a _____ (also referred to as equity _____) of stock means a _____ of ownership in a corporation (company.) In the plural, stocks is often used as a synonym for _____s especially in the United States, but it is less commonly used that way outside of North America.

In the United Kingdom, South Africa, and Australia, stock can also refer to completely different financial instruments such as government bonds or, less commonly, to all kinds of marketable securities.

a. Procter ' Gamble
b. Margin
c. Bucket shop
d. Share

14. A _____ is a private or public market for the trading of company stock and derivatives of company stock at an agreed price; these are securities listed on a stock exchange as well as those only traded privately.

The size of the world _____ is estimated at about $36.6 trillion US at the beginning of October 2008 . The world derivatives market has been estimated at about $480 trillion face or nominal value, 12 times the size of the entire world economy.

a. Andrew Tobias
b. Adolph Coors
c. Anton Gelonkin
d. Stock market

15. In finance, the term _____ describes the amount in cash that returns to the owners of a security. Normally it does not include the price variations, at the difference of the total return. _____ applies to various stated rates of return on stocks (common and preferred, and convertible), fixed income instruments (bonds, notes, bills, strips, zero coupon), and some other investment type insurance products (e.g. annuities.)

a. Macaulay duration
b. Yield
c. 4-4-5 Calendar
d. Yield to maturity

16. _____ is a form of corporation equity ownership represented in the securities. It is dangerous in comparison to preferred shares and some other investment options, in that in the event of bankruptcy, _____ investors receive their funds after preferred stockholders, bondholders, creditors, etc. On the other hand, common shares on average perform better than preferred shares or bonds over time.

a. Stock split
b. Stop-limit order
c. Stock market bubble
d. Common stock

17. _____ is typically a higher ranking stock than voting shares, and its terms are negotiated between the corporation and the investor.

_____ usually carry no voting rights, but may carry superior priority over common stock in the payment of dividends and upon liquidation. _____ may carry a dividend that is paid out prior to any dividends to common stock holders.

Chapter 14. Dividends and Dividend Policy

a. Second lien loan
b. Trade-off theory
c. Follow-on offering
d. Preferred stock

18. A _____ is a fungible, negotiable instrument representing financial value. They are broadly categorized into debt securities (such as banknotes, bonds and debentures), and equity securities; e.g., common stocks. The company or other entity issuing the _____ is called the issuer.
   a. Securities lending
   b. Tracking stock
   c. Book entry
   d. Security

19. In political science and economics, the _____ or agency dilemma treats the difficulties that arise under conditions of incomplete and asymmetric information when a principal hires an agent. Various mechanisms may be used to try to align the interests of the agent with those of the principal, such as piece rates/commissions, profit sharing, efficiency wages, performance measurement (including financial statements), the agent posting a bond, or fear of firing. The _____ is found in most employer/employee relationships, for example, when stockholders hire top executives of corporations.
   a. Principal-agent problem
   b. 4-4-5 Calendar
   c. 7-Eleven
   d. 529 plan

20. The _____, in terms of finance and investing, describes how the expected return of a stock or portfolio is correlated to the return of the financial market as a whole.

An asset with a beta of 0 means that its price is not at all correlated with the market; that asset is independent. A positive beta means that the asset generally follows the market.

   a. Beta coefficient
   b. LIBOR market model
   c. Current yield
   d. Perpetuity

21. _____ is the balance of the amounts of cash being received and paid by a business during a defined period of time, sometimes tied to a specific project. Measurement of _____ can be used

   - to evaluate the state or performance of a business or project.
   - to determine problems with liquidity. Being profitable does not necessarily mean being liquid. A company can fail because of a shortage of cash, even while profitable.
   - to generate project rate of returns. The time of _____ s into and out of projects are used as inputs to financial models such as internal rate of return, and net present value.
   - to examine income or growth of a business when it is believed that accrual accounting concepts do not represent economic realities. Alternately, _____ can be used to 'validate' the net income generated by accrual accounting.

_____ as a generic term may be used differently depending on context, and certain _____ definitions may be adapted by analysts and users for their own uses. Common terms include operating _____ and free _____.

Chapter 14. Dividends and Dividend Policy

_____s can be classified into:

1. Operational _____s: Cash received or expended as a result of the company's core business activities.
2. Investment _____s: Cash received or expended through capital expenditure, investments or acquisitions.
3. Financing _____s: Cash received or expended as a result of financial activities, such as interests and dividends.

All three together - the net _____ - are necessary to reconcile the beginning cash balance to the ending cash balance. Loan draw downs or equity injections, that is just shifting of capital but no expenditure as such, are not considered in the net _____.

a. Shareholder value
c. Real option
b. Corporate finance
d. Cash flow

22. A _____ is a profit that results from investments into a capital asset, such as stocks, bonds or real estate, which exceeds the purchase price. It is the difference between a higher selling price and a lower purchase price, resulting in a financial gain for the seller. Conversely, a capital loss arises if the proceeds from the sale of a capital asset are less than the purchase price.

a. Tax brackets
c. Payroll tax
b. Capital gain
d. Capital gains tax

23. A _____ is a tax charged on capital gains, the profit realized on the sale of a non-inventory asset that was purchased at a lower price. The most common capital gains are realized from the sale of stocks, bonds, precious metals and property. Not all countries implement a _____ and most have different rates of taxation for individuals and corporations.

a. Withholding tax
c. Tax holiday
b. Tax brackets
d. Capital gains tax

24. _____, is when a company issues common stock or shares to the public for the first time. They are often issued by smaller, younger companies seeking capital to expand, but can also be done by large privately-owned companies looking to become publicly traded.

In an _____ the issuer may obtain the assistance of an underwriting firm, which helps it determine what type of security to issue (common or preferred), best offering price and time to bring it to market.

a. Insolvency
c. Asian Financial Crisis
b. Interest
d. Initial public offering

25. In economics, business, and accounting, a _____ is the value of money that has been used up to produce something, and hence is not available for use anymore. In business, the _____ may be one of acquisition, in which case the amount of money expended to acquire it is counted as _____. In this case, money is the input that is gone in order to acquire the thing.

a. Sliding scale fees	b. Fixed costs
c. Marginal cost	d. Cost

26. The _____ duty is a legal relationship of confidence or trust between two or more parties, most commonly a _____ or trustee and a principal or beneficiary. One party, for example a corporate trust company or the trust department of a bank, holds a _____ relation or acts in a _____ capacity to another, such as one whose funds are entrusted to it for investment. In a _____ relation one person justifiably reposes confidence, good faith, reliance and trust in another whose aid, advice or protection is sought in some matter.

a. Fiduciary	b. Financial Institutions Reform Recovery and Enforcement Act
c. General obligation	d. Legal tender

27. A _____ is a pool of assets forming an independent legal entity that are bought with the contributions to a pension plan for the exclusive purpose of financing pension plan benefits.

_____s are important shareholders of listed and private companies. They are especially important to the stock market where large institutional investors like the Ontario Teachers' Pension Plan dominate.

a. Leveraged buyout	b. Limited liability company
c. Leverage	d. Pension fund

28. _____ is a Fortune 500, American multinational corporation headquartered in Cincinnati, Ohio, that manufactures a wide range of consumer goods. As of 2008, P'G is the 8th largest corporation in the world by market capitalization and 14th largest US company by profit.

a. Procter ' Gamble Co.	b. 529 plan
c. 7-Eleven	d. 4-4-5 Calendar

29. _____ is the fraction of net income a firm pays to its stockholders in dividends:

>

The part of the earnings not paid to investors is left for investment to provide for future earnings growth. Investors seeking high current income and limited capital growth prefer companies with high _____. However investors seeking capital growth may prefer lower payout ratio because capital gains are taxed at a lower rate.

a. Dividend payout ratio	b. Dividend puzzle
c. Dividend imputation	d. Dividend yield

30. In some countries, including the United States and the United Kingdom, corporations can buy back their own stock in a share repurchase, also known as a _____ or share buyback. There has been a meteoric rise in the use of share repurchases in the U.S. in the past twenty years, from $5b in 1980 to $349b in 2005. A share repurchase distributes cash to existing shareholders in exchange for a fraction of the firm's outstanding equity.

a. Stockholder	b. Trading curb
c. Stock repurchase	d. Common stock

Chapter 14. Dividends and Dividend Policy

31. In financial accounting, a _____ or statement of financial position is a summary of a person's or organization's balances. Assets, liabilities and ownership equity are listed as of a specific date, such as the end of its financial year. A _____ is often described as a snapshot of a company's financial condition.
    a. Financial statements
    b. Statement of retained earnings
    c. Statement on Auditing Standards No. 70: Service Organizations
    d. Balance sheet

32. _____ are the earnings returned on the initial investment amount.

In the US, the Financial Accounting Standards Board (FASB) requires companies' income statements to report _____ for each of the major categories of the income statement: continuing operations, discontinued operations, extraordinary items, and net income.

The _____ formula does not include preferred dividends for categories outside of continued operations and net income.

    a. Earnings per share
    b. Inventory turnover
    c. Average accounting return
    d. Assets turnover

33. In business, _____ is income that a company receives from its normal business activities, usually from the sale of goods and services to customers. Some companies also receive _____ from interest, dividends or royalties paid to them by other companies. _____ may refer to business income in general, or it may refer to the amount, in a monetary unit, received during a period of time, as in 'Last year, Company X had _____ of $32 million.'

In many countries, including the UK, _____ is referred to as turnover.

    a. Matching principle
    b. Bottom line
    c. Furniture, Fixtures and Equipment
    d. Revenue

34. A _____ or stock divide increases or decreases the number of shares in a public company. The price is adjusted such that the before and after market capitalization of the company remains the same and dilution does not occur. Options and warrants are included.
    a. Stop price
    b. Stock split
    c. Contract for difference
    d. Stop order

35. The _____ is a stock exchange based in New York City, New York. It is the largest stock exchange in the world by dollar value of its listed companies securities. As of October 2008, the combined capitalization of all domestic _____ listed companies was $10.1 trillion.
    a. 4-4-5 Calendar
    b. New York Stock Exchange
    c. 7-Eleven
    d. 529 plan

36. _____ measures the rate of return on the ownership interest (shareholders' equity) of the common stock owners. _____ is viewed as one of the most important financial ratios. It measures a firm's efficiency at generating profits from every dollar of shareholders' equity (also known as net assets or assets minus liabilities.)

Chapter 14. Dividends and Dividend Policy

a. Return of capital
b. Return on equity
c. Diluted Earnings Per Share
d. Return on sales

37. In finance, _____, also known as return on investment is the ratio of money gained or lost on an investment relative to the amount of money invested. The amount of money gained or lost may be referred to as interest, profit/loss, gain/loss, or net income/loss. The money invested may be referred to as the asset, capital, principal, or the cost basis of the investment.
   a. Doctrine of the Proper Law
   b. Rate of return
   c. Stock or scrip dividends
   d. Composiition of Creditors

38. On a stock exchange, a _____ is the opposite of a stock split, i.e. a stock merge - a reduction in the number of shares and an accompanying increase in the share price. The ratio is also reversed: 1-for-2, 1-for-3 and so on.

There is a stigma attached to doing this so it is not initiated without very good reason.

   a. Correlation trading
   b. Conglomerate merger
   c. Reverse stock split
   d. Trade date

39. A _____, securities exchange or (in Europe) bourse is a corporation or mutual organization which provides 'trading' facilities for stock brokers and traders, to trade stocks and other securities. _____s also provide facilities for the issue and redemption of securities as well as other financial instruments and capital events including the payment of income and dividends. The securities traded on a _____ include: shares issued by companies, unit trusts and other pooled investment products and bonds.
   a. 4-4-5 Calendar
   b. 529 plan
   c. 7-Eleven
   d. Stock Exchange

40. In finance, _____ is the process of estimating the potential market value of a financial asset or liability. they can be done on assets (for example, investments in marketable securities such as stocks, options, business enterprises, or intangible assets such as patents and trademarks) or on liabilities (e.g., Bonds issued by a company.) _____s are required in many contexts including investment analysis, capital budgeting, merger and acquisition transactions, financial reporting, taxable events to determine the proper tax liability, and in litigation.
   a. Share
   b. Margin
   c. Valuation
   d. Procter ' Gamble

41. The _____ is an American stock exchange. It is the largest electronic screen-based equity securities trading market in the United States. With approximately 3,200 companies, it has more trading volume per day than any other stock exchange in the world.
   a. 4-4-5 Calendar
   b. 7-Eleven
   c. NASDAQ
   d. 529 plan

42. A _____ is an equity investment option offered directly from the underlying company. The investor does not receive quarterly dividends directly as cash; instead, the investor's dividends are directly reinvested in the underlying equity. It should be noted that the investor still must pay tax annually on his or her dividend income, whether it is received or reinvested.

a. Dividend puzzle
c. Dividend decision
b. Dividend payout ratio
d. Dividend reinvestment plan

Chapter 15. Raising Capital

1. A _____ is a type of auction where the auctioneer begins with a high asking price which is lowered until some participant is willing to accept the auctioneer's price, or a predetermined reserve price (the seller's minimum acceptable price) is reached. The winning participant pays the last announced price. This is also known as a 'clock auction' or an open-outcry descending-price auction.
   - a. 7-Eleven
   - b. 529 plan
   - c. 4-4-5 Calendar
   - d. Dutch auction

2. In economic models, the _____ time frame assumes no fixed factors of production. Firms can enter or leave the marketplace, and the cost (and availability) of land, labor, raw materials, and capital goods can be assumed to vary. In contrast, in the short-run time frame, certain factors are assumed to be fixed, because there is not sufficient time for them to change.
   - a. 4-4-5 Calendar
   - b. Short-run
   - c. 529 plan
   - d. Long-run

3. The institution most often referenced by the word '_____' is a public or publicly traded _____, the shares of which are traded on a public stock exchange (e.g., the New York Stock Exchange or Nasdaq in the United States) where shares of stock of _____s are bought and sold by and to the general public. Most of the largest businesses in the world are publicly traded _____s. However, the majority of _____s are said to be closely held, privately held or close _____s, meaning that no ready market exists for the trading of shares.
   - a. Protect
   - b. Depository Trust Company
   - c. Federal Home Loan Mortgage Corporation
   - d. Corporation

4. In economics, business, and accounting, a _____ is the value of money that has been used up to produce something, and hence is not available for use anymore. In business, the _____ may be one of acquisition, in which case the amount of money expended to acquire it is counted as _____. In this case, money is the input that is gone in order to acquire the thing.
   - a. Fixed costs
   - b. Sliding scale fees
   - c. Marginal cost
   - d. Cost

5. In finance, the _____ is the minimum rate of return a firm must offer shareholders to compensate for waiting for their returns, and for bearing some risk.

   The _____ capital for a particular company is the rate of return on investment that is required by the company's ordinary shareholders. The return consists both of dividend and capital gains, e.g. increases in the share price.

   - a. Cost of equity
   - b. Net pay
   - c. Residual value
   - d. Round-tripping

6. _____ or financing is to provide capital (funds), which means money for a project, a person, a business or any other private or public institutions.

   Those funds can be allocated for either short term or long term purposes. The health fund is a new way of _____ private healthcare centers.

Chapter 15. Raising Capital

a. Synthetic CDO
b. Product life cycle
c. Proxy fight
d. Funding

7. In finance, _____ is an asset class consisting of equity securities in operating companies that are not publicly traded on a stock exchange. Investments in _____ most often involve either an investment of capital into an operating company or the acquisition of an operating company. Capital for _____ is raised primarily from institutional investors.

a. Stock valuation
b. Currency swap
c. Pecking order theory
d. Private equity

8. _____ is a type of private equity capital typically provided to early-stage, high-potential, growth companies in the interest of generating a return through an eventual realization event such as an IPO or trade sale of the company. _____ investments are generally made as cash in exchange for shares in the invested company. It is typical for _____ investors to identify and back companies in high technology industries such as biotechnology and ICT.

a. Treasury Inflation-Protected Securities
b. Venture capital
c. Tail risk
d. Probability distribution

9. In finance, a _____ is a debt security, in which the authorized issuer owes the holders a debt and, depending on the terms of the _____, is obliged to pay interest (the coupon) and/or to repay the principal at a later date, termed maturity.

Thus a _____ is a loan: the issuer is the borrower, the _____ holder is the lender, and the coupon is the interest. _____s provide the borrower with external funds to finance long-term investments, or, in the case of government _____s, to finance current expenditure.

a. Catastrophe bonds
b. Convertible bond
c. Puttable bond
d. Bond

10. _____ refinancing (in the case of real property) occurs when a loan is taken out on property already owned, and the loan amount is above and beyond the cost of transaction, payoff of existing liens, and related expenses.

Strictly speaking all refinancing of debt is '_____', when funds retrieved are utilized for anything other than repaying an existing lien.

In the case of common usage of the term, _____ refinancing refers to when equity is liquidated from a property above and beyond sum of the payoff of existing loans held in lien on the property, loan fees, costs associated with the loan, taxes, insurance, tax reserves, insurance reserves, and in the past any other non-lien debt held in the name of the owner being paid by loan proceeds.

a. Conforming loan
b. Cash-out
c. Fixed rate mortgage
d. Home equity line of credit

11. _____ is that which is owed; usually referencing assets owed, but the term can cover other obligations. In the case of assets, _____ is a means of using future purchasing power in the present before a summation has been earned. Some companies and corporations use _____ as a part of their overall corporate finance strategy.

a. Cross-collateralization
c. Partial Payment
b. Credit cycle
d. Debt

12. A _____, is a securities offering whereby one or more parties that have some connection to a new enterprise invest the funds necessary to start the business so that it has enough funds to sustain itself for a period of development until it reaches either a state where it is able to continue funding itself, or has created something in value so that it is worthy of future rounds of funding. Seed money refers to the money so invested.
    a. Product liability
    b. Seed round
    c. Debtor-in-possession financing
    d. Model risk

13. A _____ is a fungible, negotiable instrument representing financial value. They are broadly categorized into debt securities (such as banknotes, bonds and debentures), and equity securities; e.g., common stocks. The company or other entity issuing the _____ is called the issuer.
    a. Securities lending
    b. Book entry
    c. Tracking stock
    d. Security

14. Congress enacted the _____, in the aftermath of the stock market crash of 1929 and during the ensuing Great Depression. It requires that any offer or sale of securities using the means and instrumentalities of interstate commerce be registered pursuant to the 1933 Act, unless an exemption from registration exists under the law.
    a. 529 plan
    b. 4-4-5 Calendar
    c. Securities Act of 1933
    d. 7-Eleven

15. The _____ of 1934 is a law governing the secondary trading of securities (stocks, bonds, and debentures) in the United States of America. The Act, 48 Stat. 881 (enacted June 6, 1934), codified at 15 U.S.C. § 78a et seq., was a sweeping piece of legislation. The Act and related statutes form the basis of regulation of the financial markets and their participants in the United States.
    a. 7-Eleven
    b. 4-4-5 Calendar
    c. Securities Exchange Act
    d. 529 plan

16. Under a secondary market offering or seasoned equity offering of shares to raise money, a company can opt for a _____ to raise capital. The _____ is a special form of shelf offering or shelf registration. With the issued rights, existing shareholders have the privilege to buy a specified number of new shares from the firm at a specified price within a specified time.
    a. Tender offer
    b. Rights issue
    c. Market for corporate control
    d. Corporate finance

17. In the _____ contract the underwriter agrees to sell as many shares as possible at the agreed-upon price.

Under the all-or-none contract the underwriter agrees either to sell the entire offering or to cancel the deal.

Stand-by underwriting, also known as strict underwriting or old-fashioned underwriting is a form of stock insurance: the issuer contracts the underwriter for the latter to purchase the shares the issuer failed to sell under stockholders' subscription and applications.

Chapter 15. Raising Capital

a. Best efforts
c. Book building
b. Follow-on offering
d. Real option

18. A _____ or secondary offering is an issuance of stock subsequent to the company's initial public offering. A _____ can be either of two types (or a mixture of both): dilutive and non-dilutive. A secondary offering is an offering of securities by a shareholder of the company (as opposed to the company itself, which is a primary offering).

a. Capital structure
c. Shareholder value
b. Second lien loan
d. Follow-on offering

19. _____, is when a company issues common stock or shares to the public for the first time. They are often issued by smaller, younger companies seeking capital to expand, but can also be done by large privately-owned companies looking to become publicly traded.

In an _____ the issuer may obtain the assistance of an underwriting firm, which helps it determine what type of security to issue (common or preferred), best offering price and time to bring it to market.

a. Insolvency
c. Initial public offering
b. Interest
d. Asian Financial Crisis

20. A _____ or Capital increase is a new equity issue by a company after its IPO. It differs from a secondary equity offering, in which owners (not the company) sell their shares. In the latter case, the company gets no money and no ownership dilution happens, for the company does not issue new shares.

a. Seasoned equity offering
c. FATF Blacklist
b. Debt-for-equity swap
d. Sinking fund

21. In the _____ contract the underwriter guarantees the sale of the issued stock at the agreed-upon price. For the issuer, it is the safest but the most expensive type of the contracts, since the underwriter takes the risk of sale.

In the best efforts contract the underwriter agrees to sell as many shares as possible at the agreed-upon price.

a. Firm commitment
c. Rights issue
b. Participating preferred stock
d. Special purpose entity

22. Unemployment occurs when a person is available to work and currently seeking work, but the person is without work. The prevalence of unemployment is usually measured using the _____, which is defined as the percentage of those in the labor force who are unemployed. The _____ is also used in economic studies and economic indexes such as the United States' Conference Board's Index of Leading Indicators as a measure of the state of the macroeconomics.

a. Unemployment rate
c. A Random Walk Down Wall Street
b. AAB
d. ABN Amro

23. In finance, a _____ is a security that entitles the holder to buy stock of the company that issued it at a specified price, which is usually higher than the stock price at time of issue.

_____s are frequently attached to bonds or preferred stock as a sweetener, allowing the issuer to pay lower interest rates or dividends. They can be used to enhance the yield of the bond, and make them more attractive to potential buyers.

a. Clearing
b. Clearing house
c. Credit
d. Warrant

24. A _____, also known by its legal title as an 'over-allotment option' (the only way it can be referred to in a prospectus), gives underwriters the right to sell additional shares in a registered securities offering if demand for the securities is in excess of the original amount offered. The _____ can vary in size up to 15% of the original number of shares offered.

The _____ option is popular because it is the only SEC-permitted means for an underwriter to stabilize the price of a new issue post-pricing.

a. Business valuation standards
b. Green Shoe
c. Foreign Language and Area Studies
d. Supply and demand

25. The _____ is the financial market where previously issued securities and financial instruments such as stock, bonds, options, and futures are bought and sold. The term '_____' is also used refer to the market for any used goods or assets, or an alternative use for an existing product or asset where the customer base is the second market

With primary issuances of securities or financial instruments, or the primary market, investors purchase these securities directly from issuers such as corporations issuing shares in an IPO or private placement, or directly from the federal government in the case of treasuries.

a. Secondary market
b. Performance attribution
c. Financial market
d. Delta neutral

26. An _____ is a contract written by a seller that conveys to the buyer the right -- but not the obligation -- to buy (in the case of a call _____) or to sell (in the case of a put _____) a particular asset, such as a piece of property such as, among others, a futures contract. In return for granting the _____, the seller collects a payment (the premium) from the buyer.

For example, buying a call _____ provides the right to buy a specified quantity of a security at a set strike price at some time on or before expiration, while buying a put _____ provides the right to sell.

a. Amortization
b. Option
c. Annuity
d. AT'T Mobility LLC

27. In financial accounting, _____s are precautions for which the amount or probability of occurrence are not known. Typical examples are _____s for warranty costs and _____ for taxes the term reserve is used instead of term _____; such a use, however, is inconsistent with the terminology suggested by International Accounting Standards Board.

a. Money measurement concept
b. Provision
c. Momentum Accounting and Triple-Entry Bookkeeping
d. Petty cash

Chapter 15. Raising Capital

28. The term _____, also known as a waiting period is a period extended from the time a company files a registration statement with the SEC until SEC staff declared the registration statement effective. During that period, the federal securities laws limited what information a company and related parties can release to the public.'

Under the rules of the Securities Act of 1933, as modified June 29, 2005, electronic communications, including electronic road shows and information located on or hyperlinked to an issuer's website are also governed. The rules changes of June 29, 2005 also included various changes which 'liberalize permitted offering activity and communications to allow more information' for certain qualifying organizations.

a. Leasing
c. Lien
b. Quiet period
d. Duty of loyalty

29. A '_____' is a 'Charge' that is paid to obtain the right to delay a payment. Essentially, the payer purchases the right to make a given payment in the future instead of in the Present. The '_____', or 'Charge' that must be paid to delay the payment, is simply the difference between what the payment amount would be if it were paid in the present and what the payment amount would be paid if it were paid in the future.

a. Discount
c. Value at risk
b. Risk modeling
d. Risk aversion

30. The free _____ of a public company is an estimate of the proportion of shares that are not held by large owners and that are not stock with sales restrictions (restricted stock that cannot be sold until they become unrestricted stock.)

The free _____ or a public _____ is usually defined as being all shares held by investors other than:

- shares held by owners owning more than 5% of all shares (those could be institutional investors, 'strategic shareholders,' founders, executives, and other insiders' holdings)
- restricted stocks (granted to executives that can be, but don't have to be, registered insiders)
- insider holdings (it is assumed that insiders hold stock for the very long term)

The free _____ is an important criterion in quoting a share on the stock market.

To _____ a company means to list its shares on a public stock exchange through an initial public offering (or 'flotation'.)

- Open market
- Outstanding shares
- Market capitalization
- Public _____ loat
- Reverse takeover

a. Trade finance
c. Synthetic CDO
b. Golden parachute
d. Float

Chapter 15. Raising Capital

31. In finance, an _____ is the difference between the expected return of a security and the actual return. _____s are sometimes triggered by 'events.' Events can include mergers, dividend announcements, company earning announcements, interest rate increases, lawsuits, etc. all which can contribute to an _____.
   a. Abnormal return
   b. ABN Amro
   c. A Random Walk Down Wall Street
   d. AAB

32. A _____ is the price of a single share of a no. of saleable stocks of the company. Once the stock is purchased, the owner becomes a shareholder of the company that issued the share.
   a. Stock split
   b. Whisper numbers
   c. Trading curb
   d. Share price

33. _____ are expenses that change in proportion to the activity of a business. In other words, _____ are the sum of marginal costs. It can also be considered normal costs. Along with fixed costs, _____ make up the two components of total cost. Direct Costs, however, are costs that can be associated with a particular cost object.
   a. Transaction cost
   b. Cost accounting
   c. Variable costs
   d. Fixed costs

34. _____, in microeconomics, are the cost advantages that a business obtains due to expansion. _____ may be utilized by any size firm expanding its scale of operation.
   a. Articles of incorporation
   b. Uniform Commercial Code
   c. Employee Retirement Income Security Act
   d. Economies of scale

35. _____ are costs that are not directly accountable to a particular function or product. _____ may be either fixed or variable. _____ include taxes, administration, personnel and security costs, and are also known as overhead.
   a. AAB
   b. A Random Walk Down Wall Street
   c. Equivalent annual cost
   d. Indirect costs

36. _____ is a legally declared inability or impairment of ability of an individual or organization to pay their creditors. Creditors may file a _____ petition against a debtor ('involuntary _____') in an effort to recoup a portion of what they are owed or initiate a restructuring. In the majority of cases, however, _____ is initiated by the debtor (a 'voluntary _____' that is filed by the bankrupt individual or organization.)
   a. Bankruptcy
   b. 4-4-5 Calendar
   c. 529 plan
   d. Debt settlement

37. _____ is the provision of resources (such as granting a loan) by one party to another party where that second party does not reimburse the first party immediately, thereby generating a debt, and instead arranges either to repay or return those resources (or material(s) of equal value) at a later date. The first party is called a creditor, also known as a lender, while the second party is called a debtor, also known as a borrower.

Movements of financial capital are normally dependent on either _____ or equity transfers.

   a. Credit
   b. Comparable
   c. Warrant
   d. Clearing house

Chapter 15. Raising Capital

38. A _____ is an international bond that is denominated in a currency not native to the country where it is issued. It can be categorised according to the currency in which it is issued. London is one of the centers of the _____ market, but _____s may be traded throughout the world - for example in Singapore or Tokyo.
    a. Interest rate option
    b. Economic entity
    c. Education production function
    d. Eurobond

39. The _____ is an American stock exchange. It is the largest electronic screen-based equity securities trading market in the United States. With approximately 3,200 companies, it has more trading volume per day than any other stock exchange in the world.
    a. 4-4-5 Calendar
    b. 7-Eleven
    c. NASDAQ
    d. 529 plan

40. In the United States, a _____ is an offering of securities that are not registered with the Securities and Exchange Commission (SEC.) Such offerings exploit an exemption offered by the Securities Act of 1933 that comes with several restrictions, including a prohibition against general solicitation. This exemption allows companies to avoid quarterly reporting requirements and many of the legal liabilities associated with the Sarbanes-Oxley Act.
    a. 4-4-5 Calendar
    b. Private placement
    c. 7-Eleven
    d. 529 plan

41. _____ is the capital that a business raises by taking out a loan. It is a loan made to a company that is normally repaid at some future date. _____ differs from equity or share capital because subscribers to _____ do not become part owners of the business, but are merely creditors, and the suppliers of _____ usually receive a contractually fixed annual percentage return on their loan, and this is known as the coupon rate.
    a. Floating charge
    b. Debt Capital
    c. Risk-return spectrum
    d. Financial assistance

42. _____ is an arrangement with the U.S. Securities and Exchange Commission that allows a single registration document to be filed that permits the issuance of multiple securities.

    _____ is a registration of a new issue which can be prepared up to two years in advance, so that the issue can be offered quickly as soon as funds are needed or market conditions are favorable.

    For example, current market conditions in the housing market are not favorable for a specific firm to issue a public offering.

    a. Bought deal
    b. 4-4-5 Calendar
    c. Black Sea Trade and Development Bank
    d. Shelf registration

Chapter 16. Short-Term Financial Planning

1. In economics, business, and accounting, a _____ is the value of money that has been used up to produce something, and hence is not available for use anymore. In business, the _____ may be one of acquisition, in which case the amount of money expended to acquire it is counted as _____. In this case, money is the input that is gone in order to acquire the thing.
   a. Sliding scale fees
   b. Fixed costs
   c. Marginal cost
   d. Cost

2. In economics, the concept of the _____ refers to the decision-making time frame of a firm in which at least one factor of production is fixed. Costs which are fixed in the _____ have no impact on a firms decisions. For example a firm can raise output by increasing the amount of labour through overtime.
   a. 529 plan
   b. Long-run
   c. 4-4-5 Calendar
   d. Short-run

3. _____ is the task of determining how a business will afford to achieve its strategic goals and objectives. Usually, a company creates a Financial Plan immediately after the vision and objectives have been set. The Financial Plan describes each of the activities, resources, equipment and materials that are needed to achieve these objectives, as well as the timeframes involved.
   a. Corporate Transparency
   b. Performance measurement
   c. Management by exception
   d. Financial planning

4. In accounting, a _____ is an asset on the balance sheet which is expected to be sold or otherwise used up in the near future, usually within one year, or one business cycle - whichever is longer. Typical _____s include cash, cash equivalents, accounts receivable, inventory, the portion of prepaid accounts which will be used within a year, and short-term investments.

On the balance sheet, assets will typically be classified into _____s and long-term assets.

   a. Write-off
   b. Historical cost
   c. Long-term liabilities
   d. Current asset

5. In accounting, _____ are considered liabilities of the business that are to be settled in cash within the fiscal year or the operating cycle, whichever period is longer.

For example accounts payable for goods, services or supplies that were purchased for use in the operation of the business and payable within a normal period of time would be _____.

Bonds, mortgages and loans that are payable over a term exceeding one year would be fixed liabilities.

   a. Net income
   b. Closing entries
   c. Gross sales
   d. Current liabilities

6. _____ is a financial metric which represents operating liquidity available to a business. Along with fixed assets such as plant and equipment, _____ is considered a part of operating capital. It is calculated as current assets minus current liabilities.
   a. 529 plan
   b. Working capital management
   c. Working capital
   d. 4-4-5 Calendar

Chapter 16. Short-Term Financial Planning

7. Decisions relating to working capital and short term financing are referred to as _____. These involve managing the relationship between a firm's short-term assets and its short-term liabilities. The goal of _____ is to ensure that the firm is able to continue its operations and that it has sufficient cash flow to satisfy both maturing short-term debt and upcoming operational expenses.
   a. Working capital management
   b. 529 plan
   c. Working capital
   d. 4-4-5 Calendar

8. In business and accounting, _____s are everything of value that is owned by a person or company. The balance sheet of a firm records the monetary value of the _____s owned by the firm. The two major _____ classes are tangible _____s and intangible _____s.
   a. Accounts payable
   b. Asset
   c. Income
   d. EBITDA

9. _____ or financing is to provide capital (funds), which means money for a project, a person, a business or any other private or public institutions.

   Those funds can be allocated for either short term or long term purposes. The health fund is a new way of _____ private healthcare centers.

   a. Synthetic CDO
   b. Product life cycle
   c. Funding
   d. Proxy fight

10. In economic models, the _____ time frame assumes no fixed factors of production. Firms can enter or leave the marketplace, and the cost (and availability) of land, labor, raw materials, and capital goods can be assumed to vary. In contrast, in the short-run time frame, certain factors are assumed to be fixed, because there is not sufficient time for them to change.
    a. 529 plan
    b. Long-run
    c. Short-run
    d. 4-4-5 Calendar

11. _____, in bookkeeping, refers to assets, liabilities, income, and expenses recorded on individual pages of the so called book of final entry or ledger. Changes in _____ value are made by chronologically posting debit (DR) and credit (CR) entries to its page. Examples of _____s are cash, _____s receivable, mortgages, loans, land and buildings, common stock, sales, services provided, wages, and payroll overhead.
    a. Option
    b. Accretion
    c. Alpha
    d. Account

12. _____ is a file or account that contains money that a person or company owes to suppliers, but hasn't paid yet (a form of debt.) When you receive an invoice you add it to the file, and then you remove it when you pay. Thus, the A/P is a form of credit that suppliers offer to their purchasers by allowing them to pay for a product or service after it has already been received.
    a. Outstanding balance
    b. Accounts payable
    c. Accrual
    d. Earnings before interest, taxes, depreciation and amortization

Chapter 16. Short-Term Financial Planning

13. _____ is one of a series of accounting transactions dealing with the billing of customers who owe money to a person, company or organization for goods and services that have been provided to the customer. In most business entities this is typically done by generating an invoice and mailing or electronically delivering it to the customer, who in turn must pay it within an established timeframe called credit or payment terms.

An example of a common payment term is Net 30, meaning payment is due in the amount of the invoice 30 days from the date of invoice.

a. Accounting methods
b. Impaired asset
c. Income
d. Accounts receivable

14. _____ is the balance of the amounts of cash being received and paid by a business during a defined period of time, sometimes tied to a specific project. Measurement of _____ can be used

- to evaluate the state or performance of a business or project.
- to determine problems with liquidity. Being profitable does not necessarily mean being liquid. A company can fail because of a shortage of cash, even while profitable.
- to generate project rate of returns. The time of _____s into and out of projects are used as inputs to financial models such as internal rate of return, and net present value.
- to examine income or growth of a business when it is believed that accrual accounting concepts do not represent economic realities. Alternately, _____ can be used to 'validate' the net income generated by accrual accounting.

_____ as a generic term may be used differently depending on context, and certain _____ definitions may be adapted by analysts and users for their own uses. Common terms include operating _____ and free _____.

_____s can be classified into:

1. Operational _____s: Cash received or expended as a result of the company's core business activities.
2. Investment _____s: Cash received or expended through capital expenditure, investments or acquisitions.
3. Financing _____s: Cash received or expended as a result of financial activities, such as interests and dividends.

All three together - the net _____ - are necessary to reconcile the beginning cash balance to the ending cash balance. Loan draw downs or equity injections, that is just shifting of capital but no expenditure as such, are not considered in the net _____.

a. Shareholder value
b. Corporate finance
c. Real option
d. Cash flow

15. _____ is a list for goods and materials held available in stock by a business. It is also used for a list of the contents of a household and for a list for testamentary purposes of the possessions of someone who has died. In accounting _____ is considered an asset.

Chapter 16. Short-Term Financial Planning

    a. ABN Amro
    b. A Random Walk Down Wall Street
    c. Inventory
    d. AAB

16. The institution most often referenced by the word '_____' is a public or publicly traded _____, the shares of which are traded on a public stock exchange (e.g., the New York Stock Exchange or Nasdaq in the United States) where shares of stock of _____s are bought and sold by and to the general public. Most of the largest businesses in the world are publicly traded _____s. However, the majority of _____s are said to be closely held, privately held or close _____s, meaning that no ready market exists for the trading of shares.

    a. Federal Home Loan Mortgage Corporation
    b. Depository Trust Company
    c. Protect
    d. Corporation

17. _____ is the provision of resources (such as granting a loan) by one party to another party where that second party does not reimburse the first party immediately, thereby generating a debt, and instead arranges either to repay or return those resources (or material(s) of equal value) at a later date. The first party is called a creditor, also known as a lender, while the second party is called a debtor, also known as a borrower.

Movements of financial capital are normally dependent on either _____ or equity transfers.

    a. Comparable
    b. Credit
    c. Clearing house
    d. Warrant

18. An _____ (often called organization chart or organigram(me) or organogram(me)) is a diagram that shows the structure of an organization and the relationships and relative ranks of its parts and positions/jobs. The term is also used for similar diagrams, for example ones showing the different elements of a field of knowledge or a group of languages. The French Encyclopédie had one of the first _____s of knowledge in general.

    a. AAB
    b. A Random Walk Down Wall Street
    c. ABN Amro
    d. Organizational chart

19. _____ refers to a business or organization attempting to acquire goods or services to accomplish the goals of the enterprise. Though there are several organizations that attempt to set standards in the _____ process, processes can vary greatly between organizations. Typically the word '_____' is not used interchangeably with the word 'procurement', since procurement typically includes Expediting, Supplier Quality, and Traffic and Logistics (T'L) in addition to _____.

    a. 4-4-5 Calendar
    b. Purchasing
    c. 529 plan
    d. 7-Eleven

20. A _____ is an employee within a company, business or other organization who is responsible at some level for buying or approving the acquisition of goods and services needed by the company. The position responsibilities may be the same as that of a buyer or purchasing agent, or may include wider supervisory or managerial responsibilities. A _____ may oversee the acquisition of materials needed for production, general supplies for offices and facilities, equipment, or construction contracts.

    a. Stockbroker
    b. Day trader
    c. Financial analyst
    d. Purchasing manager

21. In political science and economics, the _____ or agency dilemma treats the difficulties that arise under conditions of incomplete and asymmetric information when a principal hires an agent. Various mechanisms may be used to try to align the interests of the agent with those of the principal, such as piece rates/commissions, profit sharing, efficiency wages, performance measurement (including financial statements), the agent posting a bond, or fear of firing. The _____ is found in most employer/employee relationships, for example, when stockholders hire top executives of corporations.

   a. 7-Eleven
   c. 529 plan
   b. 4-4-5 Calendar
   d. Principal-agent problem

22. _____ refinancing (in the case of real property) occurs when a loan is taken out on property already owned, and the loan amount is above and beyond the cost of transaction, payoff of existing liens, and related expenses.

Strictly speaking all refinancing of debt is '_____', when funds retrieved are utilized for anything other than repaying an existing lien.

In the case of common usage of the term, _____ refinancing refers to when equity is liquidated from a property above and beyond sum of the payoff of existing loans held in lien on the property, loan fees, costs associated with the loan, taxes, insurance, tax reserves, insurance reserves, and in the past any other non-lien debt held in the name of the owner being paid by loan proceeds.

   a. Home equity line of credit
   c. Fixed rate mortgage
   b. Conforming loan
   d. Cash-out

23. The _____ is an equation that equals the cost of goods sold divided by the average inventory. Average inventory equals beginning inventory plus ending inventory divided by 2.

The formula for _____:

$$\text{Inventory Turnover} = \frac{\text{Cost of Goods Sold}}{\text{Average Inventory}}$$

The formula for average inventory:

$$\text{Average Inventory} = \frac{\text{Beginning inventory} + \text{Ending inventory}}{2}$$

A low turnover rate may point to overstocking, obsolescence, or deficiencies in the product line or marketing effort.

   a. Earnings yield
   c. Information ratio
   b. Operating leverage
   d. Inventory turnover

Chapter 16. Short-Term Financial Planning

24. In marketing, _____ refers to the total cost of holding inventory. This includes warehousing costs such as rent, utilities and salaries, financial costs such as opportunity cost, and inventory costs related to perishibility, shrinkage and insurance.
    a. Carrying cost
    b. 4-4-5 Calendar
    c. 7-Eleven
    d. 529 plan

25. The _____ is a capital budgeting metric used by firms to decide whether they should make investments. It is an indicator of the efficiency or quality of an investment, as opposed to net present value (NPV), which indicates value or magnitude.

    The IRR is the annualized effective compounded return rate which can be earned on the invested capital, i.e., the yield on the investment.

    a. ABN Amro
    b. A Random Walk Down Wall Street
    c. AAB
    d. Internal rate of return

26. _____ or economic opportunity loss is the value of the next best alternative foregone as the result of making a decision. _____ analysis is an important part of a company's decision-making processes but is not treated as an actual cost in any financial statement. The next best thing that a person can engage in is referred to as the _____ of doing the best thing and ignoring the next best thing to be done.
    a. ABN Amro
    b. AAB
    c. A Random Walk Down Wall Street
    d. Opportunity cost

27. An _____ is an economic concept that relates to the cost incurred by an entity (such as organizations) associated with problems such as divergent management-shareholder objectives and information asymmetry. The costs consist of two main sources:

    1. The costs inherently associated with using an agent (e.g., the risk that agents will use organizational resource for their own benefit) and
    2. The costs of techniques used to mitigate the problems associated with using an agent (e.g., the costs of producing financial statements or the use of stock options to align executive interests to shareholder interests.)

    Though effects of _____ are present in any agency relationship, the term is most used in business contexts.

    The information asymmetry that exists between shareholders and the Chief Executive Officer is generally considered to be a classic example of a principal-agent problem. The agent (the manager) is working on behalf of the principal (the shareholders), who does not observe the actions of the agent.

    a. ABN Amro
    b. Agency cost
    c. A Random Walk Down Wall Street
    d. AAB

28. The _____ is the average project earnings after taxes and depreciation, divided by the average book value of the investment during its life.

    There are three steps to calculating the _____.

First, determine the average net income of each year of the project's life. Second, determine the average investment, taking depreciation into account. Third, determine the _____ by dividing the average net income by the average investment.

a. Assets turnover
b. Operating leverage
c. Information ratio
d. Average accounting return

29. In finance, _____, also known as return on investment is the ratio of money gained or lost on an investment relative to the amount of money invested. The amount of money gained or lost may be referred to as interest, profit/loss, gain/loss, or net income/loss. The money invested may be referred to as the asset, capital, principal, or the cost basis of the investment.
a. Doctrine of the Proper Law
b. Composiition of Creditors
c. Stock or scrip dividends
d. Rate of return

30. In financial accounting, the term _____ is most commonly used to describe any part of shareholders' equity, except for basic share capital. Sometimes, the term is used instead of the term provision; such a use, however, is inconsistent with the terminology suggested by International Accounting Standards Board. For more information about provisions, see provision (accounting.)
a. Treasury stock
b. FIFO and LIFO accounting
c. Closing entries
d. Reserve

31. In economics, the _____ is the proposition by Irving Fisher that the real interest rate is independent of monetary measures, especially the nominal interest rate. The Fisher equation is

$r_r = r_n >- >\pi^e$.

This means, the real interest rate (r_r) equals the nominal interest rate (r_n) minus expected rate of inflation ($>\pi^e$.) Here all the rates are continuously compounded.

a. 529 plan
b. Fisher hypothesis
c. 4-4-5 Calendar
d. 7-Eleven

32. _____ is a life of security. It may also refer to the final payment date of a loan or other financial instrument, at which point all remaining interest and principal is due to be paid.

1, 3, 6 months _____ band can be calculated by using 30-day per month periods.

a. False billing
b. Primary market
c. Replacement cost
d. Maturity

33. _____ is a fee paid on borrowed assets. It is the price paid for the use of borrowed money , or, money earned by deposited funds . Assets that are sometimes lent with _____ include money, shares, consumer goods through hire purchase, major assets such as aircraft, and even entire factories in finance lease arrangements.

Chapter 16. Short-Term Financial Planning

a. A Random Walk Down Wall Street
b. AAB
c. Insolvency
d. Interest

34. An _____ is the price a borrower pays for the use of money they do not own, and the return a lender receives for deferring the use of funds, by lending it to the borrower. _____s are normally expressed as a percentage rate over the period of one year.

_____s targets are also a vital tool of monetary policy and are used to control variables like investment, inflation, and unemployment.

a. A Random Walk Down Wall Street
b. Interest rate
c. ABN Amro
d. AAB

35. Working capital requirements of a business should be monitored at all times to ensure that there are sufficient funds available to meet short-term expenses.

The _____ is basically a detailed plan that shows all expected sources and uses of cash

a. Mitigating Control
b. Cash budget
c. Loans and interest, in Judaism
d. Rate of return

36. A _____ is an expenditure creating future benefits. A _____ is incurred when a business spends money either to buy fixed assets or to add to the value of an existing fixed asset with a useful life that extends beyond the taxable year. Capex are used by a company to acquire or upgrade physical assets such as equipment, property, or industrial buildings.

a. 4-4-5 Calendar
b. Cost of capital
c. Weighted average cost of capital
d. Capital expenditure

37. The _____ is the rate that a company is expected to pay to finance its assets. WACC is the minimum return that a company must earn on existing asset base to satisfy its creditors, owners, and other providers of capital.

Companies raise money from a number of sources: common equity, preferred equity, straight debt, convertible debt, exchangeable debt, warrants, options, pension liabilities, executive stock options, governmental subsidies, and so on.

a. Weighted average cost of capital
b. Capital intensity
c. 4-4-5 Calendar
d. Cost of capital

38. _____, refers to consumption opportunity gained by an entity within a specified time frame, which is generally expressed in monetary terms. However, for households and individuals, '_____ is the sum of all the wages, salaries, profits, interests payments, rents and other forms of earnings received... in a given period of time.' For firms, _____ generally refers to net-profit: what remains of revenue after expenses have been subtracted.

a. Annual report
b. Accrual
c. OIBDA
d. Income

Chapter 16. Short-Term Financial Planning

39. An _____ is a financial statement for companies that indicates how Revenue is transformed into net income The purpose of the _____ is to show managers and investors whether the company made or lost money during the period being reported.

The important thing to remember about an _____ is that it represents a period of time.

a. Income statement
c. AAB
b. A Random Walk Down Wall Street
d. ABN Amro

40. _____ is a form of short-term borrowing often used to improve a company's working capital and cash flow position.

_____ allows a business to draw money against its sales invoices before the customer has actually paid. To do this, the business borrows a percentage of the value of its sales ledger from a finance company, effectively using the unpaid sales invoices as collateral for the borrowing.

a. AAB
c. ABN Amro
b. A Random Walk Down Wall Street
d. Invoice discounting

41. _____ is that which is owed; usually referencing assets owed, but the term can cover other obligations. In the case of assets, _____ is a means of using future purchasing power in the present before a summation has been earned. Some companies and corporations use _____ as a part of their overall corporate finance strategy.

a. Credit cycle
c. Partial Payment
b. Cross-collateralization
d. Debt

42. _____ is a financial transaction whereby a business sells its accounts receivable (i.e., invoices) at a discount. _____ differs from a bank loan in three main ways. First, the emphasis is on the value of the receivables (essentially a financial asset), not the firm's credit worthiness.

a. Financial Literacy Month
c. Credit card balance transfer
b. Debt-for-equity swap
d. Factoring

43. A _____ is any credit facility extended to a business by a bank or financial institution. A _____ may take several forms such as cash credit, overdraft, demand loan, export packing credit, term loan, discounting or purchase of commercial bills etc. It is like an account that can readily be tapped into if the need arises or not touched at all and saved for emergencies.

a. Debt-snowball method
c. Cash credit
b. Line of credit
d. Default Notice

44. _____ is a type of credit that does not have a fixed number of payments, in contrast to installment credit. Examples of _____s used by consumers include credit cards. Corporate _____ facilities are typically used to provide liquidity for a company's day-to-day operations.

a. Reverse stock split
c. Commercial finance
b. Package loan
d. Revolving credit

45. In finance, a _____ is a debt security, in which the authorized issuer owes the holders a debt and, depending on the terms of the _____, is obliged to pay interest (the coupon) and/or to repay the principal at a later date, termed maturity.

Thus a _____ is a loan: the issuer is the borrower, the _____ holder is the lender, and the coupon is the interest. _____s provide the borrower with external funds to finance long-term investments, or, in the case of government _____s, to finance current expenditure.

   a. Catastrophe bonds
   b. Puttable bond
   c. Bond
   d. Convertible bond

46. In the global money market, _____ is an unsecured promissory note with a fixed maturity of one to 270 days. _____ is a money-market security issued (sold) by large banks and corporations to get money to meet short term debt obligations (for example, payroll), and is only backed by an issuing bank or corporation's promise to pay the face amount on the maturity date specified on the note. Since it is not backed by collateral, only firms with excellent credit ratings from a recognized rating agency will be able to sell their _____ at a reasonable price.
   a. Trade-off theory
   b. Commercial paper
   c. Book building
   d. Financial distress

47. An _____ is a loan that is not backed by collateral. Also known as a signature loan or personal loan.

_____s are based solely upon the borrower's credit rating.

   a. Unsecured Loan
   b. Event of default
   c. Intelliscore
   d. Annualcreditreport.com

48. A _____ is a fungible, negotiable instrument representing financial value. They are broadly categorized into debt securities (such as banknotes, bonds and debentures), and equity securities; e.g., common stocks. The company or other entity issuing the _____ is called the issuer.
   a. Tracking stock
   b. Security
   c. Book entry
   d. Securities lending

49. _____ exists when one firm provides goods or services to a customer with an agreement to bill them later, or receive a shipment or service from a supplier under an agreement to pay them later. It can be viewed as an essential element of capitalization in an operating business because it can reduce the required capital investment to operate the business if it is managed properly. _____ is the largest use of capital for a majority of business to business (B2B) sellers in the United States and is a critical source of capital for a majority of all businesses.
   a. 529 plan
   b. Going concern
   c. Trade credit
   d. 4-4-5 Calendar

50. In law, a _____ is a form of security interest granted over an item of property to secure the payment of a debt or performance of some other obligation. The owner of the property, who grants the _____, is referred to as the lienor and the person who has the benefit of the _____ is referred to as the _____ee.

The etymological root is: Anglo-French _____, loyen bond, restraint, from Latin ligamen, from ligare to bind.

a. Family and Medical Leave Act
b. Joint venture
c. Sarbanes-Oxley Act
d. Lien

51. In general usage, a _____ can be a budget, a plan for spending and saving future income. This plan allocates future income to various types of expenses, such as rent or utilities, and also reserves some income for short-term and long-term savings. A _____ can also be an investment plan, which allocates savings to various assets or projects expected to produce future income, such as a new business or product line, shares in an existing business, or real estate.
a. Credit repair software
b. Promissory note
c. Financial plan
d. Title loan

Chapter 17. Working Capital Management

1. The institution most often referenced by the word '_____' is a public or publicly traded _____, the shares of which are traded on a public stock exchange (e.g., the New York Stock Exchange or Nasdaq in the United States) where shares of stock of _____s are bought and sold by and to the general public. Most of the largest businesses in the world are publicly traded _____s. However, the majority of _____s are said to be closely held, privately held or close _____s, meaning that no ready market exists for the trading of shares.
   a. Protect
   b. Corporation
   c. Depository Trust Company
   d. Federal Home Loan Mortgage Corporation

2. _____ is a financial metric which represents operating liquidity available to a business. Along with fixed assets such as plant and equipment, _____ is considered a part of operating capital. It is calculated as current assets minus current liabilities.
   a. Working capital
   b. Working capital management
   c. 529 plan
   d. 4-4-5 Calendar

3. Decisions relating to working capital and short term financing are referred to as _____. These involve managing the relationship between a firm's short-term assets and its short-term liabilities. The goal of _____ is to ensure that the firm is able to continue its operations and that it has sufficient cash flow to satisfy both maturing short-term debt and upcoming operational expenses.
   a. 4-4-5 Calendar
   b. Working capital
   c. 529 plan
   d. Working capital management

4. In financial accounting, the term _____ is most commonly used to describe any part of shareholders' equity, except for basic share capital. Sometimes, the term is used instead of the term provision; such a use, however, is inconsistent with the terminology suggested by International Accounting Standards Board. For more information about provisions, see provision (accounting.)
   a. Treasury stock
   b. Closing entries
   c. FIFO and LIFO accounting
   d. Reserve

5. _____ is a measure of the ability of a debtor to pay their debts as and when they fall due. It is usually expressed as a ratio or a percentage of current liabilities.

   For a corporation with a published balance sheet there are various ratios used to calculate a measure of liquidity.

   a. Invested capital
   b. Operating leverage
   c. Operating profit margin
   d. Accounting liquidity

6. In United States banking, _____ is a marketing term for certain services offered primarily to larger business customers. It may be used to describe all bank accounts (such as checking accounts) provided to businesses of a certain size, but it is more often used to describe specific services such as cash concentration, zero balance accounting, and automated clearing house facilities. Sometimes, private banking customers are given _____ services.
   a. Profitability index
   b. Cash management
   c. Global tactical asset allocation
   d. Capitalization rate

7. The free _____ of a public company is an estimate of the proportion of shares that are not held by large owners and that are not stock with sales restrictions (restricted stock that cannot be sold until they become unrestricted stock.)

The free _____ or a public _____ is usually defined as being all shares held by investors other than:

- shares held by owners owning more than 5% of all shares (those could be institutional investors, 'strategic shareholders,' founders, executives, and other insiders' holdings)
- restricted stocks (granted to executives that can be, but don't have to be, registered insiders)
- insider holdings (it is assumed that insiders hold stock for the very long term)

The free _____ is an important criterion in quoting a share on the stock market.

To _____ a company means to list its shares on a public stock exchange through an initial public offering (or 'flotation'.)

- Open market
- Outstanding shares
- Market capitalization
- Public _____ *loat*
- Reverse takeover

a. Trade finance
c. Synthetic CDO

b. Float
d. Golden parachute

8. In banking and finance, _____ denotes all activities from the time a commitment is made for a transaction until it is settled. _____ is necessary because the speed of trades is much faster than the cycle time for completing the underlying transaction.

In its widest sense _____ involves the management of post-trading, pre-settlement credit exposures, to ensure that trades are settled in accordance with market rules, even if a buyer or seller should become insolvent prior to settlement.

a. Share
c. Procter ' Gamble

b. Clearing house
d. Clearing

9. A _____ is the principal book for recording transactions. Originally, the term referred to a large volume of Scripture/service book kept in one place in church and accessible.

According to Charles Wriothesley's Chronicle (1538):

> the curates should provide a booke of the bible in Englishe, of the largest volume, to be a lidger in the same church for the parishioners to read on.

It is an application of this original meaning that is found in the commercial usage of the term for the principal book of account in a business house, the general _____ or nominal _____ and also in the terms purchase _____ and sales _____.

Chapter 17. Working Capital Management

    a. Journal entry
    b. General journal
    c. General ledger
    d. Ledger

10. The _____ was enacted in 1987 by the United States Congress for the purpose of standardizing hold periods on deposits made to commercial banks and to regulate institutions' use of deposit holds. It is also referred to as Regulation CC or Reg CC, after the Federal Reserve regulation that implements the act. The law is codified in Title 12, Chapter 41 of the US Code and Title 12, Part 229 of the Code of Federal Regulations.
    a. Expedited Funds Availability Act
    b. ABN Amro
    c. A Random Walk Down Wall Street
    d. AAB

11. _____ is the transfer of funds from diverse accounts into a central account to improve the efficiency of cash management. The consolidation of cash into a single account allows a company to maintain smaller cash balances overall, and to identify excess cash available for short term investments. The cash available in different bank accounts are pooled into a master account. The advantages of _____ are 1) Cash control 2) Cash visibility .
    a. Conditional prepayment rate
    b. Cash concentration
    c. Capitalization rate
    d. Profitability index

12. A _____ is a system (including physical or electronic infrastructure and associated procedures and protocols) used to settle financial transactions in bond markets, currency markets, and futures, derivatives or options markets, or to transfer funds between financial institutions. Due to the backing of modern fiat currencies with government bonds, _____s are a core part of modern monetary systems.
    a. 529 plan
    b. 4-4-5 Calendar
    c. 7-Eleven
    d. Payment system

13. In finance, the _____ is the global financial market for short-term borrowing and lending. It provides short-term liquidity funding for the global financial system. The _____ is where short-term obligations such as Treasury bills, commercial paper and bankers' acceptances are bought and sold.
    a. Cramdown
    b. Consumer debt
    c. Money market
    d. Debt-for-equity swap

14. _____, in bookkeeping, refers to assets, liabilities, income, and expenses recorded on individual pages of the so called book of final entry or ledger. Changes in _____ value are made by chronologically posting debit (DR) and credit (CR) entries to its page. Examples of _____s are cash, _____s receivable, mortgages, loans, land and buildings, common stock, sales, services provided, wages, and payroll overhead.
    a. Alpha
    b. Accretion
    c. Option
    d. Account

15. A _____ is a professionally managed type of collective investment scheme that pools money from many investors and invests it in stocks, bonds, short-term money market instruments, and/or other securities. The _____ will have a fund manager that trades the pooled money on a regular basis. Currently, the worldwide value of all _____s totals more than $26 trillion.

Since 1940, there have been three basic types of investment companies in the United States: open-end funds, also known in the US as _____s; unit investment trusts (UITs); and closed-end funds.

Chapter 17. Working Capital Management

a. Mutual fund
b. Trust company
c. Net asset value
d. Financial intermediary

16. _____ are securities that can be easily converted into cash. Such securities will generally have highly liquid markets allowing the security to be sold at a reasonable price very quickly. This is a usual feature in real estate .

a. Securities lending
b. Book entry
c. Marketable
d. Tracking stock

17. _____ is a life of security. It may also refer to the final payment date of a loan or other financial instrument, at which point all remaining interest and principal is due to be paid.

1, 3, 6 months _____ band can be calculated by using 30-day per month periods.

a. Replacement cost
b. Maturity
c. Primary market
d. False billing

18. A _____ is a fungible, negotiable instrument representing financial value. They are broadly categorized into debt securities (such as banknotes, bonds and debentures), and equity securities; e.g., common stocks. The company or other entity issuing the _____ is called the issuer.

a. Securities lending
b. Book entry
c. Security
d. Tracking stock

19. In economics, the concept of the _____ refers to the decision-making time frame of a firm in which at least one factor of production is fixed. Costs which are fixed in the _____ have no impact on a firms decisions. For example a firm can raise output by increasing the amount of labour through overtime.

a. Long-run
b. 529 plan
c. Short-run
d. 4-4-5 Calendar

20. _____ is the balance of the amounts of cash being received and paid by a business during a defined period of time, sometimes tied to a specific project. Measurement of _____ can be used

- to evaluate the state or performance of a business or project.
- to determine problems with liquidity. Being profitable does not necessarily mean being liquid. A company can fail because of a shortage of cash, even while profitable.
- to generate project rate of returns. The time of _____s into and out of projects are used as inputs to financial models such as internal rate of return, and net present value.
- to examine income or growth of a business when it is believed that accrual accounting concepts do not represent economic realities. Alternately, _____ can be used to 'validate' the net income generated by accrual accounting.

_____ as a generic term may be used differently depending on context, and certain _____ definitions may be adapted by analysts and users for their own uses. Common terms include operating _____ and free _____.

Chapter 17. Working Capital Management

_____s can be classified into:

1. Operational _____s: Cash received or expended as a result of the company's core business activities.
2. Investment _____s: Cash received or expended through capital expenditure, investments or acquisitions.
3. Financing _____s: Cash received or expended as a result of financial activities, such as interests and dividends.

All three together - the net _____ - are necessary to reconcile the beginning cash balance to the ending cash balance. Loan draw downs or equity injections, that is just shifting of capital but no expenditure as such, are not considered in the net _____.

a. Shareholder value
b. Real option
c. Corporate finance
d. Cash flow

21. _____ is that which is owed; usually referencing assets owed, but the term can cover other obligations. In the case of assets, _____ is a means of using future purchasing power in the present before a summation has been earned. Some companies and corporations use _____ as a part of their overall corporate finance strategy.

a. Cross-collateralization
b. Debt
c. Credit cycle
d. Partial Payment

22. In finance, _____ occurs when a debtor has not met its legal obligations according to the debt contract, e.g. it has not made a scheduled payment, or has violated a loan covenant (condition) of the debt contract. _____ may occur if the debtor is either unwilling or unable to pay their debt. This can occur with all debt obligations including bonds, mortgages, loans, and promissory notes.

a. Debt validation
b. Vendor finance
c. Credit crunch
d. Default

23. _____ is the risk of loss due to a debtor's non-payment of a loan or other line of credit (either the principal or interest (coupon) or both)

Most lenders employ their own models (credit scorecards) to rank potential and existing customers according to risk, and then apply appropriate strategies. With products such as unsecured personal loans or mortgages, lenders charge a higher price for higher risk customers and vice versa. With revolving products such as credit cards and overdrafts, risk is controlled through careful setting of credit limits.

a. Transaction risk
b. Liquidity risk
c. Market risk
d. Credit risk

24. _____ or financing is to provide capital (funds), which means money for a project, a person, a business or any other private or public institutions.

Those funds can be allocated for either short term or long term purposes. The health fund is a new way of _____ private healthcare centers.

a. Synthetic CDO
c. Proxy fight
b. Funding
d. Product life cycle

25. A _____ s a time deposit, a financial product commonly offered to consumers by banks, thrift institutions, and credit unions.

They are similar to savings accounts in that they are insured and thus virtually risk-free; they are 'money in the bank'. They are different from savings accounts in that they have a specific, fixed term (often three months, six months, or one to five years), and, usually, a fixed interest rate.

a. Variable rate mortgage
c. Reserve requirement
b. Time deposit
d. Certificate of deposit

26. In the global money market, _____ is an unsecured promissory note with a fixed maturity of one to 270 days. _____ is a money-market security issued (sold) by large banks and corporations to get money to meet short term debt obligations (for example, payroll), and is only backed by an issuing bank or corporation's promise to pay the face amount on the maturity date specified on the note. Since it is not backed by collateral, only firms with excellent credit ratings from a recognized rating agency will be able to sell their _____ at a reasonable price.

a. Trade-off theory
c. Financial distress
b. Book building
d. Commercial paper

27. _____ mature in one year or less. Like zero-coupon bonds, they do not pay interest prior to maturity; instead they are sold at a discount of the par value to create a positive yield to maturity. Many regard _____ as the least risky investment available to U.S. investors.

a. Treasury securities
c. 4-4-5 Calendar
b. Treasury Inflation Protected Securities
d. Treasury bills

28. _____ is the provision of resources (such as granting a loan) by one party to another party where that second party does not reimburse the first party immediately, thereby generating a debt, and instead arranges either to repay or return those resources (or material(s) of equal value) at a later date. The first party is called a creditor, also known as a lender, while the second party is called a debtor, also known as a borrower.

Movements of financial capital are normally dependent on either _____ or equity transfers.

a. Clearing house
c. Warrant
b. Comparable
d. Credit

29. _____ is the method by which one calculates the creditworthiness of a business or organization. The audited financial statements of a large company might be analyzed when it issues or has issued bonds. Or, a bank may analyze the financial statements of a small business before making or renewing a commercial loan.

a. Capital note
c. Credit crunch
b. Credit report monitoring
d. Credit analysis

30. _____ is typically a higher ranking stock than voting shares, and its terms are negotiated between the corporation and the investor.

_____ usually carry no voting rights, but may carry superior priority over common stock in the payment of dividends and upon liquidation. _____ may carry a dividend that is paid out prior to any dividends to common stock holders.

a. Follow-on offering
b. Second lien loan
c. Trade-off theory
d. Preferred stock

31. _____ are those dividends paid out in form of additional stock shares of the issuing corporation or other corporation They are usually issued in proportion to shares owned (for example for every 100 shares of stock owned, 5% stock dividend will yield 5 extra shares). If this payment involves the issue of new shares, this is very similar to a stock split in that it increases the total number of shares while lowering the price of each share and does not change the market capitalization or the total value of the shares held

a. Stock or scrip dividends
b. Database auditing
c. The Hong Kong Securities Institute
d. Time-based currency

32. _____ exists when one firm provides goods or services to a customer with an agreement to bill them later, or receive a shipment or service from a supplier under an agreement to pay them later. It can be viewed as an essential element of capitalization in an operating business because it can reduce the required capital investment to operate the business if it is managed properly. _____ is the largest use of capital for a majority of business to business (B2B) sellers in the United States and is a critical source of capital for a majority of all businesses.

a. 4-4-5 Calendar
b. Going concern
c. 529 plan
d. Trade credit

33. In economics, business, and accounting, a _____ is the value of money that has been used up to produce something, and hence is not available for use anymore. In business, the _____ may be one of acquisition, in which case the amount of money expended to acquire it is counted as _____. In this case, money is the input that is gone in order to acquire the thing.

a. Cost
b. Fixed costs
c. Sliding scale fees
d. Marginal cost

34. A _____ is a payment made by a corporation to its shareholder members. When a corporation earns a profit or surplus, that money can be put to two uses: it can either be re-invested in the business (called retained earnings), or it can be paid to the shareholders as a _____. Many corporations retain a portion of their earnings and pay the remainder as a _____.

a. Dividend puzzle
b. Dividend yield
c. Special dividend
d. Dividend

35. An _____ or bill is a commercial document issued by a seller to the buyer, indicating the products, quantities, and agreed prices for products or services the seller has provided the buyer. An _____ indicates the buyer must pay the seller, according to the payment terms.

In the rental industry, an _____ must include a specific reference to the duration of the time being billed, so rather than quantity, price and discount the invoicing amount is based on quantity, price, discount and duration.

a. AAB
b. ABN Amro
c. A Random Walk Down Wall Street
d. Invoice

36. _____ is the long dimension of any object. The _____ of a thing is the distance between its ends, its linear extent as measured from end to end. This may be distinguished from height, which is vertical extent, and width or breadth, which are the distance from side to side, measuring across the object at right angles to the _____.
   a. 4-4-5 Calendar
   b. 529 plan
   c. 7-Eleven
   d. Length

37. In lending agreements, _____ is a borrower's pledge of specific property to a lender, to secure repayment of a loan. The _____ serves as protection for a lender against a borrower's risk of default - that is, a borrower failing to pay the principal and interest under the terms of a loan obligation. If a borrower does default on a loan (due to insolvency or other event), that borrower forfeits (gives up) the property pledged as _____ *ollateral* - and the lender then becomes the owner of the _____.
   a. Nominal value
   b. Refinancing risk
   c. Future-oriented
   d. Collateral

38. _____ is a list for goods and materials held available in stock by a business. It is also used for a list of the contents of a household and for a list for testamentary purposes of the possessions of someone who has died. In accounting _____ is considered an asset.
   a. A Random Walk Down Wall Street
   b. ABN Amro
   c. AAB
   d. Inventory

39. A '_____' is a 'Charge' that is paid to obtain the right to delay a payment. Essentially, the payer purchases the right to make a given payment in the future instead of in the Present. The '_____', or 'Charge' that must be paid to delay the payment, is simply the difference between what the payment amount would be if it were paid in the present and what the payment amount would be paid if it were paid in the future.
   a. Risk modeling
   b. Discount
   c. Value at risk
   d. Risk aversion

40. _____ is the level of inventory that minimizes the total inventory holding costs and ordering costs. The framework used to determine this order quantity is also known as Wilson _____ Model. The model was developed by F. W. Harris in 1913.
   a. A Random Walk Down Wall Street
   b. AAB
   c. Economic order quantity
   d. ABN Amro

41. _____ is a fee paid on borrowed assets. It is the price paid for the use of borrowed money , or, money earned by deposited funds . Assets that are sometimes lent with _____ include money, shares, consumer goods through hire purchase, major assets such as aircraft, and even entire factories in finance lease arrangements.
   a. A Random Walk Down Wall Street
   b. Insolvency
   c. Interest
   d. AAB

42. An _____ is the price a borrower pays for the use of money they do not own, and the return a lender receives for deferring the use of funds, by lending it to the borrower. _____s are normally expressed as a percentage rate over the period of one year.

Chapter 17. Working Capital Management

_____s targets are also a vital tool of monetary policy and are used to control variables like investment, inflation, and unemployment.

- a. Interest rate
- b. ABN Amro
- c. AAB
- d. A Random Walk Down Wall Street

43. A _____, referred to as a note payable in accounting, is a contract where one party (the maker or issuer) makes an unconditional promise in writing to pay a sum of money to the other (the payee), either at a fixed or determinable future time or on demand of the payee, under specific terms. They differ from IOUs in that they contain a specific promise to pay, rather than simply acknowledging that a debt exists.

The terms of a note typically include the principal amount, the interest rate if any, and the maturity date.

- a. Financial plan
- b. Credit repair software
- c. Title loan
- d. Promissory note

44. The terms _____, nominal _____, and effective _____ describe the interest rate for a whole year (annualized), rather than just a monthly fee/rate, as applied on a loan, mortgage, credit card, etc. Those terms have formal, legal definitions in some countries or legal jurisdictions, but in general:

  - The nominal _____ is the simple-interest rate (for a year.)
  - The effective _____ is the fee+compound interest rate (calculated across a year.)

The nominal _____ is calculated as: the rate, for a payment period, multiplied by the number of payment periods in a year. However, the exact legal definition of 'effective _____' can vary greatly in each jurisdiction, depending on the type of fees included, such as participation fees, loan origination fees, monthly service charges, or late fees. The effective _____ has been called the 'mathematically-true' interest rate for each year. The computation for the effective _____, as the fee+compound interest rate, can also vary depending on whether the up-front fees, such as origination or participation fees, are added to the entire amount, or treated as a short-term loan due in the first payment.

- a. AAB
- b. A Random Walk Down Wall Street
- c. Annual percentage rate
- d. ABN Amro

45. In marketing, _____ refers to the total cost of holding inventory. This includes warehousing costs such as rent, utilities and salaries, financial costs such as opportunity cost, and inventory costs related to perishibility, shrinkage and insurance.
- a. 4-4-5 Calendar
- b. 7-Eleven
- c. 529 plan
- d. Carrying cost

46. _____ or economic opportunity loss is the value of the next best alternative foregone as the result of making a decision. _____ analysis is an important part of a company's decision-making processes but is not treated as an actual cost in any financial statement. The next best thing that a person can engage in is referred to as the _____ of doing the best thing and ignoring the next best thing to be done.

a. A Random Walk Down Wall Street
b. AAB
c. ABN Amro
d. Opportunity cost

47. A _____ can require immediate payment by the second party to the third upon presentation of the _____. This is called a sight _____. A Cheques is a sight _____. An importer might write a _____ promising payment to an exporter for delivery of goods with payment to occur 60 days after the goods are delivered. Such a _____ is called a time _____.

a. Gross profit margin
b. Cashflow matching
c. Draft
d. Second lien loan

48. _____ refinancing (in the case of real property) occurs when a loan is taken out on property already owned, and the loan amount is above and beyond the cost of transaction, payoff of existing liens, and related expenses.

Strictly speaking all refinancing of debt is '_____', when funds retrieved are utilized for anything other than repaying an existing lien.

In the case of common usage of the term, _____ refinancing refers to when equity is liquidated from a property above and beyond sum of the payoff of existing loans held in lien on the property, loan fees, costs associated with the loan, taxes, insurance, tax reserves, insurance reserves, and in the past any other non-lien debt held in the name of the owner being paid by loan proceeds.

a. Conforming loan
b. Fixed rate mortgage
c. Cash-out
d. Home equity line of credit

49. _____ are formal records of a business' financial activities.

_____ provide an overview of a business' financial condition in both short and long term. There are four basic _____:

1. **Balance sheet**: also referred to as statement of financial position or condition, reports on a company's assets, liabilities, and net equity as of a given point in time.
2. **Income statement**: also referred to as Profit and Loss statement (or a 'P'L'), reports on a company's income, expenses, and profits over a period of time.
3. **Statement of retained earnings**: explains the changes in a company's retained earnings over the reporting period.
4. **Statement of cash flows**: reports on a company's cash flow activities, particularly its operating, investing and financing activities.

a. Statement of retained earnings
b. Financial statements
c. Notes to the Financial Statements
d. Statement on Auditing Standards No. 70: Service Organizations

Chapter 17. Working Capital Management

50. _____ is one of a series of accounting transactions dealing with the billing of customers who owe money to a person, company or organization for goods and services that have been provided to the customer. In most business entities this is typically done by generating an invoice and mailing or electronically delivering it to the customer, who in turn must pay it within an established timeframe called credit or payment terms.

An example of a common payment term is Net 30, meaning payment is due in the amount of the invoice 30 days from the date of invoice.

a. Accounts receivable
b. Impaired asset
c. Income
d. Accounting methods

51. _____s are goods that have completed the manufacturing process but have not yet been sold or distributed to the end user.

Manufacturing has three classes of inventory:

1. Raw material
2. Work in process
3. _____s

A good purchased as a 'raw material' goes into the manufacture of a product. A good only partially completed during the manufacturing process is called 'work in process'. When the good is completed as to manufacturing but not yet sold or distributed to the end-user is called a '_____'.

a. Finished good
b. 7-Eleven
c. 4-4-5 Calendar
d. 529 plan

52. _____ is an accounting concept used most often in mining, timber, petroluem, or other similar industries. The _____ deduction allows an owner or operator to account for the reduction of a product's reserves. _____ is similar to depreciation in that, it is a cost recovery system for accounting and tax reporting.

a. Deferred income
b. Net profit
c. Current liabilities
d. Depletion

53. In financial and business accounting, _____ is a measure of a firm's profitability that excludes interest and income tax expenses.

EBIT = Operating Revenue - Operating Expenses (OPEX) + Non-operating Income

Operating Income = Operating Revenue - Operating Expenses

Operating income is the difference between operating revenues and operating expenses, but it is also sometimes used as a synonym for EBIT and operating profit. This is true if the firm has no non-operating income.

Chapter 17. Working Capital Management

a. ABN Amro
b. A Random Walk Down Wall Street
c. AAB
d. Earnings before interest and taxes

54. In economics, and cost accounting, _____ describes the total economic cost of production and is made up of variable costs, which vary according to the quantity of a good produced and include inputs such as labor and raw materials, plus fixed costs, which are independent of the quantity of a good produced and include inputs (capital) that cannot be varied in the short term, such as buildings and machinery. _____ in economics includes the total opportunity cost of each factor of production in addition to fixed and variable costs.

The rate at which _____ changes as the amount produced changes is called marginal cost.

a. Total cost
b. 7-Eleven
c. 4-4-5 Calendar
d. 529 plan

55. The _____ is the level of inventory when a fresh order should be made with suppliers to bring the inventory up by the Economic order quantity ('EOQ'.)

The _____ for replenishment of stock occurs when the level of inventory drops down to zero. In view of instantaneous replenishment of stock the level of inventory jumps to the original level from zero level.

a. 7-Eleven
b. 529 plan
c. 4-4-5 Calendar
d. Reorder point

56. _____ is a term used by inventory specialists to describe a level of extra stock that is maintained below the cycle stock to buffer against stockouts. _____ exists to counter uncertainties in supply and demand. _____ is defined as extra units of inventory carried as protection against possible stockouts .(shortfall in raw material or packaging.)

a. Golden parachute
b. Safety stock
c. Counting house
d. Funding

57. In business and finance, a _____ (also referred to as equity _____) of stock means a _____ of ownership in a corporation (company.) In the plural, stocks is often used as a synonym for _____s especially in the United States, but it is less commonly used that way outside of North America.

In the United Kingdom, South Africa, and Australia, stock can also refer to completely different financial instruments such as government bonds or, less commonly, to all kinds of marketable securities.

a. Share
b. Procter ' Gamble
c. Margin
d. Bucket shop

58. _____ is an inventory strategy implemented to improve the return on investment of a business by reducing in-process inventory and its associated carrying costs. In order to achieve _____ the process must have signals of what is going on elsewhere within the process. This means that the process is often driven by a series of signals, which can be Kanban, that tell production processes when to make the next part.

a. Debtor-in-possession financing
b. Pac-Man defense
c. Greed and fear
d. Just-in-time

59. A _____ is a set of companies with interlocking business relationships and shareholdings. It is a type of business group.

The prototypical _____ are those which appeared in Japan during the 'economic miracle' following World War II.

   a. Relative strength Index   b. Keiretsu
   c. Zero-coupon bond   d. Stock split

Chapter 18. International Aspects of Financial Management

1. A _____, reserve bank, or monetary authority is the entity responsible for the monetary policy of a country or of a group of member states. It is a bank that can lend money to other banks in times of need. Its primary responsibility is to maintain the stability of the national currency and money supply, but more active duties include controlling subsidized-loan interest rates, and acting as a lender of last resort to the banking sector during times of financial crisis (private banks often being integral to the national financial system.)
   a. 4-4-5 Calendar
   b. 529 plan
   c. 7-Eleven
   d. Central Bank

2. An _____ is a single market with a common currency. It is to be distinguished from a mere currency union, which does not involve a single market. This is the fifth stage of economic integration.
   a. Economic and Monetary Union
   b. ABN Amro
   c. A Random Walk Down Wall Street
   d. AAB

3. An _____ represents the ownership in the shares of a foreign company trading on US financial markets. The stock of many non-US companies trades on US exchanges through the use of _____s. _____s enable US investors to buy shares in foreign companies without undertaking cross-border transactions.
   a. AAB
   b. A Random Walk Down Wall Street
   c. ABN Amro
   d. American Depository Receipt

4. A _____ is an international bond that is denominated in a currency not native to the country where it is issued. It can be categorised according to the currency in which it is issued. London is one of the centers of the _____ market, but _____s may be traded throughout the world - for example in Singapore or Tokyo.
   a. Interest rate option
   b. Education production function
   c. Eurobond
   d. Economic entity

5. _____ is the term used to describe deposits residing in banks that are located outside the borders of the country that issues the currency the deposit is denominated in. For example a deposit denominated in US dollars residing in a Japanese bank is a _____ deposit, or more specifically a Eurodollar deposit.

Key points are the location of the bank and the denomination of the currency, not the nationality of the bank or the owner of the deposit/loan.

   a. AAB
   b. ABN Amro
   c. A Random Walk Down Wall Street
   d. Eurocurrency

6. _____s are deposits denominated in United States dollars at banks outside the United States, and thus are not under the jurisdiction of the Federal Reserve. Consequently, such deposits are subject to much less regulation than similar deposits within the United States, allowing for higher margins. There is nothing 'European' about _____ deposits; a US dollar-denominated deposit in Tokyo or Caracas would likewise be deemed _____ deposits.
   a. ABN Amro
   b. A Random Walk Down Wall Street
   c. Eurodollar
   d. AAB

7. In economics, a _____ is a mechanism that allows people to easily buy and sell (trade) financial securities (such as stocks and bonds), commodities (such as precious metals or agricultural goods), and other fungible items of value at low transaction costs and at prices that reflect the efficient-market hypothesis.

Chapter 18. International Aspects of Financial Management

_____s have evolved significantly over several hundred years and are undergoing constant innovation to improve liquidity.

Both general markets (where many commodities are traded) and specialized markets (where only one commodity is traded) exist.

a. Secondary market
b. Financial market
c. Cost of carry
d. Delta hedging

8. _____ is the branch of economics that studies the dynamics of exchange rates, foreign investment, and how these affect international trade. It also studies international projects, international investments and capital flows, and trade deficits. It includes the study of futures, options and currency swaps.

a. AAB
b. ABN Amro
c. A Random Walk Down Wall Street
d. International finance

9. In political science and economics, the _____ or agency dilemma treats the difficulties that arise under conditions of incomplete and asymmetric information when a principal hires an agent. Various mechanisms may be used to try to align the interests of the agent with those of the principal, such as piece rates/commissions, profit sharing, efficiency wages, performance measurement (including financial statements), the agent posting a bond, or fear of firing. The _____ is found in most employer/employee relationships, for example, when stockholders hire top executives of corporations.

a. 4-4-5 Calendar
b. Principal-agent problem
c. 529 plan
d. 7-Eleven

10. In finance, a _____ is a debt security, in which the authorized issuer owes the holders a debt and, depending on the terms of the _____, is obliged to pay interest (the coupon) and/or to repay the principal at a later date, termed maturity.

Thus a _____ is a loan: the issuer is the borrower, the _____ holder is the lender, and the coupon is the interest. _____s provide the borrower with external funds to finance long-term investments, or, in the case of government _____s, to finance current expenditure.

a. Catastrophe bonds
b. Convertible bond
c. Bond
d. Puttable bond

11. The _____ is a financial market where participants buy and sell debt securities, usually in the form of bonds. As of 2006, the size of the international _____ is an estimated $45 trillion, of which the size of the outstanding U.S. _____ debt was $25.2 trillion.

Nearly all of the $923 billion average daily trading volume in the U.S. _____ takes place between broker-dealers and large institutions in a decentralized, over-the-counter market.

a. Fixed income
b. Bond market
c. 4-4-5 Calendar
d. 529 plan

Chapter 18. International Aspects of Financial Management

12. The institution most often referenced by the word '_____' is a public or publicly traded _____, the shares of which are traded on a public stock exchange (e.g., the New York Stock Exchange or Nasdaq in the United States) where shares of stock of _____s are bought and sold by and to the general public. Most of the largest businesses in the world are publicly traded _____s. However, the majority of _____s are said to be closely held, privately held or close _____s, meaning that no ready market exists for the trading of shares.
   a. Federal Home Loan Mortgage Corporation
   b. Protect
   c. Depository Trust Company
   d. Corporation

13. A _____ is a foreign exchange agreement between two parties to exchange principal and fixed rate interest payments on a loan in one currency for principal and fixed rate interest payments on an equal (regarding net present value) loan in another currency. They are motivated by comparative advantage.
   a. Forex swap
   b. Foreign exchange market
   c. Currency pair
   d. Currency swap

14. The _____ is where currency trading takes place. It is where banks and other official institutions facilitate the buying and selling of foreign currencies. FX transactions typically involve one party purchasing a quantity of one currency in exchange for paying a quantity of another.
   a. Foreign exchange option
   b. Spot market
   c. Floating exchange rate
   d. Foreign exchange market

15. _____ are bonds issued by the governments of the United Kingdom, South Africa, or Ireland. The term is of British origin, and refers to the debt securities issued by the Bank of England, which had a gilt (or gilded) edge. Hence, they are called gilt-edged securities, or _____ for short.

These are the simplest form of UK government bond and make up the largest share of UK government debt. A conventional gilt is a bond issued by the UK government which pays the holder a fixed cash payment (or coupon) every six months until maturity, at which point the holder receives their final coupon payment and the return of the principal.

   a. Zero coupon bond
   b. Bond fund
   c. Zero-coupon bond
   d. Gilts

16. _____ is a fee paid on borrowed assets. It is the price paid for the use of borrowed money, or, money earned by deposited funds. Assets that are sometimes lent with _____ include money, shares, consumer goods through hire purchase, major assets such as aircraft, and even entire factories in finance lease arrangements.
   a. Insolvency
   b. AAB
   c. Interest
   d. A Random Walk Down Wall Street

17. An _____ is the price a borrower pays for the use of money they do not own, and the return a lender receives for deferring the use of funds, by lending it to the borrower. _____s are normally expressed as a percentage rate over the period of one year.

_____s targets are also a vital tool of monetary policy and are used to control variables like investment, inflation, and unemployment.

Chapter 18. International Aspects of Financial Management

a. A Random Walk Down Wall Street
b. ABN Amro
c. AAB
d. Interest rate

18. An _____ is a derivative in which one party exchanges a stream of interest payments for another party's stream of cash flows. _____s can be used by hedgers to manage their fixed or floating assets and liabilities. They can also be used by speculators to replicate unfunded bond exposures to profit from changes in interest rates.
   a. Implied volatility
   b. Interest rate swap
   c. International Swaps and Derivatives Association
   d. Equity swap

19. In finance, a _____ is a derivative in which two counterparties agree to exchange one stream of cash flows against another stream. These streams are called the legs of the _____.

The cash flows are calculated over a notional principal amount, which is usually not exchanged between counterparties.

   a. Volatility swap
   b. Volatility arbitrage
   c. Local volatility
   d. Swap

20. In finance, the _____ between two currencies specifies how much one currency is worth in terms of the other. For example an _____ of 102 Japanese yen to the United States dollar means that JPY 102 is worth the same as USD 1. The foreign exchange market is one of the largest markets in the world.
   a. ABN Amro
   b. A Random Walk Down Wall Street
   c. AAB
   d. Exchange rate

21. _____ is the process of decreasing an amount over a period of time. The word comes from Middle English amortisen to kill, alienate in mortmain, from Anglo-French amorteser, alteration of amortir, from Vulgar Latin admortire to kill, from Latin ad- + mort-, mors death. Particular instances of the term include:

- _____ (business), the allocation of a lump sum amount to different time periods, particularly for loans and other forms of finance, including related interest or other finance charges.
  - _____ schedule, a table detailing each periodic payment on a loan (typically a mortgage), as generated by an _____ calculator.
  - Negative _____, an _____ schedule where the loan amount actually increases through not paying the full interest
- Amortized analysis, analyzing the execution cost of algorithms over a sequence of operations.
- _____ of capital expenditures of certain assets under accounting rules, particularly intangible assets, in a manner analogous to depreciation.
- _____ (tax law)

_____ is also used in the context of zoning regulations and describes the time in which a property owner has to relocate when the property's use constitutes a preexisting nonconforming use under zoning regulations.

- Depreciation

Chapter 18. International Aspects of Financial Management

a. Amortization
b. Intrinsic value
c. AT'T Inc.
d. Option

22. The _____ is published by The Economist as an informal way of measuring the purchasing power parity (PPP) between two currencies and provides a test of the extent to which market exchange rates result in goods costing the same in different countries. It 'seeks to make exchange-rate theory a bit more digestible'.
    a. 529 plan
    b. Divisia index
    c. Big Mac index
    d. 4-4-5 Calendar

23. _____ refers to taking advantage of a state of imbalance between three foreign exchange markets: a combination of matching deals are struck that exploit the imbalance, the profit being the difference between the market prices.

    _____ offers a risk-free profit (in theory), so opportunities for _____ usually disappear quickly, as many people are looking for them, or simply never occur as everybody knows the pricing relation.

    Consider the three foreign exchange rates among the Canadian dollar, the U.S. dollar, and the Australian dollar.

    a. Currency pair
    b. Floating exchange rate
    c. Currency future
    d. Triangular arbitrage

24. In economics and finance, _____ is the practice of taking advantage of a price differential between two or more markets: striking a combination of matching deals that capitalize upon the imbalance, the profit being the difference between the market prices. When used by academics, an _____ is a transaction that involves no negative cash flow at any probabilistic or temporal state and a positive cash flow in at least one state; in simple terms, a risk-free profit.
    a. Issuer
    b. Initial margin
    c. Efficient-market hypothesis
    d. Arbitrage

25. _____ are a currency pair that does not include USD, such as GBP/JPY. Pairs that involve the EUR are called euro crosses, such as EUR/GBP. All other currency pairs (those that don't involve USD or EUR) are generally referred to as _____.
    a. 529 plan
    b. Foreign exchange risk
    c. 4-4-5 Calendar
    d. Cross rates

26. The _____ or spot rate of a commodity, a security or a currency is the price that is quoted for immediate (spot) settlement (payment and delivery.) Spot settlement is normally one or two business days from trade date. This is in contrast with the forward price established in a forward contract or futures contract, where contract terms (price) are set now, but delivery and payment will occur at a future date.
    a. Central Securities Depository
    b. Cost of carry
    c. Market price
    d. Spot price

27. The _____ of a commodity, a security or a currency is the price that is quoted for immediate (spot) settlement (payment and delivery.) Spot settlement is normally one or two business days from trade date. This is in contrast with the forward price established in a forward contract or futures contract, where contract terms (price) are set now, but delivery and payment will occur at a future date.

a. Limits to arbitrage
b. Long position
c. Market anomaly
d. Spot rate

28. _____ refers to a business or organization attempting to acquire goods or services to accomplish the goals of the enterprise. Though there are several organizations that attempt to set standards in the _____ process, processes can vary greatly between organizations. Typically the word '_____' is not used interchangeably with the word 'procurement', since procurement typically includes Expediting, Supplier Quality, and Traffic and Logistics (T'L) in addition to _____.

a. 4-4-5 Calendar
b. Purchasing
c. 7-Eleven
d. 529 plan

29. _____ is the value of goods/services compared to the amount paid with a currency. Currency can be either a commodity money, like gold or silver, or fiat currency like US dollars which are the world reserve currency. As Adam Smith noted, having money gives one the ability to 'command' others' labor, so _____ to some extent is power over other people, to the extent that they are willing to trade their labor or goods for money or currency.

a. 7-Eleven
b. Purchasing power
c. 529 plan
d. 4-4-5 Calendar

30. The _____ theory uses the long-term equilibrium exchange rate of two currencies to equalize their purchasing power. Developed by Gustav Cassel in 1920, it is based on the law of one price: the theory states that, in ideally efficient markets, identical goods should have only one price.

This purchasing power SEM rate equalizes the purchasing power of different currencies in their home countries for a given basket of goods.

a. TED spread
b. Gross national product
c. 4-4-5 Calendar
d. Purchasing power parity

31. A '_____' is a 'Charge' that is paid to obtain the right to delay a payment. Essentially, the payer purchases the right to make a given payment in the future instead of in the Present. The '_____', or 'Charge' that must be paid to delay the payment, is simply the difference between what the payment amount would be if it were paid in the present and what the payment amount would be paid if it were paid in the future.

a. Risk aversion
b. Value at risk
c. Discount
d. Risk modeling

32. The _____ or forward rate is the agreed upon price of an asset in a forward contract. Using the rational pricing assumption, we can express the _____ in terms of the spot price and any dividends etc., so that there is no possibility for arbitrage.

The _____ is given by:

where

F is the _____ to be paid at time T
e^x is the exponential function
r is the risk-free interest rate
q is the cost-of-carry
S_0 is the spot price of the asset (i.e. what it would sell for at time 0)
D_i is a dividend which is guaranteed to be paid at time t_i where $0 < t_i < T$.

The two questions here are what price the short position (the seller of the asset) should offer to maximize his gain, and what price the long position (the buyer of the asset) should accept to maximize his gain?

At the very least we know that both do not want to lose any money in the deal.

a. Financial Gerontology
b. Security interest
c. Forward price
d. Biweekly Mortgage

33. _____ is the loss of value of a country's currency with respect to one or more foreign reference currencies, typically in a floating exchange rate system. It is most often used for the unofficial increase of the exchange rate due to market forces, though sometimes it appears interchangeably with devaluation. Its opposite is called appreciation.

a. 7-Eleven
b. 4-4-5 Calendar
c. 529 plan
d. Currency depreciation

34. _____ is a term used in accounting relating to the increase in value of an asset. In this sense it is the reverse of depreciation, which measures the fall in value of assets over their normal life-time.

_____ is a rise of a currency in a floating exchange rate.

a. A Random Walk Down Wall Street
b. Operating cash flow
c. Other Comprehensive Basis of Accounting
d. Appreciation

35. _____ is a term used in accounting, economics and finance to spread the cost of an asset over the span of several years.

In simple words we can say that _____ is the reduction in the value of an asset due to usage, passage of time, wear and tear, technological outdating or obsolescence, depletion or other such factors.

In accounting, _____ is a term used to describe any method of attributing the historical or purchase cost of an asset across its useful life, roughly corresponding to normal wear and tear.

a. Deferred financing costs
b. Bottom line
c. Depreciation
d. Matching principle

Chapter 18. International Aspects of Financial Management

36. _____ is the investment strategy where an investor buys a financial instrument denominated in a foreign currency, and hedges his foreign exchange risk by selling a forward contract in the amount of the proceeds of the investment back into his base currency. The proceeds of the investment are only known exactly if the financial instrument is risk-free and only pays interest once, on the date of the forward sale of foreign currency. Otherwise, some foreign exchange risk remains.
   a. Covered interest arbitrage
   b. Currency future
   c. Floating exchange rate
   d. Triangular arbitrage

37. The terms _____ , nominal _____ , and effective _____ describe the interest rate for a whole year (annualized), rather than just a monthly fee/rate, as applied on a loan, mortgage, credit card, etc. Those terms have formal, legal definitions in some countries or legal jurisdictions, but in general:

   - The nominal _____ is the simple-interest rate (for a year.)
   - The effective _____ is the fee+compound interest rate (calculated across a year.)

   The nominal _____ is calculated as: the rate, for a payment period, multiplied by the number of payment periods in a year. However, the exact legal definition of 'effective _____' can vary greatly in each jurisdiction, depending on the type of fees included, such as participation fees, loan origination fees, monthly service charges, or late fees. The effective _____ has been called the 'mathematically-true' interest rate for each year. The computation for the effective _____, as the fee+compound interest rate, can also vary depending on whether the up-front fees, such as origination or participation fees, are added to the entire amount, or treated as a short-term loan due in the first payment.

   a. ABN Amro
   b. AAB
   c. A Random Walk Down Wall Street
   d. Annual percentage rate

38. _____ is an economic concept, expressed as a basic algebraic identity that relates interest rates and exchange rates. The identity is theoretical, and usually follows from assumptions imposed in economics models. There is evidence to support as well as to refute the concept.
   a. Unit price
   b. AAB
   c. A Random Walk Down Wall Street
   d. Interest rate parity

39. In economics, the concept of the _____ refers to the decision-making time frame of a firm in which at least one factor of production is fixed. Costs which are fixed in the _____ have no impact on a firms decisions. For example a firm can raise output by increasing the amount of labour through overtime.
   a. Short-run
   b. 529 plan
   c. Long-run
   d. 4-4-5 Calendar

40. In economics, business, and accounting, a _____ is the value of money that has been used up to produce something, and hence is not available for use anymore. In business, the _____ may be one of acquisition, in which case the amount of money expended to acquire it is counted as _____. In this case, money is the input that is gone in order to acquire the thing.
   a. Sliding scale fees
   b. Cost
   c. Fixed costs
   d. Marginal cost

41. The _____ is an expected return that the provider of capital plans to earn on their investment.

Chapter 18. International Aspects of Financial Management

Capital (money) used for funding a business should earn returns for the capital providers who risk their capital. For an investment to be worthwhile, the expected return on capital must be greater than the _____.

a. 4-4-5 Calendar
b. Cost of capital
c. Capital intensity
d. Weighted average cost of capital

42. In economic models, the _____ time frame assumes no fixed factors of production. Firms can enter or leave the marketplace, and the cost (and availability) of land, labor, raw materials, and capital goods can be assumed to vary. In contrast, in the short-run time frame, certain factors are assumed to be fixed, because there is not sufficient time for them to change.

a. Short-run
b. Long-run
c. 529 plan
d. 4-4-5 Calendar

43. The role of the _____ is to issue accounting standards in the United Kingdom. It is recognised for that purpose under the Companies Act 1985. It took over the task of setting accounting standards from the Accounting Standards Committee (ASC) in 1990.

a. Accounting Standards Board
b. A Random Walk Down Wall Street
c. ABN Amro
d. AAB

44. _____ is the field of accountancy concerned with the preparation of financial statements for decision makers, such as stockholders, suppliers, banks, employees, government agencies, owners, and other stakeholders. The fundamental need for _____ is to reduce principal-agent problem by measuring and monitoring agents' performance and reporting the results to interested users.

_____ is used to prepare accounting information for people outside the organization or not involved in the day to day running of the company.

a. 529 plan
b. 7-Eleven
c. 4-4-5 Calendar
d. Financial Accounting

45. The _____ is a private, not-for-profit organization whose primary purpose is to develop generally accepted accounting principles (GAAP) within the United States in the public's interest. The Securities and Exchange Commission (SEC) designated the _____ as the organization responsible for setting accounting standards for public companies in the U.S. It was created in 1973, replacing the Accounting Principles Board and the Committee on Accounting Procedure of the American Institute of Certified Public Accountants. The _____'s mission is 'to establish and improve standards of financial accounting and reporting for the guidance and education of the public, including issuers, auditors, and users of financial information.'

The _____ is not a governmental body.

a. Financial Accounting Standards Board
b. KPMG
c. World Congress of Accountants
d. Federal Deposit Insurance Corporation

46. _____ is a type of risk faced by investors, corporations, and governments. It is a risk that can be understood and managed with proper aforethought and investment.

Chapter 18. International Aspects of Financial Management

Broadly, _____ refers to the complications businesses and governments may face as a result of what are commonly referred to as political decisions--or 'any political change that alters the expected outcome and value of a given economic action by changing the probability of achieving business objectives.'.

a. Political risk
c. Single-index model
b. Mid price
d. Capital asset

47. _____ is an area of finance dealing with the financial decisions corporations make and the tools and analysis used to make these decisions. The primary goal of _____ is to maximize corporate value while managing the firm's financial risks. Although it is in principle different from managerial finance which studies the financial decisions of all firms, rather than corporations alone, the main concepts in the study of _____ are applicable to the financial problems of all kinds of firms.

a. Special purpose entity
c. Corporate finance
b. Gross profit
d. Cash flow

48. _____ measures the nominal future sum of money that a given sum of money is 'worth' at a specified time in the future assuming a certain interest rate rate of return; it is the present value multiplied by the accumulation function.

The value does not include corrections for inflation or other factors that affect the true value of money in the future. This is used in time value of money calculations.

a. Discounted cash flow
c. Future value
b. Future-oriented
d. Present value of costs

49. _____ is the value on a given date of a future payment or series of future payments, discounted to reflect the time value of money and other factors such as investment risk. _____ calculations are widely used in business and economics to provide a means to compare cash flows at different times on a meaningful 'like to like' basis.

The most commonly applied model of the time value of money is compound interest.

a. Negative gearing
c. Present value of benefits
b. Present value
d. Net present value

50. An _____ can be defined as a contract which provides an income stream in return for an initial payment.

An immediate _____ is an _____ for which the time between the contract date and the date of the first payment is not longer than the time interval between payments. A common use for an immediate _____ is to provide a pension to a retired person or persons.

a. Intrinsic value
c. AT'T Inc.
b. Annuity
d. Amortization

51. _____ is that which is owed; usually referencing assets owed, but the term can cover other obligations. In the case of assets, _____ is a means of using future purchasing power in the present before a summation has been earned. Some companies and corporations use _____ as a part of their overall corporate finance strategy.

a. Cross-collateralization
c. Credit cycle
b. Debt
d. Partial Payment

ANSWER KEY

Chapter 1
1. d   2. a   3. d   4. d   5. d   6. c   7. d   8. a   9. d   10. d
11. a   12. b   13. c   14. c   15. b   16. d   17. d   18. d   19. c   20. b
21. c   22. a   23. a   24. d   25. a   26. b   27. b   28. c   29. a   30. d
31. d   32. a   33. c   34. d   35. b   36. c   37. b   38. c   39. c   40. d
41. d   42. b   43. c   44. d   45. a   46. d   47. c   48. b   49. a   50. a
51. a   52. d   53. d   54. d   55. d   56. c   57. d   58. b   59. a   60. d
61. a   62. a   63. d   64. d

Chapter 2
1. b   2. c   3. a   4. c   5. d   6. d   7. a   8. a   9. d   10. d
11. d   12. d   13. c   14. b   15. a   16. d   17. d   18. d   19. d   20. c
21. d   22. a   23. c   24. d   25. d   26. d   27. c   28. a   29. c   30. d
31. d   32. d   33. c   34. b   35. b   36. d   37. d   38. d   39. a   40. a
41. d   42. d   43. b   44. c   45. d   46. d   47. b   48. d   49. c   50. a
51. d   52. d   53. a   54. d   55. a   56. d   57. b   58. a   59. d   60. d
61. c   62. a   63. a   64. d   65. d   66. c   67. d

Chapter 3
1. b   2. d   3. a   4. d   5. a   6. c   7. c   8. d   9. d   10. b
11. b   12. b   13. c   14. d   15. c   16. d   17. c   18. d   19. a   20. b
21. c   22. d   23. b   24. d   25. b   26. a   27. d   28. c   29. a   30. d
31. b   32. a   33. c   34. d   35. a   36. a   37. b   38. d   39. a   40. b
41. d   42. c   43. d   44. d   45. d   46. c   47. d   48. c   49. a   50. a
51. a   52. d   53. d   54. c   55. b   56. d   57. d   58. b   59. a   60. b

Chapter 4
1. a   2. d   3. d   4. d   5. d   6. b   7. d   8. d   9. d   10. c
11. c   12. d   13. d   14. c   15. d   16. d   17. a   18. c   19. d   20. b
21. d   22. d   23. a   24. d

Chapter 5
1. a   2. a   3. b   4. d   5. a   6. d   7. d   8. b   9. a   10. d
11. d   12. a   13. b   14. d   15. c   16. d   17. b   18. c   19. a   20. c
21. a   22. a   23. a   24. a   25. c   26. d   27. d   28. d

Chapter 6
1. a   2. d   3. d   4. c   5. d   6. d   7. a   8. c   9. d   10. d
11. c   12. d   13. d   14. b   15. c   16. a   17. d   18. b   19. c   20. c
21. d   22. d   23. d   24. a   25. d   26. d   27. c   28. d   29. d   30. a
31. c   32. a   33. d   34. d   35. b   36. d   37. d   38. d   39. d   40. c
41. d   42. a   43. d   44. b   45. d   46. d   47. d   48. c   49. a   50. d
51. d   52. c   53. c   54. d   55. a   56. d   57. a   58. d   59. d   60. a
61. d   62. a   63. d   64. d   65. d   66. d   67. c   68. b   69. a   70. a
71. d   72. b   73. c   74. b   75. c   76. b   77. a   78. c   79. d   80. d
81. d   82. d   83. b   84. d   85. d   86. a   87. d   88. b   89. b   90. d

Chapter 7

1. d	2. d	3. b	4. d	5. c	6. a	7. d	8. d	9. d	10. d
11. b	12. d	13. b	14. b	15. d	16. b	17. d	18. c	19. c	20. d
21. c	22. a	23. d	24. d	25. c	26. a	27. d	28. d	29. a	30. b
31. a	32. a	33. b	34. d	35. c	36. b	37. a	38. d	39. b	40. d
41. d	42. b	43. d	44. a	45. d	46. c	47. d	48. d	49. a	50. b
51. c									

Chapter 8

1. b	2. c	3. c	4. d	5. b	6. d	7. d	8. d	9. d	10. b
11. d	12. a	13. d	14. d	15. d	16. c	17. a	18. d	19. d	20. d
21. b	22. c	23. d	24. b	25. d	26. b	27. d			

Chapter 9

1. c	2. d	3. d	4. c	5. d	6. d	7. d	8. c	9. d	10. c
11. d	12. a	13. a	14. a	15. d	16. d	17. d	18. c	19. d	20. a
21. d	22. c	23. b	24. d	25. a	26. a	27. a	28. a	29. d	30. b
31. d	32. a	33. d							

Chapter 10

1. d	2. d	3. a	4. c	5. d	6. c	7. a	8. c	9. b	10. d
11. d	12. d	13. b	14. a	15. b	16. c	17. d	18. a	19. a	20. b
21. c	22. d	23. d	24. a	25. d	26. d	27. d	28. a	29. d	30. d
31. a	32. c	33. a	34. b	35. d	36. d	37. d	38. d	39. d	40. d
41. c	42. d	43. c	44. d						

Chapter 11

1. c	2. d	3. a	4. a	5. a	6. d	7. a	8. d	9. d	10. d
11. d	12. a	13. c	14. d	15. c	16. d	17. d	18. d	19. b	20. b
21. d	22. b	23. a	24. d	25. c	26. d	27. d	28. d	29. d	30. d
31. c	32. a	33. c	34. d	35. a	36. c	37. c	38. d	39. d	40. b
41. c	42. b	43. d	44. d	45. a	46. d	47. b	48. c		

Chapter 12

1. d	2. b	3. d	4. d	5. d	6. d	7. d	8. d	9. b	10. d
11. d	12. d	13. d	14. d	15. a	16. d	17. d	18. a	19. d	20. d
21. d	22. c	23. a	24. d	25. d	26. d	27. a	28. b	29. d	30. d
31. d	32. d	33. d	34. d	35. b	36. d	37. d	38. d	39. d	40. c

ANSWER KEY

Chapter 13
1. d 2. b 3. d 4. c 5. a 6. a 7. d 8. d 9. d 10. c
11. b 12. d 13. a 14. d 15. d 16. d 17. d 18. d 19. d 20. d
21. a 22. c 23. d 24. d 25. d 26. d 27. d 28. d 29. d 30. d
31. d 32. c 33. c 34. d 35. d 36. a 37. d 38. d 39. d 40. a
41. b 42. d 43. d

Chapter 14
1. a 2. d 3. b 4. b 5. d 6. d 7. d 8. b 9. b 10. a
11. c 12. b 13. d 14. d 15. b 16. d 17. d 18. d 19. a 20. a
21. d 22. b 23. d 24. d 25. d 26. a 27. d 28. a 29. a 30. c
31. d 32. a 33. d 34. b 35. b 36. b 37. b 38. c 39. d 40. c
41. c 42. d

Chapter 15
1. d 2. d 3. d 4. d 5. a 6. d 7. d 8. b 9. d 10. b
11. d 12. b 13. d 14. c 15. c 16. b 17. a 18. d 19. c 20. a
21. a 22. a 23. d 24. b 25. a 26. b 27. b 28. b 29. a 30. d
31. a 32. d 33. c 34. d 35. d 36. a 37. a 38. d 39. c 40. b
41. b 42. d

Chapter 16
1. d 2. d 3. d 4. d 5. d 6. c 7. a 8. b 9. c 10. b
11. d 12. b 13. d 14. d 15. c 16. d 17. b 18. d 19. b 20. d
21. d 22. d 23. d 24. a 25. d 26. d 27. b 28. d 29. d 30. d
31. b 32. d 33. d 34. b 35. b 36. d 37. a 38. d 39. a 40. d
41. d 42. d 43. b 44. d 45. c 46. b 47. a 48. b 49. c 50. d
51. c

Chapter 17
1. b 2. a 3. d 4. d 5. d 6. b 7. b 8. d 9. d 10. a
11. b 12. d 13. c 14. d 15. a 16. c 17. b 18. c 19. c 20. d
21. b 22. d 23. d 24. b 25. d 26. d 27. d 28. d 29. d 30. d
31. a 32. d 33. a 34. d 35. d 36. d 37. d 38. d 39. b 40. c
41. c 42. a 43. d 44. c 45. d 46. d 47. c 48. c 49. b 50. a
51. a 52. d 53. d 54. a 55. d 56. b 57. a 58. d 59. b

Chapter 18
1. d 2. a 3. d 4. c 5. d 6. c 7. b 8. d 9. b 10. c
11. b 12. d 13. d 14. d 15. d 16. c 17. d 18. b 19. d 20. d
21. a 22. c 23. d 24. d 25. d 26. d 27. d 28. b 29. b 30. d
31. c 32. c 33. d 34. d 35. c 36. a 37. d 38. d 39. a 40. b
41. b 42. b 43. a 44. d 45. a 46. a 47. c 48. c 49. b 50. b
51. b

www.ingramcontent.com/pod-product-compliance
Lightning Source LLC
Chambersburg PA
CBHW082147230426
43672CB00015B/2857